ALTERNATIVE SCHOOLING AND SCHOOL CHOICE

DEBATING ISSUES
in American Education

EDITORIAL BOARD

ALTERNATIVE SCHOOLING AND SCHOOL CHOICE

VOLUME EDITORS

ALLAN G. OSBORNE, JR.
PRINCIPAL (RETIRED), SNUG HARBOR COMMUNITY SCHOOL,
QUINCY, MASSACHUSETTS

CHARLES J. RUSSO
UNIVERSITY OF DAYTON

GERALD M. CATTARO
FORDHAM UNIVERSITY

1
VOLUME

DEBATING ISSUES
in American Education

SERIES
EDITORS

CHARLES J. RUSSO
ALLAN G. OSBORNE, JR.

⑤SAGE reference

Los Angeles | London | New Delhi
Singapore | Washington DC

Los Angeles | London | New Delhi
Singapore | Washington DC

FOR INFORMATION:

SAGE Publications, Inc.
2455 Teller Road
Thousand Oaks, California 91320
E-mail: order@sagepub.com

SAGE Publications Ltd.
1 Oliver's Yard
55 City Road
London EC1Y 1SP
United Kingdom

SAGE Publications India Pvt. Ltd.
B 1/I 1 Mohan Cooperative Industrial Area
Mathura Road, New Delhi 110 044
India

SAGE Publications Asia-Pacific Pte. Ltd.
3 Church Street
#10-04 Samsung Hub
Singapore 049483

Publisher: Rolf A. Janke
Acquisitions Editor: Jim Brace-Thompson
Assistant to the Publisher: Michele Thompson
Developmental Editors: Diana E. Axelsen, Carole Maurer
Production Editor: Tracy Buyan
Reference Systems Manager: Leticia Gutierrez
Reference Systems Coordinator: Laura Notton
Copy Editor: Melinda Masson
Typesetter: C&M Digitals (P) Ltd.
Proofreader: Eleni-Maria Georgiou
Indexer: Mary Mortensen
Cover Designer: Janet Kiesel
Marketing Manager: Carmel Schrire

Printed in the United States of America.

Library of Congress Cataloging-in-Publication Data

Alternative schooling and school choice / volume editors, Allan G. Osborne, Jr., Charles J. Russo, Gerald M. Cattaro.

p. cm. — (Debating Issues in American Education vol. 1)

Includes bibliographical references and index.

ISBN 978-1-4129-8795-0 (cloth : alk. paper)

1. School choice—United States. 2. Alternative education—United States. I. Osborne, Allan G. II. Russo, Charles J. III. Cattaro, Gerald Michael

LC46.4.A58 2013
379.1'110973—dc23   2011040901

12 13 14 15 16 10 9 8 7 6 5 4 3 2 1

CONTENTS

ABOUT THE EDITORS-IN-CHIEF

Charles J. Russo, JD, EdD, is the Joseph Panzer Chair in Education in the School of Education and Allied Professions and adjunct professor in the School of Law at the University of Dayton. He was the 1998–1999 president of the Education Law Association and 2002 recipient of its McGhehey (Achievement) Award. He has authored or coauthored more than 200 articles in peer-reviewed journals; has authored, coauthored, edited, or coedited 40 books; and has in excess of 800 publications. Russo also speaks extensively on issues in education law in the United States and abroad.

Along with having spoken in 33 states and 25 nations on 6 continents, Russo has taught summer courses in England, Spain, and Thailand; he also has served as a visiting professor at Queensland University of Technology in Brisbane and the University of Newcastle, Australia; the University of Sarajevo, Bosnia and Herzegovina; South East European University, Macedonia; the Potchefstroom Campus of North-West University in Potchefstroom, South Africa; the University of Malaya in Kuala Lumpur, Malaysia; and the University of São Paulo, Brazil. He regularly serves as a visiting professor at the Potchefstroom Campus of North-West University.

Before joining the faculty at the University of Dayton as professor and chair of the Department of Educational Administration in July 1996, Russo taught at the University of Kentucky in Lexington from August 1992 to July 1996 and at Fordham University in his native New York City from September 1989 to July 1992. He taught high school for 8½ years before and after graduation from law school. He received a BA (classical civilization) in 1972, a JD in 1983, and an EdD (educational administration and supervision) in 1989 from St. John's University in New York City. He also received a master of divinity degree from the Seminary of the Immaculate Conception in Huntington, New York, in 1978, as well as a PhD Honoris Causa from the Potchefstroom Campus of North-West University, South Africa, in May 2004 for his contributions to the field of education law.

Russo and his wife, a preschool teacher who provides invaluable assistance proofreading and editing, travel regularly both nationally and internationally to Russo's many speaking and teaching engagements.

Allan G. Osborne, Jr., is the retired principal of the Snug Harbor Community School in Quincy, Massachusetts, a nationally recognized Blue Ribbon School of Excellence. During his 34 years in public education, he served as a special education teacher, a director of special education, an assistant principal, and a principal. He has also served as an adjunct professor of special education and education law at several colleges, including Bridgewater State University and American International University.

Osborne earned an EdD in educational leadership from Boston College and an MEd in special education from Fitchburg State College (now Fitchburg State University) in Massachusetts. He received a BA in psychology from the University of Massachusetts.

Osborne has authored or coauthored numerous peer-reviewed journal articles, book chapters, monographs, and textbooks on legal issues in education, along with textbooks on other aspects of education. Although he writes and presents in several areas of educational law, he specializes in legal and policy issues in special education. He is the coauthor, with Charles J. Russo, of five texts published by Corwin, a SAGE company.

A past president of the Education Law Association (ELA), Osborne has been an attendee and presenter at most ELA conferences since 1991. He has also written a chapter now titled "Students With Disabilities" for the *Yearbook of Education Law,* published by ELA, since 1990. He is on the editorial advisory committee of *West's Education Law Reporter* and is coeditor of the "Education Law Into Practice" section of that journal, which is sponsored by ELA. He is also on the editorial boards of several other education journals.

In recognition of his contributions to the field of education law, Osborne was presented with the McGhehey Award by ELA in 2008, the highest award given by the organization. He is also the recipient of the City of Quincy Human Rights Award, the Financial Executives Institute of Massachusetts Principals Award, the Junior Achievement of Massachusetts Principals Award, and several community service awards.

Osborne spends his time in retirement writing, editing, and working on his hobbies, genealogy and photography. He and his wife Debbie, a retired elementary school teacher, enjoy gardening, traveling, attending theater and musical performances, and volunteering at the Dana Farber Cancer Institute in Boston.

ABOUT THE VOLUME EDITORS

Allan G. Osborne, Jr., retired principal of the Snug Harbor Community School in Quincy, Massachusetts, also served as a special education teacher, director of special education, assistant principal, and adjunct professor of school law during his 34 years in education. He received his doctorate in educational leadership from Boston College. Osborne authored or coauthored numerous articles, monographs, and textbooks on many topics in special education and education law. A past president of the Education Law Association (ELA), he has presented at most ELA conferences since 1991. He writes a chapter titled "Students With Disabilities" for the *Yearbook of Education Law*. Osborne is on the editorial advisory committee of *West's Education Law Reporter* and is coeditor of the "Education Law Into Practice" section of that journal. In recognition of his contributions to the field of education law, Osborne was presented with the prestigious McGhehey Award by ELA in 2008.

Charles J. Russo, JD, EdD, is the Joseph Panzer Chair in Education in the School of Education and Allied Professions and adjunct professor in the School of Law at the University of Dayton. He has authored or coauthored more than 200 articles in peer-reviewed journals; authored, coauthored, edited, or coedited 40 books; and has more than 800 publications. Before joining the University of Dayton as professor and chair of the Department of Educational Administration in 1996, Russo taught at the University of Kentucky and Fordham University. He earned a BA in classical civilization in 1972, a JD in 1983, and an EdD in educational administration and supervision in 1989, all from St. John's University in New York City. He also earned a master of divinity degree from the Seminary of the Immaculate Conception in Huntington, New York, in 1978.

Gerald M. Cattaro is a professor of educational administration at Fordham University Graduate School of Education in New York City. Since 2005, he has served as chair of the Division of Educational Leadership Administration and Policy. For the past 20 years Cattaro has headed The Center for Catholic School Leadership & Faith-Based Education as executive director. He is active on three journal boards, reflecting his research interests in urban education, international education, and faith-based education. He serves on numerous national and international commissions of education. His writing appears in books, peered-review journals, monographs, and chapters. Cattaro has worked as a practitioner in the role of teacher, chair, assistant principal, principal, and district-level administration in all levels of K–12 education.

ABOUT THE CONTRIBUTORS

Letitia Basford is an assistant professor in the School of Education at Hamline University. Her teaching and research interests focus on immigrant and refugee students' equitable access to education, with a focus on culturally relevant and reform-based pedagogy. She has a PhD from the University of Minnesota.

Martha Bigelow is an associate professor at the University of Minnesota. Her research explores the schooling of immigrants and refugees, with a focus on adolescent newcomers. Her recent publications include *Mogadishu on the Mississippi: Language, Racialized Identity and Education in a New Land*, and *Literacy and Second Language Oracy*, with Elaine Tarone and Kit Hansen. She has a PhD from Georgetown University.

Carolyn A. Brown, an associate professor in the Graduate School of Education at Fordham University, teaches social theory, education politics and policy, and qualitative methods. She taught in a tribal school and has written several comprehensive literature reviews and policy briefs to inform state policy in Indian education.

Aaron Cooley received his PhD from the University of North Carolina at Chapel Hill. He teaches public policy at New England College. His work has been published in the *Southern California Interdisciplinary Law Journal, Law and Politics Book Review, Educational Studies*, and *Journal of Education Policy.*

Bruce S. Cooper is a professor of school policy and leadership at Fordham University's Graduate School of Education. He is a noted scholar on private and religious education and is editor of the *Private School Monitor*. His interests include Catholic and Jewish schools, which he has analyzed for 40 years. One of his latest books is the coedited *Handbook of Education Politics and Policy.*

Tamela J. Dixon is a cultural studies PhD student at Ohio University. Her primary scholarly research interests include race, class, and gender disparity in education and the media; at-risk youth, in particular those labeled sexual predators; and the correlation between crime and gender, race, and class.

David Dolph is a former school principal and superintendent. He is currently a clinical faculty member in the Department of Educational Leadership at the University of Dayton.

Suzanne E. Eckes is an associate professor in the Educational Leadership and Policy Studies Department at Indiana University. She has published more than

70 articles and book chapters on school law, is an editor of the *Principal's Legal Handbook*, and is a member of the board of directors for the Education Law Association. She earned her master's degree in education from Harvard University and her law degree and PhD from University of Wisconsin–Madison.

Mary I. Grilliot is currently a graduate assistant and PhD student at the University of Dayton. Her undergraduate degree is in accounting, and she holds an MBA with a finance concentration, is a Certified Management Accountant (CMA), and holds more than 250 U.S. and international patents. Her research concentration is pedagogical practices that will encourage the development of creative and innovative skill sets.

Jyllian Rosa Guerriero is a third-year law student at the University of Dayton School of Law. Prior to attending law school, she taught language arts and ethics at the high school level in Orlando, Florida.

Alex S. Hall is a visiting professor in the Department of Counselor Education and Human Services at the University of Dayton. Her research focuses on the family and organizational structures that support development of human potential. Hall has held a number of academic leadership positions, including chair of a psychology department and coordinator of a graduate program in college student personnel. She also has served as associate editor of the *Journal of Mental Health Counseling.*

Eric S. Hall is the national director of education for AMIkids, a nonprofit organization. He is a doctoral student in educational leadership at the University of South Florida, and his research interests are juvenile justice and alternative education. Hall has 20 years of teaching and administrative experience in nontraditional school models.

Vivian Hopp Gordon is an associate professor at Loyola University Chicago, and has been an administrative law judge and hearing officer in Illinois for cases involving special education, teacher dismissals, and adult disability for 20 years. Her publications include numerous book chapters, encyclopedia entries, and peer-reviewed journal articles on varied aspects of school leadership and law.

Timothy J. Ilg is an associate professor in the Department of Educational Leadership at the University of Dayton. In addition to his 13 years at the university, he had 30 years' experience in public education, including 7 years as a school superintendent.

William Jeynes, senior fellow at the Witherspoon Institute in Princeton, New Jersey, and a professor of education at California State University, Long Beach, graduated first in his class from Harvard University. He has spoken for the G. W. Bush and Obama administrations and several government departments. He was the architect of the economic and education stimulus package that the Korean parliament passed to recover from the 1997–1998 Asian economic crisis. He has more than 100 academic publications.

Michael J. Jernigan is a math and physics teacher at Miami Valley Career Technology Center in Clayton, Ohio. He received his PhD in educational leadership from the University of Dayton. His research interests include collective bargaining; school law; teacher preparation; and science, technology, engineering, and math (STEM). Jernigan currently teaches high school juniors and seniors in a variety of math classes along with physics.

Zorka Karanxha is an assistant professor at the University of South Florida in the Department of Educational Leadership and Policy Studies. Her research focuses on educational leadership preparation, education law, and charter schools.

Marc N. Kramer is the executive director of RAVSAK: The Jewish Community Day School Network. Kramer holds a BA in Near East and Judaic studies from Brandeis University, an MSW from Columbia University, an MA from the Jewish Theological Seminary of America, and both a master's and a doctorate in education from Teachers College.

Mark Littleton is a professor of educational leadership and policy studies at Tarleton State University. He serves as coordinator of the educational leadership doctoral program, and routinely writes on the topic of sexual harassment in schools.

James L. Mawdsley received his BA from Yale University, an MA in English from Kent State University, and a JD from Cleveland-Marshall School of Law. He currently is an English instructor at Stark State College. He is a member of the Education Law Association (ELA) and the Australia New Zealand Education Law Association (ANZELA). He has authored or coauthored numerous publications, including the "Employees" chapter of the *Yearbook of Education Law*.

Ralph D. Mawdsley holds a JD from the University of Illinois and a PhD from the University of Minnesota. He has authored over 500 publications on the subject of education law. Mawdsley was president of the Education Law Association in 2001 and was awarded that organization's Marion A. McChehey Award in 2004. He has received two Fulbright Awards, one to South Africa and one to Australia.

Lesley McCue is currently in the doctoral program at the University of Dayton and focusing on public school hiring practices. She began her teaching career in a K–8 charter school. She received her master's in educational leadership from Wright State University and teaches collaboratively in gifted education in a suburban public school.

Janet Mulvey is an assistant professor at Pace University in New York City. Prior to teaching at the university level, she was a school principal in the Lakeland School District for 13 years. Mulvey received her PhD at Fordham, and two master's degrees at Long Island University. Her publications include *Getting and Keeping New Teachers: Six Essential Steps from Recruitment to Retention, Blurring the Lines: Charter, Public and Religious Schools Come Together,* and *Faith Based Charter Schools.*

Dan Schroer is the superintendent for the Greene County Career Center in Xenia, Ohio. Previously, Schroer served as an agriculture education instructor at Oak Harbor and London high schools. He was also vice president at Butler Tech in Hamilton, Ohio. Schroer is a proponent for student-centered instruction and performance improvement.

Carolyn Talbert-Johnson is a professor in the Department of Teacher Education at the University of Dayton. Her research interests include issues of diversity, teacher dispositions, and school reform. Her research consistently focuses on access to quality education for students in K–12 settings.

Rachel Trimble is a senior consultant in the Education, Human Development, and the Workforce program at American Institutes for Research. She is a technical assistance provider for the Great Lakes West and North Central Regional Comprehensive Centers. Much of her work during the past decade has been with state and district teams, providing expert consultation in continuous improvement.

Paul J. Waller is the principal of Oakwood High School in Dayton, Ohio, and is working toward his PhD in educational leadership with the University of Dayton. He has been in education for 21 years and administration for 12 years. He graduated from The Ohio State University in 1991 with a BS in science education. He received his master's in education administration in 1999 from the University of Cincinnati.

INTRODUCTION

E ducation in the United States has grown significantly from its early beginnings in Colonial times. A function that was then considered to be primarily the responsibility of the family, education is now a major purpose of governments at all levels. At present there are approximately 97,000 public schools serving students in Grades K–12 in the 14,200 school systems in the United States. Those districts and the schools within them serve approximately 50 million students who are taught by over 3 million teachers. Public education has become a major source of expenditure at the federal, state, and local levels with over $519 billion being spent each year, an average of approximately $10,418 per student (National Center for Education Statistics, 2009). When public schools were first formed, the responsibility for education was borne almost exclusively by local communities. However, during the past two centuries, state and federal governments have taken on more responsibility for the running and financing of public schools.

Against this background, particularly since it is a time when there are many critics of the existing structures in public schools, the debates in this volume examine an array of practices that are designed to provide parents with alternative ways of having their children educated.

HISTORY OF AMERICAN EDUCATION

As noted, when settlers first arrived in America, education was the responsibility of the family and was undertaken mostly at home. In Colonial times, parents taught their children the basics of reading, writing, and arithmetic. Most of the skills and knowledge children were taught was based on what was needed in an agrarian society. For the most part, boys were expected to master basic vocational skills while girls learned how to run households. Nevertheless, as the United States developed and expanded, formal schooling became a more common practice, but largely took place in nonpublic institutions accommodating only those who could afford to pay tuition. Still, the Boston Latin School, the first publicly supported secondary school in Colonial New England, was established in 1635.

In the first attempt at providing a system of mandatory education, in 1642, Massachusetts enacted a law calling on "certain chosen men of each town to ascertain from time to time, if parents and masters were attending to their educational duties; if the children were being trained in learning and labor and other employments" (Baron, 1994, p. 19). However, since the law was ineffective, leaders abandoned it in five years because it did not mandate the creation of public schools.

In 1647 the residents of the Massachusetts Bay Colony enacted what is popularly referred to as the "Ye old deluder Satan" act requiring towns of 50 households to provide instruction in reading and writing and towns of 100 households to establish grammar schools to prepare children for the universities (Commager, 1965, p. 29). A major purpose of the law, and thus the origin of its name, was to combat Satan's attempts to keep people ignorant of the scriptures so as to lead them to eternal damnation. Although this statute provided for the organization and maintenance of schools, attendance was not mandatory, but rather at parental discretion. For the most part students attended school for only a few weeks during the winter in poorly equipped schoolhouses taught by untrained teachers.

Publically financed schools did not fully come into existence until the middle of the 19th century when social reformers in Massachusetts, Connecticut, and New York succeeded in enacting legislation requiring school attendance and providing for tax-supported schools. Lawmakers in Massachusetts passed the first compulsory school law in 1852, and their New York counterparts followed suit a year later. Early schools, particularly those in rural areas, were financed partly by property taxes and partly by parental tuition. Students who lived in the cities had more options because many churches in urban areas operated their own schools. Still, through the early part of the 20th century, students in many places typically attended school for less than 100 days per year, well below the current standard of 180 class days, and did not go to school during summers because they were needed to work on the family farms. As the United States has moved from an agrarian-based economy to an information-based society, and as reflected in the debates on year-round schooling, educators have raised questions about whether American schools should change this approach.

Education remained chiefly a local and state responsibility until the middle of the 20th century when Congress passed, and President Eisenhower signed into law, the National Defense Education Act of 1958 (NDEA), largely in response to the Soviet Union's launch of Sputnik, and the Elementary and Secondary Education Act of 1965 (ESEA), now reauthorized as part of the No Child Left Behind Act. The purposes of these two significant federal statutes, respectively, were to improve instruction in commonly neglected subjects such as science, mathematics, and foreign languages and to expand educational opportunities to students from low socioeconomic backgrounds.

The passage of the NDEA represented the first time the federal government directly intervened in public school policy and curriculum when Congress earmarked funds to support more intense instruction in science and mathematics. In enacting the ESEA, Congress provided funds for school districts with large numbers of children living in poverty. Among its provisions, the ESEA also established and funded Head Start, a program designed to help prepare low-income toddlers for school. Although these were not the first pieces of federal educational legislation, the NDEA and ESEA did set the stage for the federal government's increased involvement in public education. During this period of time many educators and lawmakers began to view public education as the means to individual success and the nation's prosperity.

Regrettably, public schools in many parts of the nation were still segregated and not available to all children even in the mid-20th century. This situation began to change in the latter part of the century when public schools were essential in ensuring equal opportunity to all citizens. At first changes came about because of court orders, but further change was mandated by federal legislation. In the landmark school desegregation case, *Brown v. Board of Education,* the Supreme Court in 1954 characterized education as the most important function of the government. Chief Justice Warren, writing the majority opinion, noted that education was necessary for citizens to exercise their most basic civic responsibilities:

> In these days, it is doubtful that any child may reasonably be expected to succeed in life if he is denied the opportunity of an education. Such an opportunity, where the State has undertaken to provide it, is a right that must be made available to all on equal terms. (*Brown,* 1954, p. 493)

Twenty years later the Supreme Court ruled that failing to provide remedial English language instruction to non-English-speaking students violated the Civil Rights Act of 1964 (*Lau v. Nichols,* 1974). The Court insisted that denying these students the chance to receive remedial instruction deprived them of meaningful opportunities to participate in public education. The Court stressed that Title VI of the Civil Rights Act of 1964 and a Department of Health, Education, and Welfare regulation required recipients of federal financial aid to take affirmative steps to rectify language deficiencies.

Federal involvement in public education reached new levels one year after *Lau* when Congress passed the Education for All Handicapped Children Act, currently known as the Individuals with Disabilities Education Act (IDEA). This landmark legislation requires states to provide a free appropriate public education in the least restrictive environment for all students with disabilities between the ages of 3 and 21 as a condition of receiving federal funds. The IDEA calls for school personnel to develop individualized education programs for all students with disabilities who need special education and related services. The IDEA also gives the parents of students with disabilities unprecedented rights and creates an elaborate system for the resolution of disputes that may develop over the provision of special education services. The IDEA has not only opened the doors of public schools to children who had previously been excluded, but also provides a guarantee that the education they receive is meaningful.

The 1983 publication of *A Nation at Risk: The Imperative for Educational Reform,* an extensive report on the condition of American public schools, generated significant interest and controversy regarding the quality of public schools (National Commission for Excellence in Education). In a provocative statement in its second paragraph, the authors declared that "if an unfriendly foreign power had attempted to impose on America the mediocre educational performance that exists today, we might well have viewed it as an act of war." This report went on to reveal that students from other developed countries outperformed U.S. students on international measures. In the aftermath of this report's release, most states used the preceding quote as clarion call to implement educational reform laws that mandated more frequent testing of students in core academic subjects along with more rigorous state-mandated curricular frameworks.

A Nation at Risk played a large part in congressional reauthorization of the No Child Left Behind Act (NCLB) as an expansion of the ESEA, almost 20 years later. The major objectives of the NCLB are to improve students' academic achievement; ensure that students are taught by highly qualified personnel; make school systems accountable for student achievement; require school systems to use effective, research-based teaching methods; and afford parents choices in educational programs (Raisch & Russo, 2006; Wenkart, 2003). The NCLB provides for accountability through annual testing and the use of proven instructional methods (U.S. Department of Education, 2009). The NCLB marks the federal government's most extensive participation in public education to date. Nevertheless, states have flexibility in how they set standards, choose tests, and spend federal dollars; but they must produce results.

LEGAL BASIS FOR SCHOOL CHOICE

The Supreme Court clearly established the right of parents to enroll their children in nonpublic schools in 1925 in its landmark decision in *Pierce v. Society of Sisters of the Holy Names of Jesus and Mary.* The *Pierce* dispute began when the voters in Oregon approved a ballot initiative, and the legislature subsequently passed a law, requiring students between the ages of 8 and 16 who had not completed the eighth grade to attend the public schools. The only exception was for students who required special instruction.

Two nonpublic schools, one Roman Catholic and the other a secular military academy, filed suit challenging the statute. In affirming an order enjoining enforcement of the statute, a unanimous Supreme Court first examined the right of the schools, as private businesses, to operate. The Court ruled that enforcement of the statute would seriously impair or even destroy the profitable nature of the schools and thus greatly diminish the value of their property. Noting that the Fourteenth Amendment to the U.S. Constitution protects individuals from arbitrary state actions that impair life, liberty, and property interests, the Court found that the law was not reasonably related to the state's legitimate purpose of regulating schools. The Court recognized that nonpublic schools could provide an adequate education and acknowledged that the state had the authority to supervise their operations but emphasized that it could not exercise any greater regulation over them than it did over public schools.

Much of the Supreme Court's rationale in *Pierce* focused on the right of nonpublic schools to operate. Even so, the Court in *Pierce* added that the statute was unconstitutional because it unreasonably interfered with the rights of parents and guardians to direct the upbringing and education of their children. In oft-quoted language, the Court said that the "child is not the mere creature of the state; those who nurture him and direct his destiny have the right, coupled with the high duty, to recognize and prepare him for additional obligations" (p. 535). Thus, the Court affirmed that parents had the right to enroll their children in nonpublic schools to meet the state's compulsory attendance law.

The Supreme Court reaffirmed parents' rights to send their children to nonpublic schools two years later in *Farrington v. Tokushige* (1927). The Court agreed that public officials' attempts to regulate foreign language schools violated the Fifth Amendment of the Constitution. The schools challenged a statute in Hawaii, which at that time was a territory and not a state, requiring schools conducted in languages other than English or Hawaiian to obtain permission and pay an annual fee to the education department. The statute also limited the schools' hours of instruction, subjects offered, texts, and the ages and academic levels of students enrolling. To the extent that the statute burdened and limited instruction, the Court found that it infringed on the rights of parents who wanted their children to be taught in a foreign language.

In another landmark decision, *Wisconsin v. Yoder* (1972), the Supreme Court carved out an exception to compulsory attendance laws that has significant implications for school choice. The dispute in *Yoder* began when members of the Old Order Amish community requested that their children be excused from formal education after the eighth grade. The Amish made this request after members of their community were convicted of violating Wisconsin's compulsory attendance laws, which required all children to attend school until age 16. The parents maintained that it was unnecessary for their children to attend public high schools since they provided their young with adequate practical training in their own communities to prepare them for the Amish way of life and to be self-sufficient.

The Supreme Court, relying on the Free Exercise Clause of the First Amendment to the Constitution, agreed that the traditional Amish way of life would have been endangered by requiring their compliance with the state's compulsory attendance statutes. In its analysis, the Court balanced the parents' traditional interests in the religious upbringing of their children with the state's authority to regulate education. Observing that the Amish way of life was intertwined with their religion, the Court observed that any law infringing on their way of life also limited their free exercise of religion. In doing so, the Court placed great weight on the parents' interests in preserving their religious beliefs, which could have been impacted by requiring their children to attend public high schools. However, the Court did make it clear that its ruling limited the exception to compulsory education only to Grades 9–12 and that the state could still regulate the agrarian education that the Amish provided.

ALTERNATIVE SCHOOLING AND SCHOOL CHOICE

As the above discussion points out, parents are not restricted to sending their children to public schools to satisfy compulsory attendance requirements. Today, parents have many alternatives including nonpublic religious schools, nonsectarian schools, and home schools. Many options exist even within public school systems such as charter schools, magnet schools, and career and technical schools. Further, many schools, both public and nonpublic, continue to experiment with alternatives such as year-round programming as well as single-sex schools and classes.

In this volume many distinguished authors debate the pros and cons of both traditional and innovative educational arrangements. Although the essays in this volume cover a wide array of topics, the debates can be categorized into three main themes: issues involving charter schools, questions regarding various forms of nonpublic schooling, and topics related to schools incorporating specialized curricula or methodologies. Each of these is summarized as follows.

Charter Schools

The charter school movement, which traces its origins to Minnesota in 1991, has since gained considerable momentum. Currently, over 40 states as well as the District of Columbia and Puerto Rico have legislation allowing for the establishment of charter schools. It is important to note that charter schools are autonomous public schools essentially functioning as independent schools under special rules effectively freeing them from many of the statutes and regulations applying to traditional public schools. In exchange for being able to operate under alternative sets of rules generally allowing for greater flexibility, operators of charter schools agree to have their schools held accountable for the achievement of their students as set out in their operating charters. Although charter schools are exempt from many state rules with regard to staff and curricular issues, as public schools they do remain subject to federal and state antidiscrimination laws and constitutional provisions (Russo & Cattaro, 2009).

In spite of its rapid expansion as a means of providing school choice, the charter school movement has been controversial. As noted in selected essays in this volume, charter schools reflect many aspects of the educational reform movement embraced by politicians and educators alike since the passage of the No Child Left Behind Act. In particular, charter schools allow for greater parental participation in the management of their children's schools, which many argue is essential to school improvement and the academic success of all students. In this respect, charter schools are more like nonpublic schools than public schools. Even so, it must be kept in mind that charter schools are public schools operating with public funds even though they function more like nonpublic schools in terms of managing their own budgets, establishing their curricula, and setting policy. Thus, charter schools provide a viable alternative to the public schools for many parents. Still, as reflected in the essays in this volume, many question whether the charter school movement has been successful.

In the first chapter in this volume, the authors debate the central issue of whether charter schools are, in fact, a viable educational model. As with any innovation, examples of success and failure can be found. These authors examine quantifiable data in reaching differing conclusions about the overall success of charter schools, particularly in terms of their organizational structures and student achievement. The disparity of views shows that more research is needed in this area but, more important, that much more can be learned from the charter school movement.

Other chapters in the volume debate the merits of so-called niche charter schools that have been formed for specific purposes or to attract identifiable student populations. Chapter 2 debates the development of ethnocentric charter schools. Ethnocentric charter schools can be defined as those designed around specialized curricula with the intent of attracting students from specific cultures or ethnic backgrounds. Since students attending ethnocentric charter schools have, in essence, chosen to self-segregate, these essays question their constitutionality. In addition to the constitutional questions, this chapter debates the various policy and legal issues involved with ethnocentric charter schools. As noted in the chapter overview, the Constitution may not be offended since the students and their parents have chosen to segregate themselves by attending specialized charter schools and there is no state action directing the segregation. Conversely, ethnocentric charter schools may be viewed as promoting state-sponsored segregation to the extent that they recruit specified populations.

Chapter 3 focuses on the constitutionality of faith-based charter schools. Faith-based charter schools extol the values held by the founding religious community, even though their mission is not to proselytize or advance their own religious faith and beliefs. Although religious instruction is not part of their curricula, opponents of faith-based charter schools claim that their establishment violates the First Amendment of the U.S. Constitution's separation of church and state doctrine. Yet, proponents respond that insofar as the First Amendment also protects their right to practice religion without governmental interference, they should have the freedom to send their children to schools whose teachings are in line with their own religious values and convictions. As the essays in this chapter show, the debate over whether faith-based charter schools can survive constitutional scrutiny is destined to continue until it is resolved by judicial intervention.

The final chapter on the theme of charter schools, Chapter 4, examines the question of whether culturally specific charter schools are an appropriate means of preserving Muslim identity. The essayists in this chapter look at issues such as whether these schools can support the foundation of Muslim culture and thereby provide a positive model for young Muslims. As with the debates on ethnocentric and faith-based charter schools, these debates raise constitutional issues because it may be impossible to separate the cultural values from the religious values of Muslim families.

Nonpublic Schools

As indicated earlier, nonpublic schools have operated in the United States since Colonial times. In fact, religiously affiliated nonpublic schools in America predate public schools and can trace their histories back to the 16th century when Catholic missionaries first established them in what is now Florida and

Louisiana. Initially, most nonpublic schools were established in urban areas by religious groups. In the early days of the republic, the line between public and nonpublic schools was blurred with many being a hybrid of both. In the years following the Civil War, when the movement to develop free common schools took hold, nonpublic schools went out of favor and were often considered to be un-American.

In response to religious prejudice, as a result of the Third Baltimore Council of 1884, a meeting of Catholic Bishops, parish schools were created to combat rampant anti-Catholic prejudice that permeated public schools in many parts of the United States. Following World War II, Catholic schools in particular experienced a period of unprecedented growth that peaked in the late 1960s. The years since the late 1960s witnessed the emergence of day schools established by evangelical Christians as well as members of Islamic and Jewish organizations. Home schools, which may be considered a form of nonpublic schooling, took hold in the 1980s and have experienced rapid growth since then. During this same time, enrollment in Catholic schools declined even as enrollment in other religious schools grew significantly (Russo & Cattaro, 2009). Finally, in the 1990s a new type of independent school, the proprietary or for-profit school, emerged.

Today, as data from the U.S. Department of Education's National Center for Education Statistics (NCES) (2006) indicate, there is considerable diversity among nonpublic schools in terms of orientation and affiliation. According to recent statistics, there are approximately 30,000 nonpublic schools that educate approximately 15% of the total U.S. student population. In terms of affiliation, 48% of nonpublic schools are categorized as non-Catholic religious, 28% Catholic, and 24% nonsectarian. Most nonpublic schools offer at least some elementary grades while 61% offer elementary grades only, 9% offer secondary only, and 30% offer both elementary and secondary. A vast majority (95%) of nonpublic schools are coeducational. Most nonpublic schools provide standard elementary and/or secondary programs of studies, but some offer specialized curricula such as Montessori, special emphasis, special education, early childhood, alternative, or vocational/technical programming.

Although nonpublic schools are well rooted in the United States, many aspects of their existence are subject to ongoing debate. The essays in this volume address these issues. Chapter 5, the first chapter in the volume that speaks to nonpublic school topics, debates the benefits of proprietary or for-profit schools. On the one hand, proponents of such schools claim that they must produce in order to stay in business. Other commentators, on the other hand, claim that many proprietary schools have not met the objective of providing better results than the public schools through greater efficiencies and innovation. At the center of this debate is the question of whether for-profit nonpublic schools provide parents with a viable school choice alternative. The authors of the essays in this chapter sharply disagree over the answer to that question.

Chapter 6 ponders the controversial subject of whether publically funded programs that give parents the option of where to send their children to school are an appropriate means of promoting school choice. In essence, this debate is over the feasibility of voucher and tax-credit/deduction programs. As with many other programs that may have the indirect consequence of supporting religious schools, constitutional questions arise. Even though some voucher programs have thus far survived judicial scrutiny, many opponents still argue that public funds should not be diverted to schools run by religious organizations. Conversely, proponents insist that parents who choose to send their children to religiously affiliated nonpublic schools should receive some form of assistance since they are paying taxes to support public schools without receiving any benefit.

As stated above, the practice of homeschooling has recently experienced a renaissance. Chapter 7 looks at the question of whether home schools, which are considered to be a form of nonpublic education, should be subject to greater state regulation. Although homeschooling is legal in all 50 states, the amount and degree of oversight by state and local education agencies varies from one state to another. Since states typically have minimal regulations when it comes to matters such as teacher qualifications and curricular content in home schools, many educators argue that there should be much greater supervision to ensure that children who are homeschooled receive a quality education. On the other side of the argument, many home school proponents argue that the very states that failed to provide high-quality education for their children should not be allowed to regulate home schools. The authors in this chapter disagree over whether states should regulate home schools to the same extent that they regulate public and nonpublic schools.

In Chapter 8, the authors debate the issue of whether the Jewish community should provide Jewish day schools as a means of preserving the Jewish identity of their children. These authors examine the pros and cons of Jewish day schools while exploring other alternatives for promoting Jewish identity. In the end, though, the authors differ as to whether day schools are necessary for preserving Jewish identity or whether that identity can be promoted and preserved by other means such as summer camps. The debate is not purely an academic discussion since the issue is very controversial in the Jewish community today and reflects the various perspectives on the purpose of Jewish education.

The final chapter in the volume on the subject of nonpublic education, Chapter 9, asks whether nonpublic, nonsectarian schools enhance student achievement. Although a small minority of the nonpublic schools in the United States are nonsectarian, they provide an option for parents who want their children to have a nonpublic education but not one with a religious orientation. The debate in this chapter is particularly interesting since both authors cite research studies that support their differing points of view as to whether independent schools have, in fact, enhanced student achievement. Much of the disagreement centers on how data should be interpreted, particularly when it is adjusted to allow for the fact that nonpublic school populations often differ from their public counterparts.

Specialized Schools

The six remaining chapters in the volume can best be categorized as addressing issues involving schools offering specialized curricula or methodologies or those established for special purposes. The focus of many of the debates in these chapters is on whether the specialized schools are effective in terms of student achievement.

Magnet schools emerged in the mid-20th century predominantly as one means of desegregating large urban school districts. By definition, magnet schools focus on particular disciplines or offer specialized curricula. For example, many magnet schools specialize in advanced studies in the sciences or the arts. Since many magnet schools have strict admission criteria and are highly competitive, they often attract students who are gifted and talented. As with selected other chapters in this volume, the debate in Chapter 10 centers on whether magnet schools enhance student achievement. As can be expected, the authors agree that there are both positive and negative aspects of magnet schools, but have widely differing opinions as to whether their overall effect on student achievement has been beneficial.

Many parents and educators recently expressed renewed interest in single-sex schools and classes, which were prominent, particularly in religious schools, until late into the 20th century but have largely fallen out of favor. Proponents of this organizational arrangement contend that since boys and girls learn differently, it makes sense to educate each in environments that can cater to their needs in settings with fewer distractions. Opponents argue that segregation by gender is discriminatory and indicative of an era when students were expected to assume stereotypical gender roles. Since the research on the academic advantages of single-sex schools and classes is inconclusive, it is likely that the debate over whether such arrangements better meet the needs of elementary and secondary students, which is the focus of Chapter 11, will continue.

The federal Head Start program, designed to improve the school readiness skills of preschool children from families with low incomes, has recently come under attack as many commentators question whether it is meeting its overriding goal of helping students achieve at higher levels once they enter school. At the same time, many educators are calling for the establishment of universal preschool programs for all toddlers. While few dispute that the initial benefits Head Start provides to children from low income families in terms of educational, social, health, and nutrition services are worthwhile, empirical evidence indicates that the early gains made by toddlers in the program may not translate into greater academic achievement in later years. The essayists in Chapter 12 examine the mixed evidence of Head Start's success and debate whether it is worth preserving. These authors analyze whether Head Start has helped close the achievement gap between students from families with low incomes and their more affluent peers.

The face of vocational education has changed dramatically in recent years. In fact, even its name has been modified so that it is now more commonly referred to as career and technical education to reflect the changes in the skills students now need to enter the workforce. With a marked change in the skill sets needed for 21st-century careers, high schools face many new challenges, including the task of preparing students for jobs that have not yet been created. Given the fact that workers in the future will require a higher level of skills, Chapter 13 discusses the current value and need for vocational education and apprentice programs in today's high schools. Much of the debate centers on how high school programs should be organized to best prepare students for their future careers. These authors discuss whether career and technical education can best be provided in separate but specialized school environments or as part of comprehensive high schools.

Many boards across the country have experimented with schools that are open year-round. Year-round schools offer scheduling alternatives that many educators believe are more conducive to student learning while making more efficient use of buildings and facilities. Students attending year-round schools still go to classes for the same number of days as their peers in schools operating under a traditional calendar. Advocates of year-round schools claim that this arrangement results in better student and faculty attendance and consequently greater academic achievement. Even so, setting up year-round schedules presents school officials with a new set of challenges and obstacles. Since the evidence that year-round schools produce greater student achievement is sparse, many educators are reluctant to experiment with this option. In the debate in Chapter 14, the essayists ponder the pros and cons of this alternative in terms of student outcomes. Insofar as there may also be nonacademic benefits to rearranging school calendars, it is likely that this debate will continue as policymakers continue to explore alternatives to traditional schedules as part of the overall school reform movement.

Chapter 15, the final chapter on the theme of specialized schools, asks whether Native American schools are a viable means of enhancing student achievement. Federal regulations require the Bureau of Indian Education (BIE) to provide quality educational opportunities for Native Americans from early childhood through life. Educational offerings in these schools must be in harmony with each tribe's needs for cultural and economic well-being. Moreover, offerings must consider the wide diversity of Indian tribes and Alaska Native villages as distinctive cultural and governmental entities. In an attempt to meet this goal, the BIE operates or funds schools specifically for Native Americans. Yet, statistics show that a significant achievement gap exists between students attending Native American schools and their peers in traditional public school. Thus, this chapter debates whether Native American schools can improve the achievement of their students to close the existing achievement gap.

SUMMARY

This volume looks at many alternative educational arrangements that can provide students with options to traditional public schools. Although three major themes emerged in the essays in this volume, each chapter discusses whether various educational options are good, not only for students, but for education in general.

As is made abundantly clear in these essays, many educators and policymakers alike are convinced that having these alternatives, and the competition they provide, will force traditional public schools to improve. At the crux of all the debates is the question of whether various educational arrangements result in better student achievement. While the question seems fairly straightforward, as the essays in this volume show, the answer is not always clear-cut.

Allan G. Osborne, Jr.
Principal (Retired), Snug Harbor Community School,
Quincy, Massachusetts

Charles J. Russo
University of Dayton

Gerald M. Cattaro
Fordham University

Further Readings and Resources

Baron, R. C. (1994). *Soul of America: Documenting our past, Vol. I: 1492–1870.* Golden, CO: North American Press.

Commager, H. S. (1965). *Documents of American history, Vol. I: To 1898* (7th ed.). New York: Appleton-Century-Crofts.

National Center for Education Statistics. (2006). *Characteristics of private schools in the United States: Results from the 2003–2004 private school universe survey.* Retrieved from http://nces.ed.gov/pubs2006/2006319.pdf

National Center for Education Statistics. (2009). *Fast facts.* Retrieved from http://nces .ed.gov/fastfacts/display.asp?id=372

National Commission on Excellence in Education. (1983). *A Nation at risk: The imperative for educational reform.* Washington, DC: Author. Retrieved from http:// www2.ed.gov/pubs/NatAtRisk/risk.html

Raisch, C. D., & Russo, C. J. (2006). The No Child Left Behind Act: Federal over reaching or necessary educational reform? *Education Law Journal, 7*(4), 255–265.

Russo, C. J., & Cattaro, G. M. (2009). Faith-based charter schools: An idea whose time is unlikely to come. *Religion and Education, 36*(1), 72–93.

Tayak, D. (1774). *The one best system: A history of American urban education.* Cambridge, MA: Harvard University Press.

U.S. Department of Education. (2009). *Great expectations: Holding ourselves and our schools accountable for results.* Washington, DC: Author.

Wenkart, R. D. (2003). The No Child Left Behind Act and Congress' power to regulate under the Spending Clause. *Education Law Reporter, 174,* 589–597.

Court Cases and Statutes

Brown v. Board of Education, 347 U.S. 483 (1954).

Civil Rights Act of 1964, Title VI, 42 U.S.C. §§ 2000d *et seq.* (2006).

Education for All Handicapped Children Act, 20 U.S.C. § 1400 *et seq.* (1975).

Elementary and Secondary Education Act, P.L. 89–10, 20 U.S.C. § 6301 *et seq.* (1965).

Farrington v. Tokushige, 273 U.S. 284 (1927).

Individuals with Disabilities Education Act, 20 U.S.C. § 1400–1491 (2006).

Lau v. Nichols, 414 U.S. 563 (1974).

National Defense Education Act, P.L. 85–864 (1958).

No Child Left Behind Act, 20 U.S.C. §§ 6301–7941 (2006).

Pierce v. Society of Sisters of the Holy Names of Jesus and Mary, 268 U.S. 510 (1925).

Wisconsin v. Yoder, 406 U.S. 205 (1972).

Are charter schools a viable educational model as an alternative to public education?

POINT: Eric S. Hall, *University of South Florida*
COUNTERPOINT: Zorka Karanxha, *University of South Florida*

OVERVIEW

Central to the discourse of education in the 21st century is the notion of change. A review of current educational literature shows that school improvement, reform, development, and innovation are at the top of the list of educational policy matters being researched and discussed. The summons for educational change materializes in the schoolhouse and classroom in matters of curriculum audits, participatory education, bureaucratic reform, school governance, and economic accountability. The academic, social, economic, and political networks have fostered a national discussion of such issues, the likes of which we have not seen since the Soviet Union's successful launching of Sputnik in 1957. Sputnik's launch raised concerns that the Soviet Union's school system was better than that of the United States and would produce superior scientists. Going along with the Soviet scare of the 1950s, today we are confronted by global economies and technological advances that have been placed on the steps of the schoolhouse door. These forces have led the attack on our public schools. One of the solutions is to establish a school that will be able to deliver the academic goods in an efficient and effective manner.

Charter schools mirror the many facets of educational change sweeping the nation by embracing the concerns of school reformers as top priorities. However, key to their culture, they pivot around the supposition of school control, the hypothesis being that a lesser amount of central control will provide a reduced amount of bureaucracy and that local control will enable reform vis-à-vis school improvement and consequently academic success for all students. Thus, the understanding of the organizational culture of charter schools is paramount to the underpinning of such institutions. Building on a premise that promotes the concept that less is more, they often mimic private schools. Such institutional isomorphism promotes an idiosyncratic nature allowing the genre of the charter school to highlight two contentious dynamics built upon competition and school choice. By definition, charter schools are public schools of choice in that students and faculty choose to be part of the charter school community. Using the simile of a hybrid car, charter schools should maintain a cost and bureaucratic efficiency operating on a different source of power, yet knowing full well they can go back to their original power if need be. They are hybrids of public funding and private school options. Such schools manage their own budget, curriculum, and policy while subject to academic audits. Thus, charter schools were created to diversify the academic market and promote tailored educational practice to better serve the community. It is also important to note that charter schools, while offering choice in educational concerns, are not to be confused with magnet schools, which rely on the sole bureaucracy of boards of education and school systems. Further, it may be argued that charter schools are meant to reflect community values and parental involvement within their educational system (Lubienski, 2003).

As an initial matter, it is important to note that charter schools, officially started in 1991 in Minnesota, and the related movement have been developing over the past two decades. While the initial move toward charter schools was somewhat sketchy, Albert Shanker, former president of the American Federation of Teachers, was part of their conceptualization. This indeed is ironic because charter schools started out as a liberal movement in education and were not embraced by the conservative establishment. Today, after tinkering with the model especially in the area of governance structures, charter supporters have turned ideologies upside down. Teachers' unions no longer endorse the charter school as a viable educational option (Kahlenberg, 2008).

Indeed, while no one is against school improvement, reform, and accountability, the path to allow these concepts to flourish seems to be inherent in the current academic arena leading toward august polemics and, in some instances, division. Divergent opinions such as these overlook the balanced realization of the multifaceted fabric of pluralism in the American education system.

Eric S. Hall (University of South Florida) in the point essay defends the charter school system and provides us with a qualitative analysis of organizational characteristics. He addresses the attribute of flexibility of charter schools initiating their success, citing examples of innovation in operations, small student populations, local focus, and cost-effectiveness as paramount to this success. Charter schools, Hall maintains, have evolved rapidly in their short history. Based on the data supplied by the Center for Education Reform (Allen, Consoletti, & Kerwin, 2009), they are producing strong outcomes as part of their mandated accountability measures. Hall further states that if charter schools fail, they ultimately close or are assimilated into a public school operation. The notion of organizational survival supports Hall's argument that indeed these schools are built on the foundation of success.

Conversely, in the counterpoint essay, author Zorka Karanxha (University of South Florida) takes a quantitative approach and relies heavily on various empirical studies to buttress her opposition to the concept of the charter school as a successful academic place where student achievement is paramount. Her argument cites several studies indicating no difference in student achievement in traditional public schools and charter schools. In fact, the research she cites indicates that in some instances traditional public schools surpass charter schools in student achievement, supporting former research on this topic. Interestingly, Karanxha raises the issue of equity, especially concerning students with disabilities, an issue that indeed may need further examination.

The disparity of views on the topic shows the need exists to find common ground on the main elements of all schools, opportunity for all, school choice, and responsibility for achievement. In reading the essays in this chapter, you may want to reflect on the following questions: What innovations from the charter school movement could be incorporated into traditional public schools? Will competition from charter schools cause traditional public schools to improve?

Gerald M. Cattaro
Fordham University

POINT: Eric S. Hall
University of South Florida

Charter schools are a fast-growing, innovative process for providing parents and communities with alternatives to the traditional public school options. Charter schools, due to expanding policies and an evolving legislative process, are taking center stage in the debate about education reform in the United States. They are also a point of controversy across many states and districts that have some significant resentment toward the flexibility that these nontraditional schools have acquired since 1991, when the first charter school was established.

Charter schools have grown quite rapidly since their introduction into the U.S. education system, and based on many of the federal initiatives, such as Race to the Top, the climate appears to be ideal for the continuous expansion of these schools, despite the widespread controversy they have created. What opponents have failed to accept regarding charter schools is that these nontraditional models for learning have opened the door to advanced competition in the education system. No longer are the traditional models for public education safe from their assumed proprietary rights for educating students. Now, with the rapid growth of charter school options, public school districts are scrambling to improve their own instructional programs based on increased accountability, while also being expected to embrace and support locally established charter schools, which operate independently of district guidelines.

Many advocates of charter schools point to a few well-established characteristics that make these schools both competitive and potential elements to support nationwide school reform in the coming years. These traits include flexibility and innovation in their operations, ability to maintain a local focus, decentralized operation, small student populations, and cost-effectiveness. Just a few elements that have helped to make charter schools thrive in such a restrictive system with limited and declining resources, these characteristics will now be explored in more detail in an effort to support the need for expanding this school model as part of a systemwide reform.

FLEXIBILITY AND INNOVATION IN OPERATIONS

Charter schools were founded upon several principles, two of which are the necessity and ability for flexibility and innovation. The point that early charter school organizers wanted to make was that independent schools operating with such characteristics as innovation and flexibility could exceed the student achievement outcomes produced by their public school counterparts. These traits are evident in the diverse practices in operation today across the many charter schools in the United States, by way of curriculum, scheduling, teacher performance expectations, implementation of instructional strategies, and various models for school configuration. Charter schools using flexible and innovative practices in partnership with strong commitments to their mission can help satisfy their pledge to perform at or above their public school counterparts in student achievement and overall parent and community satisfaction.

Since charter schools are not mandated to follow the same curricular frameworks as their traditional school counterparts within a district, these institutions are encouraged to create, and typically are very creative in the design of, their instructional strategies and curriculum models. This freedom allows charter schools to determine their primary focus and to target the specific mission of their operation. Some examples of targeted curriculum include schoolwide thematic practices focused on the arts, the environment, or technology and a number of other content structures that define the school's curriculum and instructional operations. Every year, more and more creative and pioneering charter school models make their way into existence using curriculum that has evolved rapidly to meet society's demand for innovation. In recent years, our nation has seen an eruption of online, virtual charter schools open with the intent of serving children completely through a web-based platform aimed at providing parents and students with greater flexibility for learning. Many charter schools are also using their innovative rights to build collaborative instructional teams where curriculum is alive and fluid to meet the ever-changing needs of the students using present-day societal issues to guide instruction. This level of innovation keeps curriculum and instruction both rigorous and relevant to the lives of the students participating in the school.

Flexibility and innovation are also evident in charter schools by the type of scheduling model that they choose to adopt or design, depending on their charter with their local sponsor, which is typically a school district. Some charter schools use year-round academic schedules to reduce the instructional gaps found in traditional public school systems where learning is interrupted in the summer months, which can lead to knowledge loss or relapse. Some charter schools also use extended-day schedules to help maintain academic focus and to help accelerate student achievement while also serving parents by providing extended care for their children. Support systems like these are often a reason why many parents want their child in a charter school. The comfort and structure provided in these types of settings offer parents a private-school-like setting without the expense, as charter schools are publicly funded.

Charter schools have one exclusive practice that truly separates them from the bureaucratic practices commonly found in the traditional model of education, which is the fact that they can quickly remove a bad teacher. All too often, teachers in the public school system are entitled to long-term positions simply because of tenure and/or extensive contracts, which are well guarded by unions within the district. This practice can lead some teachers to become complacent, with little ramification for poor performance. Charter schools, on the other hand, deemed public yet privately managed, are not bound by these agreements, and any teachers not supporting the mission of the school or the needs of students can easily have their employment terminated. This makes the stakes high for teachers working in these schools, which requires that all team members operate at high levels of performance in order to meet the goals of the school. This type of flexibility supports a charter school's operation by ensuring that only top-quality team members, in true support of the mission, are employed. This practice also allows charter schools to ensure that they are making the greatest possible impact on their students' education, since they are accountable for achievement results on high-stakes assessments.

In many public school operations, the local school district may adopt a particular school improvement model for districtwide use that is focused on specific instructional strategies. This is not the case for charter schools. Charter schools, as part of their ability to be flexible and innovative, can choose to adopt a single strategy or integrate a full menu of strategies aimed at supporting the mission and purpose of the school. It is common to see some charter schools assemble their entire operation on strategies such as service learning, experiential education, project-based learning, computer-based instruction, differentiated instruction, and other practices not solely typical in a traditional setting. The ability of charter schools to implement these diverse strategies for instruction is a great example of how these institutions can have limitless flexibility in their day-to-day operations.

Other unique elements of charter schools are the various school configurations found across the nation and the target populations that some identify for their specific mission. For example, some charter schools may decide that their target population will be inner-city youth, while others may decide to focus on gender-specific education. Some may decide to tailor their curriculum to specific ethnic groups, with others focused on special education students. This practice does create some criticism of charter schools because opponents indicate that this leads to perpetual school segregation; however, advocates would argue that charter schools designing their curriculum for specific groups of students are only working to meet the needs of the local community, which may in fact be predominantly made up of a single ethnicity. Some examples of schools working under this model may have a curriculum and mission designed specifically for Native Americans, Hispanic-Latino immigrants, or African Americans, or even a curriculum and mission based on gender. Regardless of their target population, charter schools are rising to the challenge to offer many groups of students the necessary instructional content and strategies to support their own unique needs and/or heritage, while working to ensure positive outcomes for many marginalized groups that public schools have let slip through the cracks.

Another example of innovation is found in the partnership of charter schools, where a school may partner with a college or university, thus allowing students in high school to earn both their standard credits for graduation and college credits as part of the curriculum. Some charter boarding schools are also emerging across the country, where targeted populations can reside while earning a high quality education in preparation for college. Some schools have opened day care centers for infant and prekindergarten children as part of their operation. This serves both the community's need for child care and the charter schools' need for enrollment numbers by creating a pipeline for students into their elementary charter school programs. This model provides the community with an education-focused child care facility, while guaranteeing the children in these day care programs a spot in the feeder charter school. To extend this model further, the elementary charter schools will seek incentives and support grants to expand their charter to include a middle school feeder operation and then later expand for a high school feeder program. This perpetual feeder practice creates a complete miniature school system where students could potentially go from day care all the way through to high school graduation all under the same charter school organization. This process creates a sense of community and provides parents with a complete and secure connection to their child's school and learning community. This type of structure also helps to maintain parental involvement, while reducing the transitional anxiety that some students may experience during their traditional rite of passage from elementary school to middle school and then on to high school. Charter schools, using their given right for flexibility, offer a number of options for families and communities for the education of children. These alternatives, in many cases, would not be found in a traditional school model.

LOCAL FOCUS

Charter schools are typically established based on a local community's response to a specific need or desire to offer something different. Based on this, charter schools are able to tailor their design, target population, and instructional focus based on the ambitions of the local community. Knowing the needs of the local community, it is common to see charter schools design services that address local needs and serve the sustainability of the school, as pointed out earlier with the example of the child care and feeder school configurations. In addition, charter schools must establish their own board, which serves as the guiding force linking the community and the school into a seamless, collaborative operation. This gives the community, at the discretion and direction of the board, the opportunity to provide true feedback on what it deems to be critical in the education of its children. In essence, this charter school board is the school board for this independent operation, thus making it the authorizing agent for many of the operational issues and budgetary practices at the school.

DECENTRALIZED OPERATION

Schools operating within a district are typically managed and supervised by a set of governing practices that ensure consistency and compliance for all education operations. Charter schools, on the other hand, operate as single, self-defined centers under the supervision of their own board and the overriding expectations of the state based on defined accountability measures. The fact that charter schools can create their own curriculum and establish their own identity allows them to operate fairly independent of the larger bureaucracy that has plagued the public education system in the United States. This decentralized practice allows charter schools to focus on smaller, more independent circumstances that affect the single school as opposed to the large-scale issues affecting an entire district or state.

SMALL STUDENT POPULATION

Today's public schools operate with overwhelmingly large populations of students, with some schools exceeding enrollment sizes of 2,000 children. Based on data collected by the Center for Education Reform, most charter schools average about 372 students (Allen & Consoletti, 2010). The traditional, high-enrollment dynamics in public schools are a key characteristic that makes it very difficult to create a collaborative learning community where individual students are known and not lost in the hustle and bustle of a chaotic school environment with crowded hallways and classrooms. Even the smallest of public schools are challenged at times with truly creating a learning community where productive and responsible relationships flourish between teachers, students, administrators, and parents. This dynamic is generally addressed at a charter school, where student enrollment and class sizes are typically defined at a level that embraces relationships while also providing individual students with support for instructional services. This small learning environment is also a key element that is inviting to parents and creates an atmosphere of safety and security, without the large institutional feel of an oversized and over-crowded public school.

COST-EFFECTIVENESS

Since most charter schools are small, independent operations with minute student populations, it is vital that they operate in a fiscally responsible manner to ensure their long-term sustainability. The fact that most charter schools operate with less funding per student than their counterparts in the traditional public school system, these schools must function with minimal overhead and low administrative costs. This allows a majority of the funding to go directly toward the classroom to support student instruction as opposed to sustaining large district offices with vast numbers of support personnel and capital expenses. Charter schools, because of their nonprofit designation, are also able to capitalize on several diverse grant opportunities and to organize large fund-raising events to support their initiatives.

CONCLUSION

Charter schools have evolved rapidly in their short history, and overall they are producing strong outcomes as part of their mandated accountability measures, as reported by the Center for Education Reform (Allen et al., 2009). These outcomes, as dictated by their state education agencies and legislatures, are not merely a goal for public relations and press release, but rather a requirement in order to maintain their operation. Unlike their traditional public school counterparts, charter schools must produce results that meet or exceed the mandates of their sponsoring district or state department of education in order to sustain themselves. If they fail, they ultimately end up closing or are assimilated into a public school operation. This accountability is a driving force that helps motivate charter schools and their instructional teams to tackle challenges as they arise and collaborate at a level that requires quality practices to yield quality outcomes. Their ability to meet the challenges derived from accountability, at a lower cost than their public school counterparts, allows charter schools to meet the commitments that they have made since their beginnings in the U.S. education system.

Since the inception of the U.S. Department of Education in 1867, public schools have worked to provide effective practices to support the nation's global ability to compete in the workforce and capacity to lead in innovation.

Charter schools, which have occupied less than 20 years of this history, are in most cases producing results that mirror or exceed those of their public school counterparts. Many of these outcomes include achievement rates on high-stakes assessments, with other results focused on parent/community satisfaction and overall cost efficiency. Charters also lead innovation by breaking away from the traditional shackles of bureaucracy and implementing methods focused on individual students and the local community, thus making education a local asset and not a district or state liability.

Research regarding the overall effectiveness of charter schools is very conflicting, notes Zorka Karanxha, the counterpoint author; however, a study from Harvard provides an alternative view of charter schools' impact on achievement (Hoxby, 2004). This study found that fourth graders in charter schools nationwide scored higher on state exams than fourth graders in conventional public schools. These data contradict the results cited in Karanxha's essay from the 2003 report regarding scores on the National Assessment of Educational Progress (NAEP), which indicated no variance in fourth-grade outcomes. Considering these reports and the fact that charter schools are competing well based on their student outcomes, the results are quite impressive; many charters are serving higher rates of poor, minority, and at-risk children than their counterparts. One successful model is KIPP (Knowledge Is Power Program) charter schools, which operate 99 schools across 20 states and are focused on underserved communities with a college preparatory approach resulting in over 85% of their graduates attending college. The growing popularity of charters is also evident by the vast waiting lists that have resulted in lotteries to determine student acceptance.

It is also important to note that charters are operating with revenues far below those of conventional public schools, in some cases 40% less. This funding variance in many scenarios is considered a central factor influencing the effectiveness of charter schools deemed to be underperforming, or those argued to be producing comparable results to conventional public schools. If direct comparisons in performance are to be made, then it is critical that policy be addressed to ensure equal funding.

The years ahead are fruitful for charter schools considering the current political and economic climate in the United States. With the expansion of charter-friendly laws across many states working to provide greater flexibility, with additional funding, and with the support of federal initiatives like Race to the Top, charter schools are in a strategic position to serve as competition for conventional schooling and as partners helping reshape the educational landscape. With the realization that no school, conventional or charter, produces perfect results, the future of education in our nation is becoming an open market built on competition, outcomes, and endless possibilities.

COUNTERPOINT: Zorka Karanxha
University of South Florida

Minnesota enacted the nation's first charter school law in 1991. Since then, 40 states and the District of Columbia have enacted charter school laws. Data from the Center for Education Reform (2010) show more than 5,400 charter schools operating across the United States, serving 1.7 million children as of fall 2010. Charter schools appeal to both Republicans and Democrats who see the charter school model as a solution to the bureaucratic public school system's inability to serve all children well. First, freedom from bureaucratic rules and union contracts would foster innovation and improve academic achievement, and, second, the lessons from the charters' successes will be shared in order to improve public education. Furthermore, charter schools would provide much needed competition to the monopoly of public schools that would force public schools to improve themselves. In other words, market-driven processes would determine the success or failure of public schools.

Charter schools enjoy autonomy from most state regulations (a key characteristic of charter schools) and from school districts or authorizers, which include control of budgeting and financial decisions, hiring and firing of personnel, and curriculum and instruction decisions. Charter school proponents advocate and claim that high levels of autonomy benefit the students they serve; however, research has not been able to conclude whether that is the case. Charter schools trade autonomy for accountability, which comes from two sources—markets (the ability to have students enrolled in the charter school) and authorizers (through the contracts that last from 3 to 5 years in most states, with a few states granting contracts for up to 15 years). The two areas that have received the most attention in regard to charter school accountability are increased student achievement and fiscal responsibility. Two decades of charter schools have shown that they are not more accountable than public schools in either student achievement or fiscal responsibility. In response to charter schools' inability to fulfill these promises, charter school proponents argue that charter schools should only satisfy the parents since they are their customers, and lament the antagonistic environment between charter schools and their chartering school districts.

STUDENT ACHIEVEMENT

Many supporters of charter schools see charters as vehicles to improve academic achievement of poor minority students; however, results from multiple national and some local research studies, to date, have not shown that charter school students do better than their public school counterparts. Research studies have continuously shown that charter schools do not have an advantage over public schools when it comes to student achievement. Some of the studies would illustrate this point well. They are noteworthy due to their scope, their methodology, and the sources that commissioned them. They were national studies, their methodology was rigorous, and the institutions that provided financial support for them were supporters of charter schools.

The U.S. Department of Education conducted a national study of charter school and traditional public school students in 2003. According to the findings of the study, which looked at students' National Assessment of Educational Progress (NAEP) scores, there were no differences in reading and mathematics between the fourth-grade students who attended charter schools and the ones who attended traditional public schools. Also, poor children enrolled in public schools performed better than their charter school counterparts.

In 2007, NAEP test results showed that, nationally, charter school students had lower results than traditional public school students in all categories with the exception of eighth-grade Hispanic students in mathematics. Another national study of charter school and traditional public school students in 15 states conducted by Stanford University researchers and funded by the Michael and Susan Dell Foundation in 2009 (widely known as CREDO) concluded that students in charter schools did not perform better than students in public schools. Specifically, researchers found that 37% of charter school students had significantly lower academic gains than their public school counterparts, 46% had gains that were the same as those of students in public schools, and only 17% showed gains that were significantly better than those of students in public schools. Put simply, there is a 2:1 ratio of bad charter schools to good charter schools.

The most recent national study commissioned by the federal government and conducted by Mathematica Policy Research of Princeton (U.S. Department of Education, 2010) looked at the students who won lotteries to attend charter middle schools and the ones who applied but did not gain admission to the charter schools. The researchers concluded that charter school students who were admitted through lotteries performed, on average, no better in mathematics and reading than those students who lost out in the random admission process and enrolled in the local public schools.

RAND researchers (Zimmer et al., 2009) analyzed longitudinal, student-level data from Chicago, San Diego, Philadelphia, Denver, Milwaukee, and the states of Ohio, Texas, and Florida. Their findings show that *on average, across varying communities and policy environments, charter middle and high schools produce achievement gains that are about the same as those in traditional public schools.* The achievement gains for charter elementary schools are challenging to estimate and remain unclear because elementary students typically have no baseline test scores at the time they enter kindergarten. For middle and high school levels, the RAND research team found that achievement gains in charter schools and traditional public schools were about the same, with two exceptions. First, charter schools perform worse in the first year of operation; that is, student achievement drops below the traditional public school level, and there is reason for concern about the performance of virtual charter schools, which serve their students remotely in the students' homes rather than in a school building. In Ohio, which has a sizeable number of virtual charter schools, students showed achievement gains that were significantly lower than those of students in traditional public schools and classroom-based charter schools.

The School District of Philadelphia is one of the largest urban school districts in the country that turned over many of its struggling schools to education management organizations (EMOs), hoping they would transform these public schools and increase student achievement. RAND Corporation researchers conducted two studies of Philadelphia charter school and traditional public school students, one in 2007 and the other in 2008. RAND Corporation researchers found similar results during both years of these studies. According to their conclusions, charter school students overall performed similarly to traditional public school students. A small number of schools (six elementary schools and one middle school) performed better than traditional public schools; however, 10 schools did worse. The rest of the schools in the study had no significant differences. These results led Philadelphia officials who had turned over the management of public schools to for-profit (Edison Schools) and not-for-profit organizations to state that privatization and changing schools to charter schools had not worked as initially anticipated.

Charter schools have been among the fastest-growing segments of the K–12 education sector in Chicago as well. According to RAND researchers, who conducted a study of students' achievement in Chicago's charter and public schools, on average, charter schools' performance in raising student achievement is approximately on the same level as that of traditional public schools— except that charter schools do not do well in raising student achievement in their first year of operation.

Research results of study after study show that charter schools have not achieved what most supporters expect: higher student achievement than traditional public schools. Based on data, charter schools have not been shown yet to be a viable alternative to public education. Nationally, charter school students are not outperforming public school students overall; instead, many charter schools are underperforming compared to their public school peers.

Some proponents predicted that the presence of charter schools would have a positive effect on nearby traditional public schools by applying positive competitive pressure; some opponents worried that charter schools would harm students in nearby traditional public schools by draining resources. However, RAND study findings in eight states could not support such a theory. The researchers found that the presence of charter schools did not appear to either help or harm student achievement in the traditional public schools. Overall, there are no data to support the assertion that public schools will change due to existence of charter schools or the threat of competition from charter schools; thus, any positive impact of charter schools on public schools remains to be found.

Another argument of charter schools is that market accountability will ensure charter school efficiency as well as effectiveness and parent/student satisfaction; in other words, charter schools will run the schools better and for less money. There are numerous studies that debunk this kind of assertion by charter school proponents. One research finding is that charter school teachers have, in general, lower salaries than their public school counterparts; however, lower teacher salaries are often the consequence not of greater efficiency but of lesser quality. Lower teacher salaries often result from a lower level of qualifications—especially in years of experience of teachers employed by charter schools. Another argument is that charter schools operate on a lower budget than traditional public schools; however, research shows that charter schools might have lower expenditures due to providing fewer services, not the same services at a lower cost. For example, studies show that charter schools serve (1) elementary school students who are less costly to educate, (2) fewer students classified as English language learners, and (3) a lower number of English students with special education needs, or (4) fewer students who are English language learners and have special education needs, and (5) students with disabilities who attend charter schools tend to have mild learning disabilities rather than more severe disabilities.

The most recent national study conducted by Gary Miron and Jessica Urschel (2010) found that differences in revenues and expenditures can be largely explained by higher spending by traditional public schools for special education, student support services, transportation, and food services. This study found, however, that charter schools pay more for administration, both as a percentage of overall spending and for the salaries they pay administrative personnel. So, akin to businesses, charter schools pay less for their teachers (rank and file); however, they compensate better for their administration (management).

Most choice legislation gives charter schools immunity from most of the laws, rules, and regulations that govern traditional public schools. Such freedoms are based on the theory that if schools are free of restrictions, they would be more innovative and spend most of their time on instruction without dealing with the mounting paperwork with which traditional public schools are riddled. However, charter schools still need to be held accountable to the public since they use public monies to finance their operations, and consequently local school districts and other institutions that authorize charter schools need to provide oversight and ensure that charter schools do comply with their contracts. This responsibility is shared with charter school boards whose role is to govern charter schools. However, regulation and oversight of charter schools has proved to be difficult for multiple reasons such as lack of resources necessary to oversee charter schools, expertise to conduct audits of charter schools, and lack of political will to hold charter schools accountable. Overall, the number of students in charter schools is still low, and there is concern about the disproportionate amount of resources that oversight of charter schools demands. So, instead of saving money, precious resources are spent on overseeing charter schools at public expense.

The issue of reduced regulations and autonomy has surfaced as a significant concern for charter schools. Media (newspapers, radio, and television) are replete with headlines of charter schools' managers who engage in money mismanagement, falsifying documents, theft, hiring of felons and former convicts, teaching religion, noncompliance with state regulations, and nepotism, among others. These headlines can be found across many of the 41 states with charter school laws and the District of Columbia. Such events have even led to charter school proponents joining the voices that express concern on the lack of accountability of some charter school operators.

Nationally, approximately 20% of all opened charter schools have closed. These percentages vary from state to state. The highest closure rates are in Florida (30%) and Arizona (over 23%). Arizona comes second in the number of students charter schools serve, and Florida comes third. California has the highest number of charter schools in the United States. As of 2009, 103 such schools had closed in California. Most notably, California Charter Academy, which at one time operated 60 schools serving 10,000 students, faced criminal charges from the state for misusing $25.6 million (including $2.6 million for personal expenses). The largest charter school chain went bankrupt in 2004, leaving students and their parents to look for other schools in which to place their children. To date, it is not clear how much money (the highest number stands at $100 million) the CEO, a former insurance company executive, collected from the state (Ravitch, 2010).

Only 14% of charter schools closed because of low academic performance, as many underperforming charter schools are still in operation, and many school districts are either unable or unwilling to close schools for academic reasons (Center for Education Reform, 2011). Other reasons for charter school closures include (a) financial mismanagement or distress, (b) low enrollment, (c) voluntary withdrawal of charter, (d) violation of contractual agreement, (e) poor leadership/governance, (f) lack of community or local political support, and (g) lack or loss of facility.

EQUITY AND DIVERSITY

Issues of equity and diversity have also arisen in the literature on charter schools. Several studies have identified special education as a major issue facing charter schools. Not only do charter schools enroll fewer students with disabilities than traditional public schools, but charter schools tend to enroll students who have mild or specific learning disabilities rather than children with severe disabilities who require more services. Accordingly, researchers have raised the possibility that special education students who wish to attend charter schools may suffer implicit or explicit obstacles to enrollment. Research studies have suggested discrimination against children with disabilities in Arizona charter schools. Noncompliance with the Individuals with Disabilities Education Act (IDEA) and not meeting the individual needs of students with disabilities have been reported in many states including charter schools in New York and Massachusetts. Shortages of qualified special education teachers have been raised in North Carolina due in part to lower salaries in charter schools. Some Pennsylvania schools have been found in violation of IDEA by spending money allocated to children with special needs for other charter school operations.

Another equity concern emphasized in the literature is segregation based on race and socioeconomic status. Charter schools serve children of all races and socioeconomic backgrounds that are to some extent comparable to the demographics of the local district level; however, what has surfaced by looking closely at the school level is that charter schools are more racially and socioeconomically homogeneous than the already highly segregated public schools. It appears that until now charter schools were missing an opportunity to address segregation and have a positive impact on integrating children of different racial and socioeconomic backgrounds and thus serve a greater public good. Being mindful of segregation would lead charter schools to remedy one of the ills of public schools; however, it appears that charter schools have not done so.

TEACHER ISSUES IN CHARTER SCHOOLS

Another promise of charter schools is that they would empower teachers to be involved in decision making and engage in innovative teaching. Furthermore, charter schools would be able to hire better teachers who would be different from public school teachers. Also, charter schools would be able to easily fire an underperforming teacher since the impact of a teachers' union would not be an issue. However, what has happened, especially with schools associated with larger EMOs, is that teachers are not empowered or allowed to be creative but rather have to follow a set design for curriculum and instructional techniques, and apply set student behavior programs.

Teachers are leaving charter schools at much higher rates than their traditional public school counterparts. A study by the National Center on School Choice at Vanderbilt University (Cannata, 2010) showed that charter school teachers are more likely than public school teachers to leave the profession due in part to teacher characteristics such as certification and part-time employment. However, research findings show that one of the most important reasons teachers leave charter schools is dissatisfaction with the working conditions. Also, charter school teachers are more likely to leave involuntarily due to staffing issues at the school. Additionally, teacher attrition is higher in some part due to charter school closures. Finally, the study also found little evidence that turnover is higher at charter schools because they exercise greater flexibility in personnel practices such as hiring and firing.

Charter schools burst to the national scene with great promises, many of which they have not delivered on. Even so, charter schools cannot be easily dismissed due to the wide support and popularity they enjoy with businesses, foundations, and politicians. So far, charter schools have not backed their claims with data that show they are doing a better job than public schools. Even their staunch advocates have highlighted the difficulties associated with establishing successful charter schools.

FURTHER READINGS AND RESOURCES

Allen, J., & Consoletti, A. (2010). *Annual survey of America's charter schools.* Retrieved from the Center for Education Reform website: http://www.edreform.com/wp-content/uploads/2011/09/CER_Charter_Survey_2010.pdf

Allen, J., Consoletti, A., & Kerwin, K. (2009). *2009 Accountability report: Charter schools.* Washington, DC: Center for Education Reform.

Buckley, K. E., & Wohlstetter, P. (Eds.). (2004). *Taking account of charter schools: What's happened and what's next?* New York: Teachers College Press.

Cannata, M. (2010). *School choice, school organization, and teacher turnover.* Retrieved from the National Center on School Choice website: http://www.vanderbilt.edu/schoolchoice/documents/ucea_choice_organization_turnover.pdf

Center for Education Reform. (2009). *The accountability report.* Retrieved from http://www.edreform.com/wp-content/uploads/2011/09/CER_2009_AR_Charter_Schools.pdf

Center for Education Reform. (2010). *Charter connection.* Retrieved from http://www.edreform.com/issues/choice-charter-schools/facts

Center for Education Reform. (2011). *All about charter schools.* Retrieved from http://www.edreform.com/issues/choice-charter-schools/facts

Center for Research on Education Outcomes (CREDO). (2009). *Multiple choice: Charter school performance in 16 states.* Retrieved September 22, 2011, from http://credo.stanford.edu/reports/MULTIPLE_CHOICE_CREDO.pdf

Center on Reinventing Public Education. (2009). *Choice & innovation.* Retrieved September 22, 2011, from http://www.crpe.org/cs/crpe/view/topics/1

Finn, C. E., & Kanstoroom, M. (2002). Do charter schools do it differently? *Phi Delta Kappan, 84,* 59–62.

Hoxby, C. (2004). *Achievement in charter schools and regular public schools in the United States: Understanding the differences.* Retrieved September 22, 2011, from http://www.vanderbilt.edu/schoolchoice/downloads/papers/hoxby2004.pdf

Kahlenberg, R. D. (2008). Albert Shanker and the future of teacher unions. *Phi Delta Kappan, 89*(10), 712–720.

Lubienski, C. (2003). Innovation in education markets: Theory and evidence on the impact of competition and choice in charter schools. *American Education Research Journal, 40*(2), 395–443.

Manno, B. V., Finn, C. E., Bierlein, L. A., & Vanourek, G. (1998). How charter schools are different. *Phi Delta Kappan, 79*(7), 489–498.

Miron, G., & Nelson, C. (Eds.). (2002). *What's public about charter schools? Lessons learned about choice and accountability.* Thousand Oaks, CA: Corwin.

Miron, G., & Urschel, J. (2010). *Equal or fair? A study of revenues and expenditures in American charter schools.* Retrieved from http://epicpolicy.org/publication/charter-school-finance

Ravitch, D. (2010). *The death and life of the great American school system: How testing and choice are undermining education.* New York: Basic Books.

U.S. Department of Education. (2010). *The evaluation of charter school impacts: Final report.* Washington, DC: Author. Retrieved from http://mathematica-mpr.com/publications/PDFs/education/charter_school_impacts.pdf

Zimmer, R., Gill, B., Booker, K., Lavertu, S., Sass, T. R., & Witte, J. (2009). *Charter schools in eight states: Effects on achievement, attainment, integration, and competition.* Retrieved from http://www.rand.org/pubs/monographs/MG869

Do ethnocentric charter schools unconstitutionally discriminate on the basis of race and/or national origin?

POINT: Ralph D. Mawdsley, *Cleveland State University*
COUNTERPOINT: Alex S. Hall, *University of Dayton*

OVERVIEW

Compared to traditional public schools, charter schools have been given greater flexibility to experiment concerning their curricula, length of instructional days, and missions. This increased flexibility has given leaders in charter schools more leeway to shape their educational communities (Wells, 1998). Consequently, some charter schools have been designed to attract specific populations of students, which a number of scholars suggest has led to greater racial and ethnic segregation. Yet, state charter school laws specifically prohibit discriminatory practices in charter schools and do not allow admissions policies that select students based on certain specified characteristics. Even so, leaders in charter schools may focus their recruitment plans on specific student populations as long as their doors remain open to everyone.

As a result, some charter schools, for instance, have been designed to attract male students, at-risk students, students with disabilities, or students from specific cultural groups. These specialized charter schools have sometimes been referred to as "niche charter schools" (Eckes, Fox, & Buchanan, 2011). Charter schools that are designed around specific curricula (e.g., Afrocentric) or to attract students from specific cultures are sometimes referred to as "ethnocentric" or "culture-oriented" charter schools. These charter schools focus on cultures ranging from Arabic to Hebrew to Hawaiian. Within these specialized charter schools, students choose to self-segregate based on a school's area of focus. Voluntary segregation in specialized charter schools has only begun to be documented (Carpenter, 2005; Garcia, 2008). The legal issues involved are different from previous legal cases involving de jure segregation.

In this chapter, the point and counterpoint authors debate the various policy and legal issues involved with ethnocentric charter schools. On the one hand, because students (and their parents) choose to segregate themselves within the context of these specialized charter schools, the Constitution may not be offended. Specifically, under this form of de facto (as a matter of fact) segregation, there is no state action directing the segregation. On the other hand, the schools may be perceived as the state sponsoring a form of de jure (as a matter of law) racial segregation because the charter schools directly recruit specified populations.

Indeed, charter schools that are racially segregated seem to conflict with Justice Kennedy's concurring opinion in *Parents Involved in Community Schools v. Seattle School District No. 1* (2007). Justice Kennedy wrote that "this Nation has a moral and ethical obligation to fulfill its historic commitment to creating an integrated society that ensures equal opportunity for all its children" (p. 797). He reasoned that "a compelling interest exists in avoiding racial isolation" (p. 797) and, in all cases, we should not "ignore the problem of de facto resegregation" (p. 788). In contrast, some scholars argue that segregation in charter schools should not be perceived as negative because the schools are trying to equal the playing field for low income, minority students—in an environment where they can be free from discrimination they may have experienced in traditional public schools. Nina Buchanan and Robert Fox (2004) suggest that the notion of "separate but equal" may be evolving into the belief that only through ethnocentric schools can "true equity emerge" (p. 82).

A variety of reasons exist to explain why students may choose to self-segregate into ethnocentric charter schools. For example, some students may select culture-oriented charter schools such as those focusing on Native American culture because they may have experienced discrimination related to ethnicity in their traditional public schools. Alex S. Hall (University of Dayton) argues in the counterpoint essay that ethnocentric schools are necessary to better educate our youth, because we must allow students the psychological freedom, safety, and space to establish a sense of self, a sense of self within the context of others, and a sense of self in relation to the world. Others similarly contend that ethnocentric or culture-oriented charter schools offer students of color an alternative to Eurocentric schools (Dyson, 2004). Critics claim, though, that ethnocentric charter schools create cultural enclaves within the public school system, and although they may be boosting self-esteem, it is at the expense of preparing students for the real world.

As both the point and counterpoint essays assert, some ethnocentric charter schools have raised Establishment Clause concerns under the First Amendment of the U.S. Constitution, as the schools have been accused of blurring the line between religion and culture; see, for example, *ACLU of Minnesota v. Tarek ibn Ziyad Academy* (2009). Although some specialized charter schools have already been involved in litigation involving Establishment Clause concerns, most have successfully avoided the courtroom because their focus is on culture instead of religion. As Ralph D. Mawdsley (Cleveland State University) suggests in the point essay, while these ethnocentric schools reflect the values and culture of a particular religious group, some may also reflect the values and cultures of ethnic groups.

In reading the point and counterpoint essays, try to reflect on two key questions. First, if public schooling belongs to all citizens, then what are the legal, ethical, and policy questions involved with ethnocentric charter schools? Second, should this form of voluntary segregation in ethnocentric charter schools be defended as attempting to level the playing field for marginalized groups, or should the schools be considered as a major civil rights failure?

Suzanne E. Eckes
Indiana University

POINT: Ralph D. Mawdsley
Cleveland State University

R ace and ethnicity have long played a significant role in public education in the United States. In the 19th century, for example, public schools in urban settings tended to reflect the communities in which they existed. Thus, in many cases, the culture of public schools not only reflected race and ethnicity but also was intertwined with such other factors as religion and language. However, as immigration brought more persons to the United States and the racial and ethnic nature of communities became more diverse, political leaders worried about how to create an American educational system free of strife based on differences among the various immigrant groups. The plural system of sectarian schools that existed at the country's founding was supplanted with publicly funded "common schools" by the mid-19th century (Viteritti, 1999, pp. 146–148). Nonetheless, efforts to provide secular education free from the pressures of religious and cultural differences often fell short where common schools drew their ideology from the teachings of mainline Protestantism that "was intolerant of those who were non-believers" (Viteritti, 1998, p. 666).

With black students effectively excluded, until the mid-20th century, from all public schools in the South and many in the North, the early dividing grounds in American education focused on religion. The creation of the common school did not lead to the disappearance of schools that mixed religion, language, and ethnicity, such as, for instance, Lutheran schools organized based on German- and Norwegian-speaking students or Catholic schools differentiating between Italian- and Polish-speaking students. Consequently, while Catholics perceived the Protestant influence in public schools and created what was to become the largest nonpublic school system in the United States, they, along with various Protestant schools, established the precedent by the end of the 19th century for ethnocentric schools.

In light of the differences that emerged, this point essay maintains that ethnocentric choices for students are not advisable for constitutional reasons. In addition, ethnocentric schools can have the effect of isolating students from others who have different cultural backgrounds and limiting the ability to share the viewpoints and appreciate the contributions that persons with other backgrounds have made.

DISCUSSION

In 1954, the U.S. Supreme Court, in *Brown v. Board of Education of Topeka*, changed the face of public education by prohibiting discrimination based on race in public schools. In a unanimous decision, the Court held that, "in the field of public education the doctrine of 'separate but equal' has no place. Separate educational facilities are inherently unequal" (*Brown*, p. 495).

Nineteen years later, the Supreme Court, in Norwood v. Harrison (1973), invalidated a state statute providing the provision of free textbooks to all public and private schools in the state where many of the private schools discriminated on the basis of race. "A State may not grant the type of tangible financial aid here involved if that aid has a significant tendency to facilitate, reinforce, and support private discrimination" (Norwood, p. 466). Even if one were to assume that the state's purpose was a sincere interest in an equal education of all children in the state,

> good intentions as to one valid objective do not serve to negate the State's involvement in violation of a constitutional duty. . . . The Equal Protection Clause would be a sterile promise if state involvement in possible private activity could be shielded altogether from constitutional scrutiny simply because its ultimate end was not discrimination but some higher goal. (*Norwood*, pp. 466–467)

By the end of the 20th century, school choice through charter schools significantly changed the structure of American schooling. State legislative authorization of charter schools, which at least theoretically were considered to be public schools where school organizers were given discretion to operate the schools in return for accountability for results, has resulted in a wide variance, from state to state, in the definition of charter schools and the ground rules under which they operate.

Essentially, four patterns have developed among the states: In some jurisdictions, the lax monitoring of charter schools has allowed unscrupulous school operators to commit significant fraud; in other states, the accountability requirements placed on charter schools required less than was asked of regular public schools under the No Child Left Behind Act (NCLB, 2006); among the states, many school district superintendents and staff members did not regard charter schools as public schools, which meant that positive experiences were unlikely to be replicated; and, finally, few jurisdictions required racial or socioeconomic desegregation, creating the possibility that charter schools could serve as refuges for white flight (Liu & Taylor, 2005). However, at least facially, publicly funded, privately managed charter schools have made the school offerings of many urban districts unprecedentedly diverse. Students attending urban public schools are no longer required to attend a neighborhood school or choose only between undifferentiated generalist schools; today, a menu of specialized offerings exists, from Afrocentric schools to those with a focus on art or social change.

Charter schools, though, continue to cause controversy even as their numbers increase. While each state defines them somewhat differently, the laws of most states identify charter schools as being publicly funded, privately run, and organized as nonprofits or similar entities, subject to only limited oversight and exempt from most of the state statutes and regulations governing public schools. Proponents of charter schooling see this autonomy as charter schools' main benefit, while opponents lament the loss of public accountability that accompanies privatization. Both sides debate whether charter schools improve educational outcomes or merely drain money from resource-starved traditional public schools. Generally, though, robust choice decreases enrollment in traditional public schools, diverts funds that otherwise would have flowed to those schools, and mitigates the direct influence of public regulation.

Some have questioned whether the existence of charter schools in formerly segregated urban school districts furthers desegregation. When you examine data from individual schools and school districts, charter schools are more extreme with regard to racial and social class isolation and segregation than are the districts in which they are located. These data hardly suggest that charter schools are powerful tools of desegregation (Liu & Taylor, 2005). The argument goes that

> choice within urban district boundaries does not alter the basic geography of educational inequality. That inequality, which limits the odds of finding high-quality educational opportunities through intradistrict choice, is due in substantial part to the failure of equal protection law to require the elimination of interdistrict disparities in school resources, and to the failure of desegregation law to require suburban jurisdictions, whose local autonomy exists by grace of the state, to help remedy historic state-sponsored racial discrimination in urban school districts. (Liu & Taylor, 2005, p. 803)

The result is that inner-city schoolchildren are left to choose among high-poverty, racially isolated schools, while those living in suburbs thrive in a setting where their parents can exercise "local control" to insulate their neighborhood schools racially and socioeconomically. Despite the requirement of the No Child Left Behind Act that school districts receive Title I funds to provide students in schools identified for improvement with an option to transfer to another public school in the same district, including a charter school, that has not been identified for improvement (NCLB, 20 U.S.C. § 6316(b)(1)(E)(i)), the opportunity for interdistrict transfers exists only "to the extent practicable" (NCLB, 20 U.S.C. § 6316(b)(11)). In effect, the only option for a child in a failing public school may be a public charter school where the goal of achieving Adequate Yearly Progress under NCLB trumps a larger purpose of achieving desegregation.

To the extent that charter schools provide private groups with the chance to get involved in public education, recent years have revealed religious groups seeking to provide educational services both to their own adherents and to others at public expense. The growth of Afrocentric charter schools has tended to owe its impetus to traditionally black churches, which, while attempting to "demonstrate a unique purpose and comprehensive plan" so as not to appear to be a church school, nonetheless present to students "an organized mass base and meeting place, for African Americans to strategize their moves in the fight against racial segregation and oppression" (Flynt, 2010, pp. 107–108).

The Afrocentric charter movement presents a double dilemma for such schools in their potential for violating the Equal Protection Clause under *Brown* or *Norwood* if the admission and treatment of black students is given preference. Questions may arise under the Establishment Clause in the First Amendment of the U.S. Constitution if the religious identity of a school results in the coercion or intimidation of students belonging to other faiths under such Supreme Court precedents as *Lee v. Weisman* (1992) and *Santa Fe Independent School District v. Doe* (2000) if the public charter schools have the effect of appearing to be sponsored by the religion or have the effect of coercing students, not members of the sponsoring church's faith, to follow or adopt that faith. One author has suggested that Afrocentric charter schools violate the Equal Protection Clause as constituting "unconstitutionally re-segregated" institutions in an era where "judicial paternalism views itself as a surrogate for informed parental determinations thereby vouchsafing school quality in an era of increased educational standards and school accountability where the voluntary choice of African-American parents are not to be trusted" (Dyson, 2004, p. 2).

Other charter schools, more overtly religious in nature, have also sprung up. While these schools reflect the values and culture of a particular religious group, some, such as those that are Muslim or Jewish, can also be said to reflect the values and cultures of ethnic groups. However, these religious charter schools have come under attack as violating the Establishment Clause. The Ben Gamla Charter School in Florida, featuring "a unique bilingual, bi-literate, and bi-cultural curriculum, which prepares students to have an edge in global competition through the study of Hebrew as a second language" (Note, 2009, p. 1750), has thus far avoided breaching traditional barriers between church and state because of its careful emphasis on culture. Similarly, the Tarek ibn Ziyad Academy in Minnesota, recognized as a pioneer in efforts to communicate respect for Muslim culture and knowledge of the Arabic language alongside the traditional cornerstones of a public school education, has survived an Establishment Clause challenge because of its emphasis on Muslim culture, rather than only religion (Note, 2009, p. 1756).

The distinction between religion and culture is not always readily discernible. In *Skoros v. City of New York* (2006), the Second Circuit held that a municipal display in the public schools that featured a menorah and star and crescent, but not a nativity scene, was not an Establishment Clause violation because the menorah and star and crescent had the actual and perceived secular purpose of promoting pluralism and tolerance and respect for diverse customs through holiday celebrations. As cases such as *Skoros* suggest that charter schools that present an ethnocentric image may be able to skirt Establishment Clause requirements for public schools by making their schools available to persons of other religions, religious charter schools raise difficult constitutional, social, and political questions.

Insofar as Americans have long been suspicious of public funding for religious education, allowing religious groups to become charter school providers complicates this controversy where, since the mid-19th century, the record of state constitutional requirements has been against public funding. The social and constitutional anxieties stirred by the presence of state-funded religious charter schools stem from the fear that, by giving charters to religious organizations, such will undermine the notion of public schools being common schools, the incubators of democracy. Injecting religion into charter schools raises the legitimate concern these schools will be able to indoctrinate students with religious dogma under the guise of teaching values and culture, something that would be impermissible in the regular public schools. At the same time, the infusion of religion into charter schools raises the specter that these schools will explicitly or tacitly engage in conduct that promotes intolerance, oppresses nonadherent teachers and students, discriminates against potential attendees and employees, and segregates public schooling along religious lines.

CONCLUSION

While ethnocentric charter schools pose administrative problems with constitutional implications, the argument can be made that they provide a broad range of choices in urban districts with failing schools. However, once states and local school boards permit charter schools to be organized on ethnic or religious grounds, rejecting other requests raises constitutional questions. The extent to which school district officials have an obligation to monitor ethnocentric schools for racial, ethnic, or religious discrimination is not clear, nor do criteria exist to determine whether charter schools are complying with consti-tutional and statutory requirements concerning discrimination. The notion that failing urban school districts can close the door on all charter school requests has been made more uncertain under NCLB where parents of stu-dents in failing schools are entitled to a range of options.

The fact that urban school districts are the most likely to be ethnically diverse and, thus, to have students who could take advantage of ethnocentric charter schools begs the question as to whether such schools are advisable. To suggest that all students whose parents are interested in charter schools would benefit from the energy fostered by religiously/racially/ethnically diverse groups ignores the reality that such groups will come with their predetermined agendas. To afford parents the opportunity of organizing their own groups if displeased with those available may well be an empty gesture. If an insufficient number of students exists to warrant a new charter school, parents face the Hobson's choice of keeping their child in a failing public school or placing their child in an ethnocentric setting where the child faces isolation.

As attractive as the notion of school choice may seem, offering students an option where their racial/ethnic/religious difference may cause them to stand out may not be a real option at all. In the end, all that may have happened is that groups of students will have their own segregated settings, and the purpose of furthering diversity will have been undercut.

COUNTERPOINT: Alex S. Hall
University of Dayton

This counterpoint essay not only addresses multifaceted and complex issues but also encapsulates an urgent federal and state cornerstone con-cern: freedom to choose. The controversy associated with whether ethnocen-tric charter schools unconstitutionally discriminate on the basis of race and/or national origin has the potential to be both rancorous and ugly, because the stakes associated with the conclusion to this question are quite high. Essentially, the stakes are these: Given our penchant for freedom, for religious expression, and for the rights of citizens to participate in how they are governed, and also given our nation's struggle in attempting to share power with marginalized populations, how can we abrogate the rights of free citizens and at the same time further marginalize oppressed populations by continuing to call those actions noble educational public policy?

In order to thoughtfully address this topic, we need to look at and discuss the following in relation to education: our emerging national epistemology, our set of laws and precedents that govern this issue, our national educational goals and mandates, and our global economy. The lens through which we will view this topic simultaneously satisfies ideological, legal, and reasonable person standard perspectives. As the following paragraphs illuminate this controversy, I hope to convince you that this topic as a whole deserves a second look within the legal, educational, and national communities of interest because as it currently stands, case law and precedent do not adequately respond to our emerging need to educate well our citizenry, as evidenced by the fact that centric charter schools currently can be seen as potentially discriminatory, when public schools generally are themselves by default and de facto separatist in practice.

In short, in order to better educate our youth, we must allow them the psychological freedom, safety, and space to establish first a sense of self, then a sense of self within the context of others, and finally a sense of self in relation to the world. This discovery of self as a prerequisite for interacting with others is a simple, normal, and necessary developmental process. The best way to accomplish this identity work, according to ethnic identity theory (Helms), is for youth first to become ensconced within their own ethnic group, second to appreciate and embrace "the Other," and third to freely choose to navigate their way in mainstream society, potentially embracing our national agenda. Ethnocentric charter schools provide a uniquely appropriate environment for such identity work.

As we move through this topic, I will address each concern or issue, in order, that I have listed in the above paragraphs. Then, I will show how these concerns and issues inform the question of whether or not ethnocentric charter schools unconstitutionally discriminate based on race or national origin. Finally, I will conclude that ethnocentric charter schools do *not* violate constitutional intent and that they *do* provide protection for race and ethnicity rights related to citizenship, including especially the right to an equal education under the law.

DISCUSSION

Epistemologically, American schools are, to a large extent, not only a microcosmic reflection of the community in which they reside but also an isomorphic image of the zeitgeist, the time in history in which they operate. Our schools have always been shaped by the discourse of our dominant epistemology, or ideology—our articulation of how we see an individual's worth and contribution to American society and to our nation as a whole. For example, our schools began as sectarian, religiously based institutions, then evolved into publicly funded "common schools," and now are entrenched in racial segregation and inequality, in stark contrast to the intent of the landmark ruling in *Brown v. Board of Education of Topeka* (1954). From the 1960s to the 1970s, Americans witnessed a narrowing of the black-white student achievement gap as a result of affirmative action efforts in higher education, corporate America, and the military; in the past 40 years, however, those hard-won achievement gains have attenuated (Saltman & Scapp, 2005). Today, the goal of educational equality is elusive, and the idea of desegregated schools is unrealized. In fact, segregated schools increasingly appear to be the de facto condition, especially in densely populated urban and sparsely populated rural environments. Any curious and kindhearted person must wonder, "What is the source of this educational disparity, and what can we do to prevent its persistence?"

We have laws and precedents that must be satisfied in relation to ethnocentric charter schools. One source of guidance to schools in relation to discrimination and charter schools can be seen in our country's legal legacy, both in what we've accomplished historically and in what we have yet to accomplish. So far, this is what we have accomplished, in brief: We achieved a national understanding when the U.S. Supreme Court ruled in *Brown* that discrimination based on race in public schools is prohibited, that the doctrine of "separate but equal" cannot stand, and that separate educational facilities are inherently unequal (p. 495). We achieved progress when the Equal Protection Clause under *Brown* or *Norwood v. Harrison* (1973) articulated that equality is the standard for admission and treatment of all students for all schools.

Many would say that we achieve progress when ethnocentric charter schools are able to freely express their religious views within the educational process. Religious expression is seen by many as both a right and a natural extension of one's cultural experience. Instead of an exclusive focus on culture, religion is often perceived as an indivisible aspect of its culture. Yet, critics might argue that these schools appear to be too closely entangled with religion. Clearly, culture and religion are intertwined in ways that are complex and sometimes irreducible.

Along these lines, the Establishment Clause clarified that a school's religious identity cannot coerce or intimidate students of one faith into believing or performing acts associated with another faith. We achieved progress when the U.S. Supreme Court ruled in *Norwood v. Harrison* (1973) that a state may not grant tangible financial aid (e.g., free textbooks to private and public schools) where that aid results in private discrimination based on race, even when the overall intent is positive (providing an equal education for all). We achieved clarity regarding school prayer when the U.S. Supreme Court ruled in *Lee v. Weisman* (1992) that it may appear to the nonbeliever as coercive and in *Santa Fe Independent School District v. Doe* (2000) that it violates the Establishment Clause of the First Amendment of the U.S. Constitution as it would be seen as stamped with the school's seal of approval. To date, we clearly see that judicial intervention is a necessary but not sufficient condition for bringing about educational reform and racial and social justice in the United States.

What we have yet to accomplish is a proper legal consensus on school issues related to centric charter schools (established on the basis of religion or ethnicity) that demonstrates sufficient respect and voice for dissenting opinions related to the above cases. For example, regarding *Brown,* separate *and* equal circumstances can and do exist in many educational settings where de facto segregation occurs, yet such circumstances are not seen as either unconstitutional or illegal examples of discrimination. Further, regarding *Lee v. Weisman* (2000), Justice Scalia's dissent clearly articulated that nonsectarian prayer to God at public cerebrations is a longstanding American tradition, and that using the Establishment Clause to prohibit the same is a case of the Court acting as an instrument of prayer's destruction and as a social engineer by way of the manipulability of the test of psychological coercion (505 U.S. 577, 632). Scalia reminded the Court of the tradition of our presidents to call upon divine guidance (e.g., Washington when he proclaimed the Thanksgiving holiday in 1789; Madison and Jefferson in their inaugural addresses). Scalia said that an Establishment Cause violation could only occur if official penalties were assigned to students refusing to adhere to a particular religion. Finally, regarding *Santa Fe Independent School District v. Doe* (2000), which struck down student-led prayers before public football games as violating the Establishment Clause of the First Amendment, Justices Rehnquist, Scalia, and Thomas saw striking down prayer in school as hostile to all things religious in public life. Rehnquist saw prayer as a private statement delivered by a speaker, rather than as a public, school-sponsored speech. Obviously, school prayer is an ongoing controversy, but it seems that for all men to be seen as equal under the law, the right of a citizen to express one's faith in public life would be as valued as the right of a citizen to express no faith in public life.

Ethnocentric charter schools have experienced some constitutionally related success as seen in *Zelman v. Simmons-Harris* (2002), where school vouchers are allowable in the face of the Establishment Clause of the First Amendment. Specifically, it was determined by the U.S. Supreme Court that a voucher is constitutional when it has a valid secular purpose, when aid goes to parents and not to the schools, when a broad class of beneficiaries is covered, when the program is neutral with respect to religion, and where there are adequate nonreligious options. The Court ruled that the Ohio program met the five-part test because the valid secular purpose was that poor children were failing in the public school system and needed educational assistance, that the vouchers were given to parents, that the "broad class" included students enrolled in currently failing programs, that parents receiving the vouchers were not compelled to enroll in a religious-based school, and that other schools in adjoining districts, including nonsectarian private schools in the area, would benefit from and receive vouchers as well. In this case, Chief Justice Rehnquist's position was that the intent of the law was the important thing, and that as long as parents could choose whether to attend a private, public, or secular school with a religious mission and the government did not advocate a particular choice, the voucher system was constitutional. Justice Thomas believed that we needed some remedy for failing urban public schools because they disproportionately affect minority children. Thomas believed that choice is necessary in order for the core purposes of the Fourteenth Amendment to be satisfied, even if, on the face of it, such choice would contradict the precedent established in *Everson v. Board of Education* (1947). The same arguments that apply to the five-part test with the voucher system could readily adapt to the charter schools generally, and by extension to ethnocentric charter schools as well.

Charter schools and ethnocentric charter schools in particular meet the standard for both the Establishment Clause and the Equal Protection Clause as outlined in the Fourteenth Amendment. In *Skoros v. City of New York* (2006), the Supreme Court utilized the three-prong test from *Lemon v. Kurtzman* (1971) to show consistency with the Establishment Clause related to government and religion, in which there must be a secular purpose, an effect that neither advances nor inhibits religion, and no excessive entanglement of government with religion (Id. at 612–12). So, it would seem that as long as charter schools respect these guidelines, they would be both constitutionally consistent and legal. The Equal Protection Clause essentially states that all people are equal, and that all people are equally protected under the law. Again, as long as charter schools treat all students equally, it appears that they would be operating consonant with the Constitution and in compliance with the law.

In actual practice, ethnocentric charter schools might result in de facto segregation, as a consequence of being established for a particular purpose and for a particular population of interest, even when they do not seek to discriminate, and when they actively maintain an open admission policy. However, as long as people can freely select into or out of the centric charter school, such homogeneity would be both nondiscriminatory and legal, in the way that public schools escape scrutiny when their populations are similarly homogeneous based on residence and socioeconomic status. For whatever reasons, U.S. public schools today are de facto segregated, with the percentage of black students in mostly minority school districts returned to what it was in the late 1960s (Orfield, 2001). As long as the enrollment policies in charter schools do not have a discriminatory intent, there would be no constitutional violation. If policies are in place to ensure equal opportunities to participate in the charter school, then the school policies would be in concordance with the Equal Protection Clause of the Fourteenth Amendment.

Ethnocentric charter schools are one solution to the problem of meeting national and global exigent conditions. We must find a better way to educate our marginalized youth for future careers, for solving complex environmental and economic crises, and for engaging in critical thinking and problem solving associated with being good citizens generally, all within a zeitgeist of emerging pluralism within the educational context. Further, in order to educate our youth, we must respond to their need to navigate through their identity, ethnicity, and morality challenges so that they might successfully participate in the pulse of national politics, the dignity of economic self-sufficiency, the opportunity to properly care for and rear children in their families, and the skill to participate in a national conversation that strives to peacefully resolve international conflicts while realizing global opportunities. If we are to move forward as a nation, we need to meet youth where they are and respond educationally to their emerging sense of self so that they will become fully educated and able to competently assume adult roles in our society today.

We live in a global economy. As such, we need to remember that the purpose of education is to prepare free citizens to participate in our society as self-sufficient, moral, and intelligent people who are equipped to meet our increasingly complex local, national, and global challenges. Educating people involves providing a context where they can safely explore their identity, ethnicity, and morality in order to maximize their talents and assume adult roles as multiculturally competent citizens. We Americans are a free people who expect to be able to worship freely in both our public and our private lives, to learn in equivalent educational and social environments, to compete fairly for jobs and for meaningful work, and to live in a legal climate of justice irrespective of race, ethnicity, or national origin.

CONCLUSION

Whether or not ethnocentric charter schools discriminate must be considered within the framework of both our goal and our role as a global leader.

With that in mind, and based on the evidence provided in the paragraphs above, I conclude that ethnocentric charter schools do *not* violate constitutional intent and that they *do* provide protection for race and ethnicity rights related to free citizenship, including especially the right to an equal education under the law.

FURTHER READINGS AND RESOURCES

Buchanan, N., & Fox, R. (2004). Back to the future: Ethnocentric charter schools in Hawaii. In E. E. Rofes & L. M. Stulberg (Eds.), *The emancipatory promise of charter schools* (pp. 77–106). Albany: SUNY Press.

Carpenter, D. M. I. (2005). *Playing to type: Mapping the charter school landscape.* Washington, DC: Thomas B. Fordham Institute.

Dyson, M. R. (2004). Putting quality back into equality: Rethinking the constitutionality of charter school enabling legislation and centric school choice in a post-*Grutter* era. *Rutgers Law Journal, 36*(1), 1–52.

Eckes, S., Fox, R., & Buchanan, N. (2011). Legal and policy issues regarding niche charter schools: Race, religion, culture and the law. *Journal of School Choice, 5*(1), 85–110.

Flynt, M. L. (2010). The new generation of civil rights advocacy: The charter school movement in African American communities in the South. *Southern Region Black Law Students Association Law Journal, 4,* 100–116.

Garcia, D. (2008). Academic and racial segregation in charter schools: Do parents sort students into specialized charter schools? *Education & Urban Society, 40*(590), 590–612.

Liu, G., & Taylor, W. L. (2005). School choice to achieve desegregation. *Fordham Law Review, 74,* 791–823.

Note: Church, choice, and charters: A new wrinkle for public education? (2009). *Harvard Law Review, 122,* 1750–1771.

Orfield, G. (2001). *Schools more separate: Consequences of a decade of resegregation.* Retrieved from http://www.eric.ed.gov/ERICWebPortal/search/detailmini.jsp?_nfpb=true&_&ERICExtSearch_SearchValue_0=ED459217&ERICExtSearch_SearchType_0=no&accno=ED459217

Saiger, A. J. (2007). School choice and states' duty to support "public" schools. *Boston College Law Review, 48,* 909, 961.

Saltman, K. J., & Scapp, R. (2005). *Corporate schooling and the assault on public education.* Abingdon, Oxon, UK: Taylor & Francis.

Viteritti, J. P. (1998). Blaine's wake: School choice, the First Amendment, and state constitutional law. *Harvard Journal of Law & Public Policy, 21,* 657–718.

Viteritti, J. P. (1999). *Choosing equality: School choice, the Constitution, and civil society.* Washington, DC: Brookings Institution Press.

Wells, A. S. (1998). *Beyond the rhetoric of charter school reform: A study of ten California school districts.* Los Angeles: UCLA Charter School Study.

Court Cases and Statutes

ACLU of Minnesota v. Tarek ibn Ziyad Academy, 2009 U.S. Dist. LEXIS 62567 (D. Minn. July 21, 2009).

Brown v. Board of Education of Topeka, 347 U.S. 483 (1954).

Everson v. Board of Education, 330 U.S. 1 (1947).

Lee v. Weisman, 505 U.S. 577 (1992).

Lemon v. Kurtzman, 403 U.S. 602 (1971).

No Child Left Behind Act, 20 U.S.C. § 6301 *et seq.* (2006).

Norwood v. Harrison, 413 U.S. 455 (1973).

Parents Involved in Community Schools v. Seattle School District No. 1, 551 U.S. 701 (2007).

Santa Fe Independent School District v. Doe, 530 U.S. 290 (2000).

Skoros v. City of New York, 437 F.3d 1 (2d Cir. 2006).

U.S. Constitution, Amendment 14.

U.S. Declaration of Independence.

Zelman v. Simmons-Harris, 536 U.S. 639 (2002).

Should faith-based charter schools survive constitutional scrutiny?

POINT: Bruce S. Cooper, *Fordham University*
COUNTERPOINT: Janet Mulvey, *Pace University*

OVERVIEW

Charter schools are autonomous public schools that operate under a unique set of rules that essentially free them from some of the statutes and regulations that apply to traditional public schools. Charter schools have been established at the elementary, middle, and secondary levels. In exchange for being able to operate under a relaxed set of rules, charter school founders agree that their schools will be held accountable for the achievement of their students as set out in their charter. Students attend charter schools by choice, and such schools provide parents and students with an alternative to traditional public schools.

Charter schools first emerged in the early 1990s when Minnesota and California passed the first charter school legislation in 1991 and 1992, respectively. Since that time, the movement has spread throughout the country with more than 40 states, the District of Columbia, and Puerto Rico now having some form of charter school statute. It is estimated that currently close to 1.5 million students attend approximately 4,700 charter schools throughout the country (U.S. Department of Education, 2011).

How and by whom charters are granted varies by state. In many states charters are issued by the state board of education, but in others local school districts are authorized by statute to grant charters. In some states a special agency has been established for the purpose of issuing charters. Depending on state law, charters may be issued to a variety of entities including public school districts, universities, nonprofit organizations, and even for-profit corporations. Since charter schools are essentially autonomous, they may implement a specialized curriculum or one that is different from that adopted by the local school district.

Regardless of whether charters are issued by the state, the local school board, or another agency, charter schools are neither administered by the school district nor accountable to it. Charter schools usually are governed by their own independent boards, and parents often have a greater role in decision making and running the school than do parents in traditional public schools. Charter schools are often exempt from the provisions and restrictions of collective bargaining agreements. Thus, those teaching and working in charter schools frequently are subject to different salary schedules, benefits, working conditions, or professional qualifications than their counterparts in the traditional public schools.

As the debates over charter schools in this and other volumes will show, charter schools have not been without their controversy. Particularly controversial is the establishment of charter schools that are operated by groups affiliated with religious organizations or a particular religious sect. Many of these charter schools are not overtly religious. That is, while they may extol the values held by the founding religious community, their mission is not to proselytize or advance their own religious faith and beliefs. Religious instruction is not necessarily part of the curriculum. Nonetheless, opponents of faith-based charter schools claim that their establishment violates the First Amendment of the U.S. Constitution's separation of church and state doctrine. Proponents, on the other hand, pointing to the fact that the First Amendment also protects an individual's right to practice religion without governmental interference, feel that parents should have the freedom to send their children to a school whose teachings will be in line with their own religious values and convictions. Such advocates often claim that the public schools not only do not do this, but even promote values that are inconsistent with and hostile to their religious beliefs.

The debate in this chapter focuses on the constitutionality of faith-based charter schools. Bruce S. Cooper, a professor in the Graduate School of Education at Fordham University, argues that such schools should survive constitutional scrutiny. Cooper states that it should not be a surprise that some of the publicly funded independent charter schools organized since 1991 would promote religious values. Noting that the United States is a religious society, Cooper reminds us that helping children in sectarian schools is not forbidden by policy or law. Cooper acknowledges that public funding cannot be used to support a particular religious ideology, activity, or program, or otherwise endorse religion. Even so, he questions why tax money cannot go to support the educational choices of families whose children attend schools that promote religious values. He concludes that few can argue with the fact that faith-based charter schools serve a vital purpose by ensuring that all children are educated, learn right from wrong, and grow up to be productive, dedicated, active, and moral people.

In the counterpoint essay, Janet Mulvey, a clinical professor in the School of Education at Pace University, takes the opposite position that as public entities charter schools should not be associated with religion. She argues that using public funds to support faith-based charter schools is illegal and will undermine the existence and purpose of the public schools in the United States. Mulvey insists that the U.S. Constitution and church and state separation cases decided by the courts have made it clear that public institutions should not be the conduits for religious influence. Further, she feels that faith-based charter schools do not fulfill one of the purposes of charter schools, which is to provide more integrated settings for students, but rather tend to create new avenues of segregation and fractionalization.

The debate over whether faith-based charter schools will pass constitutional muster will continue until definitive rulings come down from the courts to resolve the question. As you read the essays in this chapter, you may want to think about a few questions. Do faith-based charter schools teach more than just values, and do they, in fact, proselytize students and promote the religious teachings of their sponsors? Should the United States use tax dollars to support sectarian schools as is the case in many other countries? Is it a small leap from giving religious schools tax-exempt status and providing remedial services to parochial school students to financially supporting charter schools run by religious organizations?

Allan G. Osborne, Jr.
Principal (Retired), Snug Harbor Community School,
Quincy, Massachusetts

POINT: Bruce S. Cooper
Fordham University

I n a free, religious society, families should be able to join and support charter schools that are religiously motivated, formed, and affiliated/supported. The United States is a free, active religious society with approximately 65% of Americans now affiliated with a formal religion, and over 9% of American children attending private and religious schools. And religious values are deemed important to the growth and spiritual and moral development of our children.

Thus, it's no real surprise that when 44 states passed laws to have publicly funded independent charter schools, some of these new schools would teach religious values, and some of the founders and supporters of these schools would be religious or religiously affiliated associations. Knowing the history of education and religion in the United States, one could have predicted it. The rationale for religious freedom and charter schools rests on six interlocking arguments:

1. The United States is a religious society where education and religion have always been connected, and charter schools should be no different—connections are clearly present.

2. The U.S. Supreme Court, in *Zelman v. Simmons-Harris* (2002), a case originating in Cleveland, Ohio, ruled that families could legally "cash in" their publicly funded vouchers at religious schools without violating the First Amendment's "separation of church and state" provision of the U.S. Constitution.

3. Schools in these tough economic and demographic times are struggling to provide space and quality education for all; so having religious associations become active in creating and expanding new schools is a blessing, not a religious conspiracy.

4. Personal values and morality help students to learn and grow; so why not imbue some charter schools with religious values—and best practices—to help children learn to be good people, and good citizens?

5. Short of Gestapo tactics, how can the government possibly police, inspect, and control every school, and every classroom, to make sure that teachers are not teaching religious beliefs, practices, and values? Part

of being a free society is allowing parents to select a good school, religious or otherwise, for their children, without having to pay privately.

6. We might be one step away from issuing publicly funded vouchers to all families for their children's education; parents and guardians could then "cash in" their vouchers at a school of their choice, even a charter school with a religious program and religious sponsorship and support.

ARGUMENT 1: THE UNITED STATES AS A FREE, RELIGIOUS SOCIETY

Like it or not, citizens of the United States have a strong set of religious beliefs: Church membership, attendance at religious workshops, and Bible study are extensive; thus, practices are so widespread that religious holidays have become virtually national holidays. Since 1923, when the state of Oregon passed a law requiring all students of school age to attend only a public school in their community, the issue of religious freedom in education went to court, ending with the critical case, *Pierce v. Society of Sisters.* The U.S. Supreme Court ruled in 1925 that outlawing private or religious school attendance was unconstitutional, a violation of the parents' rights to direct the upbringing and education of their children.

By 1965, over 11% of American children were attending private K–12 schools, with 80% of these students enrolled in schools run by the Catholic Church. But these religious schools were being privately financed through student tuition and fees, donations, diocesan support, fund-raising (e.g., raffles, Christmas card sales, and Bingo), and some private endowments, as well as receiving public recognition, being tax-free institutions, and taking their place alongside the major public schools.

It's a short step, then, from being legally recognized, publicly valued institutions—these religious schools—and getting tax-free status, federal aid, and other public benefits (e.g., free bus transportation, handicapped education services, and free educational equipment for low income pupils in their schools under the Elementary and Secondary Education Act [ESEA], Section II-A).

Thus, while direct public funding of religious schools was still not allowed, the major federal school legislation, the ESEA of 1965, passed during the liberal Democratic administration of the New Frontier under President Lyndon B. Johnson, did assign public school teachers and free educational resources to service impoverished children attending private religious schools. For without the political support of the U.S. Conference of Catholic Bishops, President

Johnson might have never built the powerful Democratic coalition that he needed to get the ESEA passed through Congress in the first place.

So, helping children in religious schools was not unknown or forbidden by law and policy; on the other hand, the courts had ruled continuously that the church and state separation doctrine meant no "direct" public dollars could pay for religious education, at least at the K–12 level. (However, the nation had always allowed military chaplains to offer religious services to military personnel; and college resources for religion classes and religious-affiliated colleges under programs such as the GI Bill for military veterans and Pell Grants to help pay tuition were not against the law.)

Thus, we see a growing, critical trend in U.S. public-private-religious education, as more and more states are "chartering" schools with a religious connection, and paying tuition for these students. In fact, a study by Marcia Harr Bailey and Bruce S. Cooper (2009) determined,

> In recent years, charter schools have focused interest on the cultures experienced by Muslims, Jews, Christians, Greek Orthodox, Hmong, and other groups in several states as these religious groups have successfully applied for public charters to open what we are calling *religious charter schools* (for want of a better term). . . . The avowed mission of these schools helps to provide a framework that is culturally relevant to that group. (pp. 272–273)

Currently, such public funding is still not legal for K–12 schools. Public tax dollars may not be used to support a particular religious ideology, activity, or program. In effect, public tax money cannot be used to endorse ("establish") religion. Hence, salaries for elementary and secondary school teachers of Bible, Koran, or catechism could not be paid from the public purse, if this teacher were endorsing these religious beliefs. However, in the United States, a growing number of charter schools are being opened, supported, and governed/managed by religious groups. For, as Robert Michaelsen (1970) explained in his book, *Piety in the Public School,* "public education has been expected to transmit beliefs supposedly common to most Americans or what school scholars have called our 'civil religion'" (Carper & Hunt, 2008, p. 3).

ARGUMENT 2: FUNDING RELIGIOUS CHARTERS MAY BE LEGAL

A landmark case was decided before the U.S. Supreme Court in 2002 in *Zelman v. Simmons-Harris,* which is different from the legalization of religious charter schools but is, in some important ways, related. The *Zelman* decision found that families, receiving publicly funded vouchers, could cash them in at a local private-religious school, without violating the First Amendment separation clause. That is, the court determined that the grant was/is to the *family*—not to the school of choice that happens to be religious—and thus is not direct public aid to religion.

An analogy would be a family, receiving a $100 federal tax refund, deciding to buy a Bible with the money. So, at the bookstore, the dollars are signed over to the owner, and the family picks up its Bible. Government is not funding religion. The choice of where to spend the money is the citizens'—just as cashing a voucher is a parental decision, not a government subsidy to any particular group or sect.

By analogy, vouchers can go to families who can use them for religious education at a private school of their choice. Direct funding of religiously related charter schools is different, but the principle may be much the same. Why should all tax money have to go to public schools, if the parents want a private/religious experience for children? Private (religious, parochial) schools already receive tax-free status at all levels (local, state, and federal); their students are granted a state and local (publicly recognized) diploma; and students with a private school background can attend a public (or private/religious) university or college without penalty.

ARGUMENT 3: PUBLIC EDUCATION NEEDS HELP FROM THE PRIVATE SECTOR

Another argument is more general. Public education needs everyone's help; public schools could hardly absorb the 4.7 million children currently attending private and religious schools, plus the 1.4 million children, often for religious reasons, who are homeschooled (Cooper, 2008). Someone once argued that the best way to get help and equal treatment for private schools, particularly in larger districts and cities, would be to announce that on Monday next, all nonpublic schools will close, because the millions of pupils would then be knocking on their neighborhood public schools to enroll. How could the U.S. public schools absorb an increase in enrollment of more than 11%? In fact, in New York City, children (kindergarteners and up) are on waiting lists to be admitted to their local, neighborhood public schools under state compulsory education laws.

The United States needs private schools, and could use a range of good charter schools as the number of charter schools grows nationally. So, why not permit some of these charter schools to be affiliated with a religious association? What's wrong with that? Families chose these schools voluntarily; for, according to Caroline M. Hoxby (2007), "publicly funded, privately-managed charter schools have made school offerings of many urban districts unprecedentedly diverse" (p. 11). So, besides these private and charter schools providing choice and diversity, they also take children whom the public schools might have trouble enrolling.

As Martin Carnoy, Rebecca Jacobsen, Lawrence Mishel, and Richard Rothstein (2005) explain in their *Charter School Dust-Up,* "competition from charter schools improves outcomes in a regular public school because educators in the regular public schools are motivated to be more effective in order to avoid losing students to charter schools" (p. 4). While their book, based on national comparative data, fails to show any significant difference, the "market forces" (which they didn't examine) were and are still there. This book also fails to mention the differences in founders of charter schools, and the potential for religious groups, perhaps in church-owned buildings, to organize charters and to test the legality of public funds going to private, religious-related institutions.

Times are tight. Religious groups, and their sponsorship of charter schools, can help relieve the pressures and provide more choice—assisting and not threatening the public schools!

ARGUMENT 4: A RELIGIOUS ENVIRONMENT TEACHES VALUES AND ETHICS

Education has always been about values, although the terminology changes: *good citizenship, moral behavior,* and so on. So if some charter schools are founded on, supported by, and focused on religious values, who are the losers? Case studies are always illustrative. A Muslim group in Brooklyn received a New York state charter, and appointed a principal whose family was Muslim (from Yemen), Ms. Almontaser.

The state ordered her removed, mainly for religious reasons, succumbing to the very bias that the creation of the school was intended to dispel. In the process, a small segment of the public succeeded in imposing its prejudices on her employer." The commission said that the Department of Education had discriminated against Ms. Almontaser, a Muslim of Yemeni descent, "on account of her race, religion and national origin" (*Almontaser v. New York City Department of Education,* 2010, p. 8).

ARGUMENT 5: A FREE SOCIETY EMPOWERS TEACHERS AND SCHOOLS TO USE RELIGIOUS EXAMPLES TO TEACH MORALITY AND GOOD BEHAVIOR

We know that education in the United States is about more than just ABCs and 2+2s. Teachers, and their schools, have a moral obligation to teach children good behavior, ethics, and to distinguish right from wrong. If funding religiously related and value-rich schools can help teachers and schools do the job better, how can one object? Only good can come out of it, since religion-related charter schools are voluntary, free, and growing—and bring to bear all the best of society. Bailey and Cooper (2009) found,

> Even though they have a particular religious identity, these charter schools do admit children and hire teachers from other faiths and cultures. Since these charter schools teach the values of religion—but do not require prayer or Bible/Koran/Torah teaching—they apparently do not as yet violate the 1st Amendment of the US Constitution—and are therefore being publicly aided under various states' charter legislation. (p. 274)

ARGUMENT 6: FUND THE CHILD AND FAMILY

A final step in making schools available, active, and right for each child and family would be to issue a voucher, say for $12,000, to every child of school age in the United States, and let the family (if it wishes) choose a private or charter school, or the children could simply attend their local "public" school. Charter schools, religious or otherwise, could be the recipient of these vouchers—which is legal under the *Zelman* (2002) decision, and education would become a tax-supported, universal, and accessible opportunity for all.

Vouchers or Scholarships

Several states and Washington, D.C., currently have authorized voucher programs while seven states provide vouchers for students with disabilities, according to the New York Foundation for Education Reform and Accountability (FERA), to transfer to another school system. Targeted scholarship programs would then aid students in low-performing school districts, students in federally designated "persistently lowest achieving" schools, and students from low income households. Voucher programs are receiving serious considerations in several states, including Pennsylvania, Florida, and Indiana. In Indiana, policies now will offer up to 15,000 education vouchers to school-age children, to be phased in over 2 years.

The United States has a long and noble tradition of endeavoring to educate every child to the highest possible level, regardless of race, color, ethnicity, spoken language, creed, or geographic location. At the same time, Americans have always been and remain a deeply religious people, with 65% professing a belief in God, the highest level in the modern world (Newport, 2011).

Balancing Religion and Public Educational Needs

Enacting policies to expand and strengthen charter and private educational opportunities, including religious schools, would build this "balance point" and give benefits to both private and public schools. As more children remain in, or are added to, the ranks of private and religious schools, only modest marginal educational costs will be imposed on taxpayers. As more children attend private schools, neighboring public schools will be relieved of the costs of educating more students.

And we now see that, with the closing of over half of U.S. Catholic schools since the peak year, 1965—from a high of 5.6 million students to a current low of 2.2 million in Catholic schools (Cattaro & Cooper, 2007)—these students in most cases attend local public schools, in crowded urban systems. So, the decline of one sector can often place greater pressure on the other sector, another good reason to reverse the declining private-religious school sector and to maintain both sectors—public and private—in the interest of parents and their communities.

CONCLUSION

We thus need to consider and support religious charter schools and other funding for children in private and religious schools (vouchers) to help all children, regardless of background or beliefs. How do our increasingly diverse schools—public, private, and religious—compare to the organization and funding of schools in other countries, which have long supported public *and* private schools with public funding—since they all serve the public "good"?

Finding a common center point could mean, in the future, that private and public schools shed light on each other's practices, and help to improve education on both sides of the divide. This middle point would mean that the best qualities and practices of both private/religious and public schooling would help make education better overall.

The publicness of public schools teaches private schools about public responsibility and earns private schools general support and funding—as with vouchers, charters, and government aid—while the private, religious values-centeredness of private schools can inspire public schools to compete, teach values, appeal to families, and build support. Public and private schools become two sides of the same coin, the same high quality, responsive education equation, best exemplified by religious charter schools and the vouchers that free funding to follow parent needs and aspirations.

Many nations do this already, as most public, private, and religious schools in nations like England, France, and Sweden, and even Canada, receive tax support, depending on how many students select that school. It would open the market, free the family, and enliven the education process (sector) like nothing else. After all, families who need and receive food stamps can turn in their food stamps to a private supermarket, and even buy kosher or halal food, without breaking the law. The important process is to make sure that people don't starve.

Similarly, the purpose of open access to charter schools, and other types of schools, is to ensure that no child goes uneducated, that children learn right from wrong, and that children grow up to be productive, dedicated, active, and moral people. Who can object to that?

COUNTERPOINT: Janet Mulvey
Pace University

C harter schools are public domains and should not be affiliated with religions, religious practices, cultural homogeneity, or curricula influenced by one defined belief. Charter schools should not be affiliated with religious institutions but must remain schools of choice for all denominations, the non-religious, and all ethnic groups. The use of public funds for religious and ethnically homogeneous charter schools not only is illegal, unethical, balkanizing, discriminatory, and undemocratic but also undermines the existence and purpose of public education in the United States.

BACKGROUND

Faith-based schools have a role in U.S. history and were, in fact, the primary source of education in the Colonial era. School access was limited to the more affluent who were able to support their education through private means. The common (public) school became the mainstay of education in the United States in the 1830s, when it was decided that the American populace should have the knowledge necessary to support the democratic process. Schools were soon mandated ("compulsory") for children ages 8–15, and parents were fined if they did not send their children to school. Although the moral basis was always important and standards for curricula were based on the Protestant faith and culture of the time, and the Lord's Prayer opened every school day, religion as such was not formally taught in schools.

Some states such as Oregon made attempts to eliminate all religious, primarily Catholic schools, through compulsory, mandated public education. The Society of Sisters, an order of nuns, challenged the mandate by suing Oregon governor Walter Pierce, bringing the case to the Supreme Court in 1925 in *Pierce v. Society of Sisters* in Oregon. The Court sided with the Society of Sisters, granting parents the right to choose the type of education they wanted for their children. This right allowed choice of schooling without government interference but did not authorize public funding for sectarian education.

LEGAL ARGUMENT

Schools, both public and private, give parents the right to choose the preferred education for their children. Public schools are funded, for the most part, through taxes and other public resources from federal and state government, and local municipalities, while parochial and other private institutions are supported through tuition payment and often from private donations and fund-raising. The funding process has ensured that private schools remain independent from much government influence, traditionally adhering to the First Amendment doctrine of the "separation of church and state" of the U.S. Constitution.

Indeed, the "separation" rationale has a long history that allowed all groups to practice, or not, religious traditions in their own ways. James Madison, often referred to as the Father of the U.S. Constitution, states the importance of separation through the following:

> I must admit . . . it may not be easy to trace the line of separation between the rights of religion and the civil authority with such distinction as to avoid collision and doubts on unessential points. The tendency to usurpation on one side or the other or to a corrupting coalition or alliance between them will be best guarded against by the entire abstinence of the government. (quotation taken from Alley, 1985, pp. 37–94)

Church and state separation cases decided by the courts have made it clear that public institutions should not be the conduits for religious influence. The U.S. Constitution is very clear in its wording and intent: "Congress shall make no laws respecting the establishment of religion, or prohibiting the free exercise thereof."

Reasons

Established in 1789, the Georgia State Constitution declared that every person had the right to worship in his own fashion but also included no obligation to pay tithes, taxes, or "any rate for the building or repairing of any place of worship or for the maintenance of any minister or ministry." Established places of worship are therefore exempt from taxation and do not contribute to the public funds. The government does not benefit from collections and donations given to any place of worship. However, contributions and donations to charitable organizations, including religious establishments, can be used as a deduction on personal income taxes. Thus, it remains resolved that public funds should not be legally used to fund schools that have religious affiliations or partnerships.

ETHICAL ARGUMENT: DILEMMAS AND RELIGIOUS ESTABLISHMENT
Resolve

Charter schools have become a possible choice for parents concerned with the lack of quality education that their children may be receiving in some public schools. Originally, the policy was intended to provide an environment for educational excellence, would be publicly funded, and would operate under the guidelines of the state; now, however, we see that an increasing number of publicly funded charter schools have begun to affiliate with religious and ethnic interests within communities and are receiving support from mosques, churches, and synagogue groups.

Perhaps, one of the most alarming intentions of the unethical use of charter schools is the coalition to eliminate schools. Roxane Premont (2000), director of the North Carolina Education Reform Foundation (NCERF), has proposed that all charter schools become private institutions—using vouchers and tax credits. Premont is quite emphatic in her plan when she states, "We must eliminate public education as it is structured today." In her presentation at the annual Road to Victory, a Christian Coalition conference, in September 2009, Premont outlined the plan to eliminate public schools by

1. establishing charter schools that operate independently of local boards of education;

2. easily converting these schools, after they open, to private and religious schools, once voucher laws are passed; and

3. having those who support religious education initiate the conversion of these charter schools into private schools.

Premont has encouraged Christian Coalition members to use their influence to convert key values taught in religious education to existing public schools. She has argued for weakening teachers' unions or eliminating them altogether by giving teachers the power to deny the need for union affiliation or representation. Once converted, the new charter schools would be able to create their curricula with values that are aligned with religious principles. She has also encouraged her members to run for local school boards and to kill corporate sponsorship, thus conserving power for the cause. In the words of Premont and the Christian Coalition:

> What is called for is an incremental strategy that helps acclimatize the public to school choice readying them for phase two—vouchers. Converting all current existing public schools to charter schools is the necessary transition. The creation of large numbers of charter schools will weaken our union-led opposition—giving us the chance of passing vouchers.

"Once we convert substantial numbers of traditional district-run public schools to charter schools," Premont continued, "the majority of Americans will start to change their paradigm of how schools can be created, where they can be located, and who can run them."

Interestingly, the movement is called an ethical coalition to eliminate schools. How ethical is it to destroy the foundation of education in the United States, the public school, and to attempt to break down the wall of separation that allows all to choose public or religious institutions?

FRACTIONALIZING SOCIETAL STRUCTURES ARGUMENT
Resolved

On January 15, 2009, Richard Kahlenberg wrote,

> For many years liberals were strong supporters of economically, racially and ethnically integrated public schools—schools that would provide equal opportunity to children of all backgrounds and would teach students to be tolerant citizens in a democracy. It was entirely appropriate for parents to instill pride in their ethnic or religious heritage, but the public schools were meant to counterbalance that tendency with efforts to teach children what united us as Americans.

When the New York charter school law was passed in 1998, the statute expressly stated the following mandates: Charter schools (1) may not charge tuition, (2) may not limit the admission of any student on any basis, and (3) may not base their curricula on denominational principles.

Argument

The reality is, too, that many charter schools have disregarded the public choice requirement and have embraced a focus on religion, language, and ethnicity as purposes for creating publicly funded but biased charter schools. Presently, we are beginning to see schools created to address the desires of ethnic and cultural groups to maintain their uniqueness in an otherwise pluralistic society.

Schools representing specific religious groups, ethnic backgrounds, and particular cultural beliefs have been established across the American landscape, changing and challenging the ideals of a common bond and social cohesiveness as a political goal. Although historically the charter school movement has roots in the desire to offer choice as a means for reforming public education—through site-based management and control, magnet schools, community-parent involvement, and empowerment—the loose interpretation of these reforms should not also mean fractionalizing society into homogenous religious enclaves.

Charter schools are one of the fastest-growing reform movements in education today. The support for charters crosses party lines and enjoys approval from federal, state, and local government. Former President Bill Clinton first publicly announced the support for charter schools, calling for the creation of 3,000 charter schools by 2002. In 2002, former President George W. Bush called for $200 million in federal funds to support charter schools and another $100 million for a new Credit Enhancement for Charter School Facilities Program. President Barack Obama continues the rhetoric for education reform and charter schools. In his education plan speech (March 10, 2009), Obama argued clearly that "state limits on numbers of charter schools aren't good for our children, our economy or our country."

The general support for charters is contained in their original intent and promise: to allow parents and students to escape failing public schools. It was hoped that improved programs and educational opportunities would help diversify the demographics of segregated schools and communities. How, then, can we justify stratification and fractionalization along ethnic and religious lines?

A review by the National Alliance for Public Charter Schools found that of 4,600 charters nationwide, at least 113 are specifically targeted toward language, ethnic, and cultural themes. Many of these schools have come under scrutiny; some have been or are being challenged in the courts as religious, publicly funded schools.

For example, both the Amber Charter School in Manhattan and the Eugenio María de Hostos Charter School in Rochester, New York, focus on the Spanish culture and language. In Hollywood, Florida, the four Ben Gamla Charter Schools teach Hebrew and Jewish culture, while the Tarek ibn Ziyad Academy (TiZA) stresses modern Arabic and is supported by Islamic organizations in Minnesota. The Pioneer Valley Chinese Immersion Charter School teaches Chinese, and the Hellenic Classical Charter School focuses on modern Greek language and culture.

Many of these schools, while they claim "open" enrollment, are, in fact, more homogenous than not, and have religious overtones in their curricula. As new charter schools continue to emerge that are supported by sectarian and ethnic interests and political agendas, one wonders how the landscape of a diverse society will really become more fractionalized and focused on narrow ideals and how this change can serve the greater interest of the United States.

Reviews on the emergence of new charters have found specific alignment with religious, ethnic, or cultural ideals. The evidence is clear that the promise for choice of more integrated schools has been broken and we are seeing cultural, language, and religious belief systems that segregate themselves into enclaves that prohibit the integrative quality for which they were first intended.

Take, for example, the Khalil Gibran International Academy in Brooklyn. Registered as a public school, it includes Middle Eastern studies and focuses on the Arabic culture. The intent in opening the school was to make Arab students feel at home in the United States. Ben Gamla in Florida defends its charter status by denying the charges of homogeneity and religious affiliation, claiming a focus on Hebrew and Jewish culture. A demographic study reveals the school does, in fact, enroll a small number of black and Hispanic students; but the school's students are not representative of the population in the county. Ben Gamla does enroll more than 86% white students of Jewish background, contradicting its declaration of real cultural and religious diversity.

Tarek ibn Ziyad Academy in Minnesota and Nampa Classical Academy in Idaho offer two more examples of balkanization through the creation of charters that focus on defined populations with narrow perspectives on culture and beliefs. TiZA describes its mission on its website, stating that it "recognizes and appreciates the traditions, histories, civilizations and accomplishments of the eastern world (Africa, Asia and Middle East)." Mandated dress codes, special dietary requirements, and worship offer insight into the intent of the school that is in direct contradiction to the public, nonsectarian purposes of charter schools.

Nampa Classical Academy, one of the largest charter schools in Idaho, offers a similar situation by adopting the Bible as its main text and following the tenets from the Hillsdale Academy, a private Christian day school in Michigan. Bewailing the works of renowned educators such as John Dewey, Jean Piaget, and Howard Gardner, the founder of the school, Isaac Moffett, explains his philosophy: "We are not a liberal school, we're not . . . liberal may be too strong a word. We are a *conservative* school" (Hoffman, 2009). Moffett strongly defends the academy's curricula of Latin texts and Bible and explains that

> teachers will also discuss where America has failed to live up to its principles and to explore why Native Americans were conquered so easily. Reading into his remarks and background, one is convinced that those who embrace the Evangelical belief system are welcome into the school. (Hoffman, 2009)

Discrimination in Charter Schools

Deborah Meier (2002) remarks, "Variety (among schools) needs to be balanced by the acknowledgement that there exist a larger community . . . it is in our public schools that we learned the art of living together as citizens" (p. 176). Schools in the public sector are already segregated, especially in urban areas. The 1954 *Brown v. Board of Education* Supreme Court decision to integrate schools has been eroded to the point where apartheid is alive and well in many of America's schools. Washington, D.C., Chicago, Cleveland, and New York are just some of the cities where schools are so segregated that diversity is like the proverbial needle in a haystack.

For example, Gary Orfield (2002) wrote, "American public schools are now 12 years into the process of continuous resegregation . . . During the 1990s, the proportion of black students in majority white schools has decreased . . . to a level lower than in any year since 1968." And, the active creation of charter schools in the United States has, unfortunately, exacerbated the segregatory nature of the education, with separation occurring by race, ethnicity, culture, and religion. Charter schools based on homogeneous principles attract like-minded participants and decry the fact that they often discriminate because they claim to allow open enrollments. Common sense argues, however, that non-Jews, non-Muslims, and/or non-Christians are unlikely to be attracted to schools identified with specific philosophies, ethnicities, and religious cultures. Charter schools attempt to circumvent the original intent of charters with questionable practices that seem acceptable in application but are discriminatory in reality.

If the intent of charter schools is to destroy the public school system, as proposed by the Christian Coalition and political leaders Jerry Falwell and Pat

Robertson, what is the result for our democracy? How can tolerance and acceptance be actually fostered in communities segregated by race, ethnicity, culture, and religion? Can we grow as a society while disenfranchising and disassociating with each other? What would be the result if we took all the money granted to charter school laws and reinvested it in a public school system for all? By continuing to embrace private institutions' rights to continue free exercise of choice, but without public funding, would we resolve the legal, ethical, and discriminatory practices? Would we return to the true ideals of democracy?

President Barack Obama in his speech to the graduating class in Ann Arbor, Michigan (May 1, 2010), asked, "And so now, class of 2010, the question for your generation is this: How will you keep our democracy going? At a moment when our challenges seem so big and our politics seem so small, how will you keep our democracy alive and vibrant; how will you keep it well in this century?" Is excellence in public schooling part of the answer, without diverting resources to divisive ventures?

FURTHER READINGS AND RESOURCES

Alley, R. S. (Ed.). (1985). *James Madison on religious liberty.* New York: Prometheus Books.

Bailey, M. H., & Cooper, B. S. (2009). The introduction of religious charter schools: A cultural movement in the private school sector. *Journal of Research on Christian Education, 18*(3), 272–289.

Carnoy, M., Jacobsen, R., Mishel, L., & Rothstein, R. (2005). *The charter school dust-up: Examining the evidence on enrollment and achievement.* Washington, DC: Economic Policy Institute and New York: Teachers College Press.

Carper, J., & Hunt, T. (2008). *The dissenting tradition in American education.* New York: Peter Lang.

Cattaro, G. M., & Cooper, B. S. (2007). Developments in Catholic schools in the USA: Politics, policy, and prophecy. In G. R. Grace & J. O'Keefe (Eds.), *International handbook of Catholic education: Challenges for school systems in the 21st century* (pp. 61–83). London & New York: Springer.

Cooper, B. S. (2008). *Home schooling in full view.* Charlotte, NC: Information Age.

Cooper, B. S., McSween, R., & Murphy, P. (in press). Finding a golden mean in education: Centering religious and public schools. *Peabody Journal of Education.*

Frankenberg, E., & Lee, C. (2003). Charter schools and race: A lost opportunity for integrated education. *Education Policy Analysis Archives, 11*(32). Retrieved from http://epaa.asu.edu/ojs/article/view/260

Hoffman, N. (2009, July 8). Charter school walks church, state line. *Boise Weekly.* Retrieved from http://www.boiseweekly.com/boise/classical-class/Content?oid=1098884

Hoxby, C. M. (2007, June). *The effects of New York City's charter schools on student achievement.* Cambridge, MA: New York City Charter Schools Evaluation Project.

Kahlenberg, R. (2009). *Taking note: The problem with ethnic charter schools.* Retrieved from http://takingnote.tcf.org/2009/01/the-problem-with-ethnic-charter-schools.html

Meier, D. (2002). *In schools we trust: Creating communities of learning in an era of testing and standardization.* Boston: Beacon Press.

Michaelsen, R. (1970). *Piety in the public school.* New York: Macmillan Press.

Mulvey, J., Cooper, B. S., & Maloney, A. (in press). *Blurring the lines between church and state in education.* Charlotte, NC: Information Age.

National Alliance for Public Charter Schools: http://www.publiccharters.org

Newport, F. (2011, June 3). *More than 9 in 10 Americans continue to believe in God.* Princeton, NJ: Gallup Poll.

Nord, W. A. (1995). *Religion and American education: Rethinking a national dilemma.* Chapel Hill: University of North Carolina Press.

Orfield, G. (2002). *The Civil Rights Project.* Retrieved from http://www.civilrightsproject.ucla.edu

Premont, R. (2000). As quoted in "*Charter schools*" *a ruse for destroying public education?* Retrieved from http://www.sullivan-county.com/nf0/nov_2000/char_sch.htm

Remarks by the President at University of Michigan Spring Commencement. (2010). Retrieved from http://www.whitehouse.gov/the-press-office/remarks-president-university-michigan-spring-commencement

U.S. Department of Education, National Center for Education Statistics. (2011). *The condition of education 2011.* Washington, DC: Author. Retrieved from http://nces.ed.gov/pubs2011/2011033.pdf

COURT CASES AND STATUTES

Almontaser v. New York City Department of Education, EEOC Charge No. 520-2008-02337 (March 9, 2010).

Brown v. Board of Education of Topeka, 347 U.S. 483 (1954).

Elementary and Secondary Education Act, P.L. 89–10, 20 U.S.C. § 6301 *et seq.* (1965).

Georgia State Constitution. (1789). Retrieved from http://www.boldhearts.com/georgia.htm

Pierce v. Society of Sisters, 268 U.S. 510 (1925).

Zelman v. Simmons-Harris, 536 U.S. 639 (2002).

Are culturally specific charter schools an appropriate means of preserving Muslim identity?

POINT: Letitia Basford, *Hamline University*

COUNTERPOINT: Martha Bigelow, *University of Minnesota*

OVERVIEW

"Tradition vs. Modern Education," reads the headline of a *New York Times* article (Yardley, 2011). It refers to two factions of Muslim students on either side of a dusty road in Akkalkuwa, India. On one side are a group of skullcapped youngsters studying ancient Muslim texts; on the other side, only 50 feet away, are a group of young professionals who are hunched over their computers preparing for what they call the real world. The divergence lies in the hermeneutical understanding of what a Muslim education ought to provide: Should education of young Muslims make available a curriculum that is existential, or would a more moderate curriculum be appropriate as these young people take their place in this world? The paradox of bridging the divide between a traditional religious education and modern education is a quagmire that many faith-based institutions face as they enter into the charter school world. In the case of religious schools, there must be justification as to what requirements must be addressed and what the cost will be to a religious identity. The argument lies in culture versus intentionality. The culture of the school may indeed reflect the philosophical components of the expectations of a Muslim education, but the intentionality will address the theology of the school. Educational goals such as good citizenship, learning to get along with others, developing skills in reading, and developing skills for work are generic objectives that may fold into a philosophical expectation of such schools. The question then becomes whether proponents of Muslim charter schools seek to provide a madrassa, that is, a religious-based school, or whether they simply want to provide a school that emphasizes the philosophy of Muhammad. The quest is crucial to the debate concerning culturally specific charter schools as an appropriate means of preserving Muslim identity. If the school is to teach the Koran as a canon, then religious identity of the school is paramount. In fact, "for Muslim teachers, the primary motive for engaging in teaching ought to be reflecting a sense of seeking the pleasure of God as they are emulating one of His actions and fulfilling His orders" (Mogra, 2010, p. 319).

The religious identity then becomes a distinctive quality that enables the school to share in the belief system by fostering the faith of those in attendance. This becomes evidenced in the physical environment and climate of the school and in all of the practices and policies that direct the daily activities and operation of the school and imbue it with its confessional identity.

The initial openness of religious leaders, to convert some of their schools into faith-based charter schools, may well have been propelled by the superficial similarities between the two systems and the positive assistance, which both can continue to offer in local faith-based communities. Along with these attributes, other external structures in the organization of public charter schools such as adaptability and flexibility find a greater fit in the religious school culture while likewise adding to their isomorphic natures. In this regard, an argument may be made that charter schools are flexible enough to offer religious objectives in educational programming.

On closer examination, though, it appears that the external organizational features of proposed faith-based charter schools only mimic the organizational domains of religiously affiliated nonpublic schools. Such a situation creates a false panacea for those who wish to serve underrepresented populations in faith-based institutions since they might be described as "religious schools lite," schools constructed around religious themes broadly but that, based on the judicial analyses, cannot include teaching of a particular faith as long as they receive public funds. Faith-based charter schools cannot operate "with no strings attached." Moreover, as legal controversies emerge, conflicts will arise in such key areas as governance and curricular content.

Charter schools may offer a secular education; the question then becomes, what is a Muslim culture? The Muslim faith, as lived out in Morocco, Malaysia, Pakistan, India, Saudi Arabia, and so on, is a different experience in each of the cultural paradigms. The global encounter of the Muslim faith has blurred identity lines similar to the question, who is a Jew? *Sirat al-Mustaqeem*, also known as "the straight path" (Zine, 2001, p. 399), is a challenge to today's Muslim youth as it presents a struggle that is both spiritual and existential (Zine, 2001). Living in two worlds is highlighted in the tension expressed in *The New York Times* article (Yardley, 2011), in which Shahid Siddiqui, editor of *Nai Duniya,* an Urdu language newspaper, is quoted as saying, "People are tired of the old ways," compounded by a statement of the economist Abusaleh Shariff, who has coauthored a major study of Muslims in defense of secular schools. Shariff professes that Muslims do not want ghettoism in education.

The debate by our contributing authors, Letitia Basford (Hamline University) and Martha Bigelow (University of Minnesota), becomes paramount on what normally may appear as a nonissue. Basford, who supports culturally sensitive schools, bases her argument on Muslim youth who are counterculture to many Western fads. She also explores the important issues of self-concept and identity. Her essay points to the fact that such Muslim charter schools are indeed needed as they support the foundation of Muslim culture, thus providing a positive model for young Muslims. Her observations are geared not only to the United States but to the diaspora in Anglo countries espousing Western thought. Accordingly, based upon her own research, she cites that building a good self-concept is tandem to the experiences in culturally sensitive Muslim schools whose culture reflects and is sensitive to the Muslim faith.

Conversely, Bigelow notes in her essay that the concept of Muslim culturally specific schools is not the way to go if we are to develop a healthy identity among young Muslims. She states that the charter school, because of its true nature, is a public school and, therefore, not the way to go as it does not allow the students to construct a deep understanding of their faith. If need be, she writes, the students should look to role models within their family and religious community.

As you read these essays, you should think about issues of separation of church and state that would restrict a charter school in its mission of preserving Muslim identity. Is it possible to separate the cultural values from the religious values of Muslim families? What safeguards would need to be put in place to ensure that the line from accommodation to proselytizing is not crossed?

Gerald M. Cattaro
Fordham University

POINT: Letitia Basford
Hamline University

Since the first charter school was established in the United States in 1991, support for charter schools has grown rapidly. A charter school is an independent public school of choice, freed from the rules of traditional mainstream public schools but held accountable for results. In other words, in exchange for having a great deal of curricular and structural independence, charters may be revoked if they do not meet certain performance goals, which vary from state to state. Unlike most mainstream public schools, charter schools are typically created around a particular educational purpose (e.g., technology, medical careers, arts), and often cater to the specific interests of a community.

A growing phenomenon in the United States is culturally specific charter schools, which seek to integrate the celebration of cultural, ethnic, linguistic, or philosophical concepts into the educational process. In Minnesota, for example, more than 30 of the state's 138 charter schools are culturally specific in orientation. For an increasing number of minority or immigrant groups, what makes these schools appealing is that, unlike public schools, charter schools can be created by almost anyone and are specifically chosen by the families of children who attend. These communities can therefore create schools that better accommodate their cultural values and beliefs. In addition, they might hope that these schools accommodate their religious practices, as well. This is especially appealing to Muslim communities who may be uncomfortable with the culture or curriculum of mainstream public schools. Some Muslim communities would like to foster a Muslim identity among their children partially through their schooling experiences. While these charter schools, by law, cannot offer religious instruction, culturally specific charter schools can offer an "Islamic" environment by virtue of the students they serve.

All charter schools, as public schools, are strictly bound to the Establishment Clause in the First Amendment of the U.S. Constitution and thus cannot offer parents the choice of religious orientation in schooling. So, while a culturally specific charter school may call itself "religiously supportive," school administrators and teachers may *not* organize, enforce, or even encourage students to, for example, pray, eat, act, or dress in a specific way. That said, the Establishment Clause allows for the government, and therefore *all* public schools, to "reasonably" accommodate religious beliefs (*Board of Education v. Grumet*, 1994, p. 706). Therefore, students are permitted to engage in religious practices when not engaged in school activities or instruction.

It is important to note that many of the culturally specific charter schools that draw Muslim students are simultaneously drawing students from a particular culture or immigrant group. It is difficult to separate culture from religion for Muslims when so many daily practices of eating and prayer, holidays, and ways of dressing are explained by religious doctrine. That said, it is important to note that cultural practices vary across regions of the world and among nations with large Muslim populations. For example, a Muslim woman from Malaysia may dress differently than a Muslim woman from Somalia. While they share a common religion, their religious practices vary across cultures. A culturally specific charter school that serves primarily Muslim children might, for example, be created by an East African community with the specific intentions of serving mostly, but legally not exclusively, Somali Muslim youth. The school might have a Somali-led school board, a Somali coadministrator, and several East Africa–born teachers and educational assistants. Some of the religious accommodations the school might offer to its students are *halal* meals, gender-segregated gym and health classes, prayer times and facilities, presence of community members and elders sitting in the hallways, and Arabic lessons. None of these accommodations violates the Establishment Clause as long as school personnel are not mandating religious practices among students. In fact, these accommodations follow the Establishment Clause because they permit students the freedom to practice their religion.

For this debate, this essay focuses on charter schools that primarily draw Muslim students and argue that such a culturally specific charter school helps students develop a Muslim identity.

DEVELOPING A MUSLIM IDENTITY

Culturally specific charter schools are an appropriate means of preserving Muslim identity. Research has continued to show that traditional public schools in the West are failing Muslim youth. Muslim youth find themselves in schools that offer them little to no support with which to nurture their religious identities—identities that continue to be largely scrutinized and unaccepted by teachers and peers alike in a post–9/11 society. A culturally specific charter school for Muslim youth promotes positive socialization where students are able to build a good self-concept and be comfortable with who they are as Muslims. By attending a school that is supportive of and sensitive to students' religious practices, youth are better able to maintain their faith and moral values, improve their academic success, preserve their ties to their family and community, and develop confidence in a healthy Muslim identity.

Muslim Youth in Traditional Public Schools

Studies from around the Western world reveal that Muslim youth are experiencing an identity crisis in schools. Schools in Canada are described as "alienating" to Muslim adolescents, and students feel confused and dissonant in them. British schools have been described as "unfriendly" and "intimidating" toward Muslim students, leaving youth to feel segregated and silent. Belgian schools are reportedly excluding their Muslim youth, who feel ostracized and discriminated against. Yemeni Muslim immigrants in U.S. schools are portrayed as "depressed," "desperate," and "living in ambiguity." David Gilbert (2004) summarizes these perspectives about the failing relationship between Western schools and Muslim students by stating that "schools and teachers maintain a powerful prejudicial discourse, immersed in unequal power relationships, where [Muslim] students are, at best, misunderstood, and, at worst, deliberately discriminated against" (p. 253). What lies behind this distressing consensus?

A place to start answering this important question surrounds the nature of how Muslim youth find themselves in direct conflict with the dominant status quo culture within Western society and schools. While rapidly changing student demographics have challenged the relevance and efficacy of long-standing administrative, curricular, instructional, and evaluative practices, many of which were developed for homogeneous nation-states, schools in the West continue to be predominantly oriented toward students who are white and Christian. Based on Western values, Western schools expect that all students be treated equally, that all children be given the same mainstream curricula, and that all students behave and respond to schools' practices in the same way—regardless of culture. In this way, schools become key sites for the production of culture and reproduction in American society—places where white, Christian dominant cultures and values are transmitted, and where the freedom to express and practice a nondominant religion, like Islam, is resisted.

Many Muslim immigrant groups locate their primary identities in their religion, not their countries of origin. While understanding that Muslim youth practice Islam to varying degrees, religious traditions are often strongly reinforced by the parents in the home, and youth are often raised to practice Islam as a comprehensive way of life. By practicing an Islamic faith-centered lifestyle, certain practices are expected, for example, adhering to modest dress, prayer time, and fasting during Ramadan. (During the month of Ramadan, otherwise known as *Sawm,* Muslims are to fast from dawn to dusk, express their gratitude and nearness to God, be mindful of their sins, and think of the needy.) In their desire to live in accordance to the literal rules of the Koran, Muslim youth are often portrayed in the literature as conflicted about the social norms and culture of schools in the West. Muslim youth have been found to be in a precarious position, where conforming to Muslim cultural values constitutes a deviation from dominant cultural norms in the West, yet conforming to dominant cultural norms challenges Eastern cultural values. Surrounded by religious discrimination and ignorance, and struggling to deal with the perceptions of their peers, teachers, family, community, and dominant society, as well as their own perceptions of themselves, Muslim youth may feel forced to compromise their Islamic values when confronted daily by the pressures to assimilate to Western cultural norms and expectations. These norms and expectations that play out in dominant societal discourses at work in mainstream schools often leave Muslim youth feeling misunderstood and marginalized. As a result, school adjustment continues to be one of the greatest challenges for Muslim youth.

Muslim Youth in Culturally Specific Charter Schools

As a response to these challenges and in an effort to maintain their religious and ethnic identity, Muslim communities have begun to create specialized schools, such as "culturally specific" charter schools, that give attention to youths' culture, religion, language, and history. While culturally specific charter schools for Muslim youth are a relatively new phenomenon and have been minimally studied, positive reports have been published thus far. *The New York Times* reported that these kinds of charter schools are offering Muslim parents a stronger voice in their children's education (Rimer, 2009). Parents see these charter schools as "safe havens" from traditional public schools, a place where youth are protected from rapid and sometimes negative assimilation. The article highlighted that culturally specific schools allow students to maintain both an American and a Somali/Muslim identity.

A study conducted at an East African charter high school in Minnesota revealed similar findings. Reporting on a two-year qualitative case study, Letitia Basford (2010a, 2010b) found that Kalsami Charter High School (a pseudonym) promoted positive socialization where students were able to build a good self-concept and find comfort in who they are as East African immigrants and as Muslims while they also established their identity as American citizens. The study's participants described feeling ostracized and discriminated against in traditional schools for taking part in practices such as praying, fasting, and wearing a hijab. Viewed through a deficit lens by both teachers and peers, youth were perceived as culturally "different," as religiously "oppressed" or "fanatic," and as suspicious and threatening beings. Some participants came to internalize these messages and reflect such images in their own behavior. With little motivation to do well or stay in school, and with dwindling faith in U.S.

society's ability to see them as hardworking, honest, valuable contributors, these youth became ostracized by the dominant American society, as well as by their own community.

This destructive process appeared to reverse when youth transferred to the culturally specific charter school. By attending a school that was supportive of and sensitive to students' cultural and religious practices, youth at Kalsami were able to maintain their faith and moral values, maintain their ties to their family and community, and develop confidence in their abilities to become full and equal members of U.S. society. In other words, the school appeared to serve as a kind of buffer between the values, beliefs, and practices of their culture and the overwhelming process of trying to fit in with the dominant society. This buffer served to slow down the pressure on youth to rapidly assimilate into the more dominant culture of mainstream schools. Instead of feeling shame about their Muslim-ness, this religiously supportive learning environment allowed youth to instead embrace and explore their religion and culture in healthy, meaningful ways. As a result, youth felt better able to preserve their Muslim identity than they did while attending traditional public schools.

Similar to current observations that people in schools choose to speak as though race does not matter, religious differences are also frequently muted in traditional public schools. In an environment where teachers and peers feel hesitant or reluctant to talk about issues of religion, the potential of a worsened acceptance becomes likely because religious accommodations and important discussions about religion remain misunderstood and unexamined. In a culturally specific charter school, youth are more likely to be given the opportunity to safely share their religion and religious views with others. For example, teachers may design curricula that give youth the opportunity to explore their history, culture, and religion. The school may provide students with a daily schedule that includes optional breaks for prayer, designated prayer rooms, *halal* meals, and gender-segregated gym and health classes. Students can openly and comfortably practice their religious and cultural ways while in school without fear of scrutiny from peers or school staff. When students perceive that their religion and culture is both accepted and understood, youth are more likely to feel like they truly belong and are valued in their school. As a result, a culturally specific charter school can offer Muslim youth a milieu where they can develop a strengthened confidence and autonomy about their religious identity.

The Benefits of a Religious Identity

Based on standardized test scores, grades, and continuation rates in school, research has shown that a stronger religious identity has positive effects on academic achievement. Studies have shown that religious involvement predicts higher educational expectations, less truancy, and lower dropout rates. Religious involvement appears to reinforce and further develop the kinds of skills and character traits that translate to improved school behavior. For example, a child who learns how to show respect for his religious tutor may use those same skills toward his K–12 teacher. A dedicated religious practice may transfer to a strong work ethic in school. Furthermore, the mosque or church serves as an advocate for schools, reinforcing the message that education is important and children should stay in school.

These positive religious effects are especially important for youth living in high-poverty/high-crime neighborhoods. Youth in these neighborhoods are more susceptible to developing oppositional attitudes and behaviors that work against academic success. Research has shown that maintenance of one's cultural and religious identity plays an important role in the academic success and attitudes of students (Qin-Hillard, 2003). A culturally specific charter school that supports a student's religious identity may offer youth a kind of refuge from deviant peer pressure and negative influences. Students are more likely to reduce contact with oppositional peers and spend more time with religiously engaged and academically challenged youth. The Kalsami study revealed that several participants from high-poverty backgrounds were able to shed their previous images as oppositional youth when they transferred to the culturally specific charter school. Youth were offered a second chance to succeed academically because Kalsami provided them with a safe and religiously supportive environment away from the negative influences in their neighborhoods.

A strengthened religious identity also improves youths' relationships with their parents and community. Shared religious participation serves as a connection between children and their parents/community and, as a result, serves to close an intergenerational gap. In turn, this provides youth with social capital, defined here as one's access to resources through reciprocal social networks. Social capital has been shown to contribute to academic achievement.

By attending a culturally specific charter school for Muslim youth, students are attending a school that includes a strong sense of shared mission and values by parents, teachers, and administrators. Parents and community members are more likely to feel invested in their child's school and, as a result, become more actively involved in their child's education. Because some youth may attend the same mosque and school, parents and community members may feel an increased social control over their child and an enhanced socialization into the religious values they share. They may also feel like they have better ties to their children, as well as their children's friends.

CONCLUSION

Schools are central places for youth to explore the meaning of their own identities. Public schools are faced with enormous challenges of educating all students while demonstrating necessary ways to accommodate their cultural and religious identities. While almost all adolescents face a varying amount of social pressure in school, Muslim youth face even greater pressures that include religious misunderstanding and discrimination. This additional pressure puts Muslim youth at great risk for academic failure, social alienation, and oppositional behavior. Many Muslim communities are deciding, at least for now, that culturally specific charter schools may be better able to meet their children's needs. By attending a school that is supportive of, and sensitive to, students' cultural and religious practices, youth are better able to develop confidence in their academic abilities, maintain their ties to their family and community, and feel like a valued member of their school community. Youth are able to feel confident and secure in their religious identity, and better able to challenge and assert themselves in U.S. society.

COUNTERPOINT: Martha Bigelow
University of Minnesota

There are numerous ways culturally specific charter schools can offer Muslim students a powerful and effective schooling experience, but they cannot preserve a Muslim identity. This stance assumes that culture and religion can somehow be separated—a tall order when cultures that are predominantly of a single religion intertwine everything from daily routines to major holidays with their belief system. However, in a formal school setting, if religion and preserving/developing a religious identity is not part of the mission of the school, the school setting is a far more unlikely place for the difficult identity work to occur than home or community settings where religion is fully sanctioned, debated, and practiced.

Students who are religiously minoritized in a large mainstream school may find positive adult role models in a culturally specific charter school. Additionally, these charter schools may have more parental involvement because parents may be more comfortable talking with school personnel about their child's academic work, communicating with school personnel in languages other than English, and volunteering at school in a range of capacities. In these nontraditional settings, students and parents may be able to use any or all of the languages they speak because they are in school with same-culture peers and adults who speak their languages and understand their culture(s). In many ways, being in a culturally specific school can be a relief to children and their families who have felt extremely minoritized in mainstream schools due to their religion. In a culturally specific charter school, Muslim youth and families tend to feel at ease because they are no longer culturally different from their peers and are given the environment to focus on their academic development, not on, for example, what they eat or what they wear. These schools can be very good academically for children who have been ignored, marginalized, or mistreated in mainstream schools. The educational community and the wider public should view culturally specific charter schools as places where much learning can take place. These schools are, however, not appropriate places to support a Muslim identity. Muslim students and families should not expect to develop or sustain a Muslim identity in a charter school that is geared toward students from a culture in which Islam is practiced.

ARGUMENTS AGAINST CULTURALLY SPECIFIC CHARTER SCHOOLS

The arguments against culturally specific charter schools as sites for supporting a Muslim identity are multiple. First, charter schools are publicly funded and are not legally permitted to sponsor religious teaching of any sort. (Of course, students' rights to practice their religion are protected under this same constitutional provision.) Second, the development of a Muslim identity is not the responsibility of a school. The belief that identity can be formed in school is narrow. Rather, religious identity is developed mainly in contexts outside of school, and over long periods of time. Third, because culturally specific charter schools are typically formed by leaders in immigrant communities, there is a risk that they are seeking a particular sort of schooling that provides the context for a particular sort of Muslim identity. Thinking of culturally specific charter schools as places where Muslim identity is a predetermined and static category does not leave room for youth to construct their own identities. Fourth, a context in which most students share a religion does not guarantee the development of a religious identity. While it is recognized that such schools may support conformity to religious practices such as not eating pork and wearing modest attire, these practices may not link to deep and meaningful religious beliefs, upon which an identity must be based. These arguments will now be explored in greater depth.

DEVELOPING MUSLIM IDENTITY AND THE SEPARATION OF CHURCH AND STATE

The role of schools in supporting a Muslim identity can only be tacit in nature due to the strict separation of church and state in the United States. If we give credit to schools for participating in the development of a religious identity, this may be a violation of the Establishment Clause in the First Amendment of the U.S. Constitution. Often it is misunderstood that the Establishment Clause focuses on preventing religion from influencing the state, but, in fact, it is the reverse. The Establishment Clause keeps the government out of religious affairs and prevents it from establishing one religion over others (as was done in England). As such, government-run public schools are not in a position to promote any one religion, nor do they have adequate background to influence religious values. It is beyond the capacity of the public school and should not be attempted. This does not mean that religious understanding, study, respect, and even tolerance of religious observances must be restricted. However, as a caveat, a close analysis may find that in practice the separation of church and state doctrine singles out minoritized religions, because mainstream religions (such as those following any of the branches of Christianity) are accommodated by mainstream public schooling (e.g., Christmas is a holiday, no school on Sundays). While publically funded schools cannot promote religion, they can play an important role in constructing other sorts of identities such as academic and vocational identities through students' experiences in learning. However, with regard to religion, schools are permitted to only accommodate students if they wish to practice their faith.

Accommodating Muslim students in their right to pray at specific times, wear modest clothes, or eat only religiously permitted foods does not support the complex work of developing a religious identity. A Muslim identity is multifaceted and is shaped over time in myriad ways over the span of an individual's life. Muslim youth may embrace an Islamic way of life and develop a Muslim identity through activities such as Koranic study, personal introspection, family role models, participation in religious holidays, and a wide range of community religious practices. Some youth have the experience of returning to their countries of origin or other Muslim countries to explore or regain this sense of being Muslim. Being Muslim, believing in the tenets of Islam, and living an Islamic lifestyle are all rights protected under U.S. law;

however, a Muslim identity is far too complex to be left to the responsibility of a culturally specific, but secular, charter school. Publically funded schools are charged with delivering a standards-based curriculum, not a religious identity. The formation of a Muslim identity is acquired through (inter)personal activities associated with being Muslim, being a member of a Muslim community, and being a part of a Muslim family.

One may wonder, then, if a private Islamic school would be able to foster a religious identity. If school, in general, only has partial influence on the development of a child, and if religion is only part of the schooling mission, how could any school foster a religious identity? It seems that a private Islamic school has the potential to play a greater role in developing a religious identity because it can freely and wholly embrace and advocate for religious views and practices. Islamic perspectives and practices are also espoused as part of the schooling mission, and families and students are made aware of the religious mission of the school. In a private Islamic school, religious beliefs and practices can be explicitly promoted. For example, a private Islamic school in Texas (Al-Hadi School of Accelerative Learning) names the following as part of its mission on the front page of its website:

> We aim to provide an Islamic environment for all students, enabling them to acquire academic excellence and Islamic morals to prepare them to become viable individuals able to meet the challenges of our changing world.

In contrast, a public charter school cannot promote this mission and therefore is unable to create a coherent and effective vision for promoting a religious identity. The following is an example from the website of an East African charter school (Minnesota International Middle School):

> This public charter school ultimately seeks to prepare students for successful and productive lives as United States citizens while allowing them to retain their unique cultural heritage.

There is a vast difference between acquiring "Islamic morals" and retaining a "unique cultural heritage." The private school can focus its mission on religion in thoughtful and deliberate ways while the publically funded charter school can only attempt to respond to the general and amorphous cultural heritage of its students. In sum, schools of any sort are only one of the many contexts Islamic children and youth occupy in the course of their daily routines, and therefore have varying and possibly haphazard potential to influence students. But when compared to a private school, charter schools have decidedly weak leverage or potential to promote Muslim identities.

SHAPING A MUSLIM IDENTITY

Muslim identities may be shaped by more powerful discursive means than simply a tacit school climate. For example, Muslim identity is also shaped among young people as they see themselves represented in and by the media. Unfortunately, the media can be a powerful source of anti-Islamic views and even Islamophobia. Muslim youth understand that there are many images and (mis)conceptions of them and their families in the wider public. Muslim children's identity can be shaped by their interactions with people in their daily lives. These interactions are informed by the wider society, including the media coverage of "the Muslim world." Positive and negative representations of Islam and Muslims in the media facilitate the development of a Muslim identity either in opposition to or through embracing images of Muslim identity. For instance, a Muslim woman in the West who formerly chose not to veil may choose to veil in the current political climate, which is anti-Muslim. This choice may be due in part to the desire to educate non-Muslims about Islam and dispel stereotypes. Conversely, a Muslim woman in the West who veiled before the attacks of September 11, 2001, may choose not to veil after the attacks because of fear of discrimination. These larger discourses are powerful delimiters of Muslim identity and reach far beyond the experiences they may have in culturally specific charter schools, which are mandated by law to not sponsor religion.

Given the powerful role of family, community, and society in shaping the varied and politically contextualized identities of Muslim youth, it is not feasible to rely on culturally specific charter schools to enact this process of identity development. It often seems that community leaders and parents are at the nexus of the creation of culturally specific charter schools. In the case of culturally specific charter schools in Muslim communities, it is important to consider whether the founders of the charter schools have a limited, traditional, or constrained view of what it means to be Muslim in the United States. Are their motivations and views based on how they grew up in a largely Muslim society or as a member of a minoritized and possibly feared religious or cultural group? It is important to question who is invested in the preservation of a Muslim identity in the consideration of whether a charter school can foster a Muslim identity. An adult agenda does not necessarily transpose easily to an agenda youth are willing to endorse or authorize.

Identity in individuals is multiple by nature. The identity of an individual may include a primary identity marker that could be imposed or selected (e.g., American, Mexican, Somali) and often includes race, class, and gender, in addition to a religious identity. If a culturally specific charter school is designed to promote a Muslim identity, how do these other identity markers intersect with religion? Which identity markers prevail over others in terms of significance in a young person's life? Does the conceptualization of Muslim identity include new views or ways of being Muslim that blend cultures and identities? Identity is something that is multidimensional and situational. The identity markers that youth choose to highlight shift across settings. Youth may wish to highlight a religious identity at school, but not at work, or in the community, but not at school. This may cause them to dress or act differently even during the course of one day. Identity changes over time as youth embrace, transform, and reject different parts of who they want to be and who they were. Immigrant youth, for example, may come to the United States with a strong sense of national identity (e.g., Kenyan), and this may shift to a more racialized identity (e.g., African American).

ROLE OF CHARTER SCHOOLS

Public charter schools are places where students should develop identities as capable learners, as producers of knowledge, as readers, as thinkers. This is the role of publicly funded schools in the United States, including culturally specific charter schools; and this is a role that is within their expertise to enact. Fostering an academic identity can be part of a mission statement, part of focused staff development, and promoted through the school curriculum. This sort of identity formation has the potential to result of outcomes. Promoting a religious identity in this learning context does not have the potential to materialize, at least not in any planned way. The complicated nature of identity and the potential for an adult-imposed religious identity of a particular type that does not include the actual lives of youth are major barriers to promoting a religious identity in a culturally specific charter school. Furthering a Muslim identity only through the fact that the learning environment includes students from Muslim families (not the curriculum, not the mission of the school) is likely to be ineffectual.

The assumption that being with other Muslim students will help youth hold on to or develop a Muslim identity places too much emphasis on the power of peer pressure to make a person more Muslim. While peer pressure undoubtedly exists at culturally specific schools, as it does everywhere, this is not sufficient for preserving a Muslim identity. One may feel pressured to eat, pray, or dress a certain way because everyone else is doing it, but this alone is not enough to shape anything more than an action or a practice. In culturally specific Muslim schools, nobody can be forced or coerced into praying, following a dress code, or not eating certain food. If students follow these religious practices because of peer pressure, there is no guarantee that these practices translate into a healthy and well-developed religious identity. Part of a strong religious identity is based on powerful convictions, affiliations with others of the same religion, and many personal decisions that align with religious beliefs and communities. While the freedom to carry out religious practices at school without fear of being ostracized is a characteristic of culturally specific charter schools, one cannot argue that by enacting these religious practices one is developing a deep, multifaceted, informed religious identity.

Finally, and importantly, does being with classmates only from one ethnicity or culture prepare students for work or further schooling in an increasingly diverse society? Or, perhaps more urgently, does this setting prepare students for a society with power structures based on structures of the majority groups in terms of social class and racial privilege? It is essential for marginalized groups to acquire the tools of power that belong to the white middle class of U.S. society. While immigrant communities are quickly acquiring these tools of power (e.g., how institutions work, English language skills), it is reasonable to assume that many of these tools lie outside the realm of their families and communities. Many immigrant youth will benefit from being members of communities that go beyond their home culture. Being isolated in culturally specific schools may bring comfort, bilingualism, and academic rigor for students who may otherwise fail; however, students may also leave their culturally specific school without the skills needed to negotiate life in a diverse, competitive, and global society.

CONCLUSION

Developing a religious identity is an intensely personal exploration that reaches far deeper than merely being "allowed" to practice Islam or display Islamic religious practices at a culturally specific charter school. The process of becoming or staying Muslim in U.S. society must be contextualized in larger sociopolitical and historical narratives and, therefore, include actors and institutions beyond the schools. The process of becoming Muslim occurs in homes and communities, through exposure to the media, and while interacting with Muslims and non-Muslims in everyday life. Becoming Muslim occurs, in part, through investment in family or community activities such as memorization of the Koran, learning and following religious practices, and participating in Muslim holidays. Immigrant Muslim families are living transnational lives that involve travel to Muslim countries as well as back to the homeland. These actions are all part of the family or community's investment in youth developing or retaining a Muslim identity. The work of developing a Muslim identity is complex and must include the intersection of other identities and the possibility that youth conceptualize their religious identity differently than their elders do.

Culturally specific charter schools may serve as appropriate places for Muslim youth to be educated and develop an academic identity, but they should not be given credit for or charged with helping youth develop a Muslim identity. Government institutions should not co-opt the role of the family and community in this process. Charter schools are not authorized to carry out the complex task of developing a Muslim identity and are ill equipped to do so in a meaningful, long-lasting way.

FURTHER READINGS AND RESOURCES

Ajrouch, K. (2004). Gender, race, and symbolic boundaries: Contested spaces of identity among Arab American adolescents. *Sociological Perspectives, 47*(4), 371–391.

Al-Hadi School of Accelerative Learning: http://www.alhadi.com

Basford, L. (2010a). Assessing the intercultural competence of K–12 schools for East African Muslim youth. *Proceedings of the 2010 Developing and Assessing Intercultural Competence Conference.* Tucson, AZ, January 29–31.

Basford, L. (2010b). From headphones to hijabs: Cultural and religious experiences of Somali youth in U.S. schools. *Proceedings of Intercultural Competence Conference, 1*(August), 1–26. Retrieved from http://cercll.webhost.uits.arizona.edu/lib/exe/fetch.php/conferences/2010/proceedings/basford_from_headphones.pdf

Gilbert, D. (2004). Racial and religious discrimination: The inexorable relationship between schools and the individual. *Intercultural Education, 15*(3), 253–266.

Haw, K. (1998). *Educating Muslim girls.* Buckingham, UK: Open University Press.

Minnesota International Middle School: http://mninternationalmiddleschool.org

Mogra, I. (2010). Teachers and teaching: A contemporary Muslim understanding. *Religious Education, 105,* 317–329.

Qin-Hillard, D. B. (2003). Gender expectations and gender experiences: Immigrant students' adaptations in schools. *New Directions for Youth Development, 100*(Winter), 91–109.

Rimer, S. (2009, January 9). Immigrants see charter schools as a haven. *The New York Times.* Retrieved September 23, 2011, from http://www.nytimes.com/2009/01/10/education/10charter.html?n=Top/Reference/Times%20Topics/People/R/Rimer,%20Sara

Sarroub, L. K. (2005). *All American Yemeni girls: Being Muslim in a public school.* Philadelphia: University of Pennsylvania Press.

Yardley, J. (2011, March 21). Akkalkuwa journal; Tradition vs. modern education, and a Mullah who is caught in the middle. *The New York Times.* Retrieved from http://query.nytimes.com/gst/fullpage.html?res=9C0DE6DC1431F932A15750C0A9679D8B63&partner=rssnyt&emc=rss&pagewanted=1

Zine, J. (2000). Redefining resistance: Towards an Islamic subculture in schools. *Race, Ethnicity and Education, 3*(3), 293–316.

Zine, J. (2001). Muslim youth in Canadian schools: Education and the politics of religious identity. *Anthropology and Education Quarterly, 32,* 399–423.

COURT CASES AND STATUTES

Board of Education v. Grumet, 512 U.S. 687 (1994).
U.S. Constitutional Amendment I (1791).

Is there any benefit to proprietary for-profit schools?

POINT: Lesley McCue, *University of Dayton*

COUNTERPOINT: Mary I. Grilliot, *University of Dayton*

OVERVIEW

As the name implies, proprietary for-profit schools (PFPSs) are privately owned and controlled institutions that have been established, in part, for purposes of earning money and making a profit. As profit-making businesses, proponents argue, PFPSs must produce results in a competitive market in order to survive. Advocates of school choice contend that private schools, whether they are for-profit or nonprofit, provide an alternative to failing public schools. In theory, the existence of private schools and the competition they provide, particularly when parents are given tuition tax credits or vouchers that can be applied to private school, serves to improve the public schools. PFPSs, it is often claimed, by following a business model that introduces greater efficiencies and innovations, can offer better results at the same or lower costs than public schools. Opponents, however, contend that in reality many PFPSs have not met these objectives.

In 2007–2008, the latest school year for which statistics are available, there were 33,740 private elementary and secondary schools in the United States (U.S. Department of Education, n.d.). Private schools have a long history in the United States. In fact, publicly financed schools did not materialize until the mid-19th century when social reformers in Massachusetts, Connecticut, and New York were successful in having legislation enacted that required school attendance and provided for tax-supported schools. Even so, early schools, particularly those in rural areas, were financed through a combination of property taxes and tuition paid by parents. More options existed in urban areas where many church-run schools existed (Osborne & Russo, 2011). Private schools, particularly sectarian schools, experienced unprecedented growth in the mid-20th century but became involved in legal controversies. Much of the debate, which is discussed thoroughly in the volumes in this series on *School Law* and *Religion in Schools,* involved the extent to which government entities could provide aid to private school students.

The right of private schools to exist and even earn profits, along with the right of parents to send their children to private schools, was clearly established by the U.S. Supreme Court in *Pierce v. Society of Sisters of the Holy Names of Jesus and Mary* (1925). The dispute began when Oregon enacted a statute that required all students in the state between the ages of 8 and 16 to attend public schools. The rationale of the law, which was enacted after a voter referendum, was that public school attendance was necessary to produce good citizens. The law was challenged by the proprietors of a Roman Catholic school and a secular military academy. After examining the property rights of the private schools, the Court ruled that the statute, if enforced, would have the effect of seriously impairing or even destroying the businesses' profitability and greatly diminishing their property values. Further, the Court held that the Oregon legislation was unconstitutional because it "unreasonably interfere[d] with the liberty of parents and guardians to direct the upbringing and education of children under their control" (pp. 534–535). Two years later the Court affirmed private schools' right to exist and parents' right to send their children to nonpublic schools in *Farrington v. Tokushige* (1927). Here the Court rejected attempts by government officials in Hawaii to impose strict controls to regulate foreign language schools.

The debate in this chapter centers on the benefits, if any, of PFPSs. In the point essay Lesley McCue, a doctoral assistant in educational leadership at the University of Dayton, contends that there are many benefits to PFPSs. Noting that their for-profit status means that to survive in a competitive environment they must focus on effectiveness while embracing a business model that addresses their customers' needs, she states that PFPSs need to adopt instructional models that are proven, well researched, and supported by investments in capital and human resources. In this respect, McCue feels that PFPSs better recognize the value of professional development for teachers. Also, consistent with their business model and need to demonstrate results, PFPSs often adopt proven research-based curricula. Acknowledging that PFPSs are controversial, McCue nonetheless argues that they are a viable alternative for parents who want more for their children than the public schools offer.

In the counterpoint essay Mary I. Grilliot, a doctoral assistant in educational leadership at the University of Dayton, claims that PFPSs do not offer any real benefits and have actually delivered a significant negative performance. Grilliot, who has a background in management and accounting, contends that data suggest that educational management organizations have not reduced costs and the schools they operate have not produced higher academic achievement. She points out that since education is a labor-intensive industry, PFPSs reduce costs in this area by employing less experienced teachers. Further, they often rely on packaged curricula that do not allow teachers to individualize or tailor their instruction to student needs. While such a scripted curriculum may compensate for inexperienced teachers, Grilliot insists that the overall effect of student learning is negative. After reviewing the data, Grilliot concludes that there is no documented support for claims of improved student performance at PFPSs or that competition with such schools makes the public schools better. She adds that education is a national trust that should not be left to firms whose first loyalty must be to profit.

While the right of PFPSs to exist and earn a profit is not in question, the debate over the benefits they provide is far from settled. In reading this chapter you may want to reflect on a number of issues. Does an institution whose main objective is to earn a profit for its proprietors have a place in American education today? Can PFPSs reduce the costs of educating children while still maintaining a high degree of quality? Is the competition PFPSs provide good for the public schools?

Allan G. Osborne, Jr.
Principal (Retired), Snug Harbor Community School,
Quincy, Massachusetts

POINT: Lesley McCue
University of Dayton

Striving to meet the demands of educating students and operating under the constraints of educational decrees, proprietary for-profit schools (PFPSs) offer reform in an age of challenges. Public schools continue to face an increase in demands with diminishing support from local communities. How can success be achieved with dwindling resources? As the pendulum swings back and forth from focusing on student individual needs to school achievement scores, a provocative solution has been proposed in the form of PFPSs. Creating a climate of student achievement as a top priority, with financial support to encourage reform and structure that local districts can only dream of, PFPSs have appeared on the scene as a potential alternative for individual and collective student success; their role is designed to meet the demands of educating students within a local area. Structure and design of schools are based on business models that capitalize on success as a driving force. Pushing aside the status quo of protecting failing schools, PFPSs offer a choice for consumers, both parents and students.

EDUCATIONAL REFORM

Schools have traditionally been designed as top-down management facilities, with one or a few individuals at the central office making decisions that impact all aspects of daily operation at individual school buildings. The constant struggle to follow top-down created policies and procedures comes in contrast to teachers and building-level administrators attempting to meet the needs of individual students and buildings. Absent from the day-to-day operations, central office staff offer limited opportunity for input from staff at the building, and parents are not regularly polled or included in decision-making processes. All of these ingredients—top-down directives, avoidance of parental input, and limited teacher leadership—combine to create a bureaucratic, closed system that exists in traditional schools.

External interaction by parents and community is often absent due to the school's desire to establish and maintain control. Conflict avoidance through limited external interactions has helped to shape schools that are unresponsive to the needs, demands, and contributions of parents. This traditional view of schools has been designed to keep parents outside of their doors, offering them little influence in the decision-making process. More often the structure of schools, as well as the success of academic programs, has been held hostage by administrators. Consideration for making decisions has been centered on the cost rather than the impact on learning or the creation of a bridge from school to home to community.

The political monopoly created by public schools with little competition from private schools has also helped maintain the status quo. Schools have been left to their own devices, seldom forced to reconsider their structure based on the input of stakeholders outside of the central office. One solution to this problem is competitive schools that offer opportunities for structure and design with students and families in mind and without monetary constraints such as PFPSs.

THE CHALLENGE

The challenge is to design and operate a school that will implement teachers as leaders, address community needs, and strive to create educational opportunities for students beyond the traditional curriculum. These ideal schools must maintain a focus on effectiveness and yet embrace a business model to create a climate of decision making that addresses customer needs. Emphasis must be placed on creating an open system to promote interaction. Leadership must not be placed only in the hands of a few; rather, it should be shared with those who make a difference—teachers. Models for instruction must be proven, researched, and invested in, both with capital and with human resources.

Taking on the challenge, stepping up as an ideal school, PFPSs recognize the demands and offer an option for parents wanting more for their children. These schools go beyond the traditional bureaucratic, closed system to create a culture of investment. Stakeholders are involved in the process, from working directly with students to engaging in professional development that increases teacher knowledge and effectiveness.

Teachers as Leaders

The concept of teachers as leaders is often mentioned in academic programs at the university level, yet this has not translated into practice from academia to school districts. Teachers in traditional school districts are leaders only when they enter into the administrative realm. Traditional K–12 districts operate in a centralized manner with teachers following orders and directives from top-level administrators. Leadership opportunities for teachers rest primarily in job titles, such as team leader, that include superficial management chores, such as counting and reporting numbers of supplies. Aside from making the jump from teacher to principal, limited opportunities remain for those educated and experienced in the classroom.

PFPSs open the doors to teachers as leaders within their home school and across the nation. Teachers are selected and encouraged to take on roles as specialists in academic fields, as well as utilizing their strengths to attempt new roles as leaders. Absent from traditional districts are leadership trainings and programs. There, teachers are expected to spend their own time and resources to attend graduate-level classes. In contrast, for-profit schools offer programs to those individuals who show potential for leadership, sending their future leaders to programs across the country that focus on leadership and that are not the financial responsibility of the individual teacher.

Breaking the Union

Traditional schools continue to wage war during contract negotiations with one side representing the teachers within the district, while the administration and school board bear the role of opposition. A divide is drawn that stretches from the negotiating table to the classroom. Teachers spend many hours working with union representatives to help develop appropriate points for negotiating contract issues, working conditions, and filing of grievances, all of which take away from time spent elsewhere. How can schools continue to function with teachers and administration struggling to come to agreement on contracts? How can districts strive to recruit and maintain top-notch teachers in a system that treats all educators as equal bodies rather than individuals?

Breaking the tradition of unions and opening the doors to contracts that come without strings attached, PFPSs offer an opportunity for individual teachers to control their contracts. Signing bonuses, retention bonuses, competitive salaries, and other perks reflective of business models allow for charter schools to recruit and maintain top-notch teachers. No longer are contracts and raises awarded based on years of experience and education. Instead, teacher pay is reflective of teacher performance. Those who are willing to sign on for extended contracts (3 or more years) are rewarded with signing bonuses. PFPSs apply business concepts in developing contracts for individual teachers rather than for a body of employees viewed as equal members.

Impact on Learning

One of the greatest factors in predicting success in the classroom is professional development. These opportunities outside of the classroom, allotting time and providing expertise to teachers, help shape in-classroom instruction and learning for students. Conflict often emerges from the traditional schools' manner of structuring professional development and the shifting continuum of support for teachers who want more. In many districts limited funds are set aside for professional development, plus these funds are the most likely cutbacks during times of financial struggle. Even in stable financial situations, reserves of money designated for continuing education remain low, and teachers are directed to fill out paperwork that does not guarantee them support or reimbursement for their individual expenses.

In contrast, PFPSs have recognized the need for professional development, both on the whole staff side and for the individual teacher. Following a business model that recognizes the impact of teachers on the final product, financial support and an overall appreciation for the importance of professional development have changed the landscape in for-profit schools. A range of programs, from early academies designed for training to blocked-off times each school day for continuous professional development and mentoring programs, have allowed PFPSs to capitalize on their investments in teachers.

Following the Business Model

Operating at a level of cost similar to their traditional school counterparts, for-profit schools are designed on an inputs-to-outputs model. The law requires students to choose the school they wish to attend in order for the PFPS to receive funding and stay in business. As with any business, customers have to want to come back. PFPSs recognize that parents and students must choose to attend their schools, and a relationship is forged based on the understanding that schools are striving to offer the best opportunity for students. In contrast, local tradition K–12 schools have operated on a monopoly model. Being the only free public school in the area meant that they could tell students to change to fit their culture and expectations; PFPSs instead adapt to fit the needs of the students; learning is designed with the student in mind. As with any business, methods and productions are dependent on the inputs and the outputs. All schools strive to achieve a level of production of outputs, that is, students who are successful. PFPSs are no exception. Programs are implemented that research demonstrates are best for students.

Extending the business model, schools must rise up to meet the needs of the clientele. Schools still functioning under traditional hours and length of school year continue to maintain a minimal standard based on minimal hours and minimal days of instruction. Unable to deviate from union-negotiated contracts that put teachers first, traditional schools have not evolved to meet the needs of their customers, both students and families. PFPSs are not designed to meet minimums or to appease unions. Keeping the needs of customers in mind, school hours and days are extended to increase hours of instruction and keep children in a safe environment. The length of the school year is based not on union contracts or minimal standards, but rather on the needs of the students and the interests of families.

Curriculum

Running rampant in the news are issues of traditional schools struggling under financial constraints to maintain levels of excellence in their instruction. Tools necessary for effective instruction can only be purchased on a rotating basis due to the low level of budget priority in most districts. In contrast, for-profit charter schools have prioritized the purchasing of instructional programs and materials to support learning. The shift in for-profit schools has focused on three areas of importance: curriculum, technology, and innovation.

Selection and purchasing of curriculum in PFPSs is based more often on proven research than on price. These schools select programs that have research to support success with students. In contrast, traditional K–12 schools often base their program selections on lower prices and flashy presentations rather than research addressing student success.

Curriculum support for traditional school districts generally is centered through a curriculum director located at a central office. Only in larger districts are directors specific to academic fields, most often reading, math, science, and social studies. The responsibility of the director of curriculum varies from district to district, with some positions holding multiple responsibilities in addition to the title of curriculum director, such as gifted coordinator, testing director, or assistant superintendent.

CONCERNS

Concerns continue to be raised in regard to PFPSs. Ignoring those concerns ultimately means ignoring potential success. Although for-profit schools recognize the importance of teachers and maintain programs to support them, teacher turnover rates remain high. Some would argue that the demands of PFPSs drive teachers away. However, the same argument could be raised that only those teachers who are able to meet the demands, embrace the philosophy of for-profit schools, and achieve success should be in the classroom. Those voluntarily choosing to leave may have done so because they did not meet the necessary standards to help students achieve success.

Student retention and selection of education settings remain controversial. Although the schools are designed to meet the needs of the students, some do not find an ideal setting. Parents must weigh the options for their children in examining PFPSs that offer choice. Parents and students must decide if they believe that the traditional K–12 or the for-profit schools will best serve them.

In demonstrating student success, there are many variables that must be addressed. Testing students has been seen as a measure of school success. If the students achieve high scores, then the school receives high scores. However, a constantly changing student population may not appropriately reflect test scores achieved. The assumption of testing students is that they have attended the same institution for an extended period of time, perhaps for their whole educational career.

Problems arise when that assumption is applied to reality. For example, students being administered a test may have only been enrolled in the PFPS for a few days, and thus their testing data would be reflective of the education they experienced at another institution prior to attending the for-profit school. Also, little attention is given to any other variables that could exemplify success. Teachers in classrooms can attest that success for students is not always shown on paper. Rather, for many students acts of success are not measurable by tests, but are revealed in classroom interaction, in processing and developing solutions to posed problems, or through portfolio evaluation.

The most popular argument against PFPSs is that enrolling students in charter schools compounds financial problems at already failing schools by pulling funds away. This is an inarguable point that must be redirected toward a core question—what is being valued? It is correct that when students and parents voluntarily choose to enroll in charter schools, financial support is moved from the traditional K–12 district to the charter schools. The common phrase is applicable, "The money follows the student." However, the question must then be raised as to what society is more concerned about preserving: the failing school districts or student learning? By maintaining the argument that charter schools contribute to the deterioration of traditional K–12 schools, the emphasis is put on saving or protecting school districts that are failing. Better said, districts that have already proven failure are being protected at the expense of student learning. If the philosophy of encouraging student learning is the priority, then the location of where this event occurs is indifferent. Those contending this inarguable point are interested more in focusing on protecting and maintaining failing schools than in the student's right to learn.

IN RESPONSE

PFPSs are not popping up everywhere. They are predominantly located in urban areas where traditional schools have been deemed to be failing. The charter school movement largely has emerged as a response to failing schools in urban areas. Entering onto the scene, charter schools offer a different option for parents and students. PFPSs have raised the bar by maintaining a position of striving to produce educational opportunities for children that offer a chance for success. Learning lessons from those schools in the areas that are failing, the for-profit schools are addressing the needs of students through opportunities for curriculum, innovation, and technology beyond the offerings of traditional school settings or schedules.

There are some who would contend that PFPSs are failing; however, this remains to be seen. Limited research is present that compares the long-term impact of these schools. Also, the comparisons of PFPSs tend to be absent of research conducted that compares for-profit schools to their urban counterparts. The birth of the PFPS was to address failing schools, and offer parents choice. Parent choice is present when for-profit schools open. They offer opportunities for students that are absent from the traditional K–12 schools, predominantly due to funding constraints.

CONCLUSION

PFPSs are designed with the business model in mind. From the major priority of student learning to recruitment of teachers, professional development, and customer feedback, all aspects of education are considered part of the final product. As with any business, a final product is the greatest measure of success. The first step to success begins with design of the school to meet the community needs. All additional steps revolve around the student. Able to function outside of the realm of local politics while still remaining under the umbrella of support from parents in the community, PFPSs have entered onto the scene. They remain a viable option for parents who demand more for their children.

Although arguments about teacher retention, students' success, and impacts on failing districts can be raised, these issues are all addressable when the main objective of setting the stage for achieving student learning is the goal and priority of the discussion. As student learning remains at the center stage for education, PFPSs offer an opportunity to address the needs of the population with an emphasis on business practices. The focus is on producing a successful product by means of research-proven instruction and materials.

For-profit schools continue to raise controversy over the role and responsibility of educating students. Pushing aside local politics to get at the heart of the task and create a shared goal of helping each child learn, regardless of the location, must become a responsibility for all educators. Creating a school designed to prioritize learning with an emphasis on producing a quality product remains a major advantage of PFPSs.

COUNTERPOINT: Mary I. Grilliot
University of Dayton

There is some benefit to any experience. Even a mistake can teach important lessons, but in balance both logic and actual experience suggest that for-profit schools do not offer real benefits. In fact, for-profit schools have delivered significantly negative performance in even the exact and key areas where they were claimed to offer benefits. Specifically, the reasoning behind for-profit schools is that they would bring professional business management models to education and provide the following positive outcomes as a result:

- Lower overall costs

- Higher student performance

- Greater access for minorities and disadvantaged student populations to higher quality educational opportunities

- Better public, nonprofit, school performance as they competed with the for-profits for students

- Positive returns for for-profit shareholders, encouraging further private investments in education

ASSESSMENT OF FOR-PROFIT PERFORMANCE ON ANTICIPATED ADVANTAGES

Lower Overall Costs

The data suggest that for-profit education management organizations (EMOs) have not reduced overall costs. For-profit EMOs have two large cost centers that nonprofit school districts do not have to contend with:

1. The investors that provided capital require a return on their investment, in other words: profits. Without an adequate return, investors, unlike taxpayers, will demand their money back, and the for-profit EMO will cease to exist.

2. For-profit EMOs are "selling" a different approach to education. They have to make a case to their "customers" that this new approach offers advantages. In short, they must advertise and absorb the costs of that advertising.

The theory was that the for-profit schools could overcome these extra burdens to deliver lower-overall-cost educational programs, based on greater efficiencies and innovations. But education is an extremely labor-intensive industry, and many school districts report that wages make up 80% or more of the budget. That means for-profit EMOs must look to personnel costs in order to have any hope of delivering lower-cost offerings. Studies show that for-profit EMOs tend to use less experienced teachers. For instance, Arizona for-profit charter teachers had 12 years of average experience versus 20 years for teachers at traditional schools in the state (Garcia, Barber, & Molnar, 2009, p. 1356). These less experienced for-profit teachers earn significantly lower salaries. As an example, from 2000 to 2008, teachers at for-profit charters in Michigan earned 33% less on average than their colleagues in traditional public schools (Garcia et al., 2009, p. 1356). For-profit EMOs also tend to have higher class sizes, and rely more on part-time faculty and staff as compared to public school districts. Inexperienced teachers and higher class sizes typically correlate with lower student performance.

Another way to reduce effective labor costs is to develop a standardized package of educational services across a large number of schools. Research has shown that for-profit EMOs tend to use structured, standardized curricula such as Success for All or Direct Instruction, which rely on drill and practice–oriented pedagogy. For-profit teachers have reported that they are literally given a script they are required to recite without any modifications, and every few months their classrooms are inspected to ensure the required displays (and no others) are on view. Teachers told the *San Francisco Bay Guardian* that such practices violate their professionalism by not allowing them to tailor lessons for individual students and groups of students (Woodward, 2000). The impact on teacher morale, student diversity, and teacher development was extremely negative. Over half of the for-profit teaching staff in San Francisco at the district's for-profit EMO-managed school left every year from 1999 to 2002. Similarly between 2000 and 2004, almost half of the teachers in Ohio charter schools (overwhelmingly for-profit) quit as compared with only 12% of the teachers in high-poverty, urban Ohio district schools in the same period and 8% of the teachers in conventional schools overall (Levin, 2006, p. 24).

Even using the highly controversial, and usually deleterious, operational adjustments discussed above to reduce costs, for-profit EMOs still find it very difficult to overcome their extra operational costs. EdisonLearning educated 37,574 students in the 2008–2009 school year, making it the largest for-profit K–12 provider. One of Edison's largest accounts was to manage 20 schools enrolling 13,000 students in Philadelphia. Edison's cost-based request for tuition in 2001 was originally $1,500 *more* per student than the district cost to educate those students. Ultimately, Edison and the Philadelphia school board agreed to a contract that paid Edison $750 more per pupil than the district cost. After that accommodation, Edison laid off 211 employees and refused delivery of new textbooks it had ordered, due to financial issues. Similarly, in Texas's Sherman Independent School District, Edison had a 5-year contract to run Washington Elementary School. The Board of Trustees ultimately allowed the contract to expire, in 2001, because it had incurred $4 million in "hidden costs" involved in Edison's management of Washington Elementary and another district school, Dillingham Intermediate. The district also charged that Edison did not reimburse it as promised for certain expenses, such as service costs for students with disabilities and a portion of district administrative costs (Molnar, 2006, p. 627).

A further cost challenge for the for-profit EMOs is that while promising to reduce their administrative costs to levels lower than the average 27% of total budget costs seen in district schools, their administrative costs have tended to run *higher* as a percentage of total budget. The main reason for this seems to be that most students are already in educational organizations that are large enough to undermine further economies of scale. This is particularly problematic for for-profit schools since they promised *lower* percentile administrative costs (in some investor offerings, as low as 8%) based on the theory that economies of scale would allow such efficiencies. Decades of study, however, show there are very low real economies of scale in education since the minimum levels needed for the base economies are met in almost all schools today. Education cost is, as noted above, overwhelmingly variable in nature as opposed to fixed costs that can be divided over more and more students.

Edison, as one of the first and largest EMOs, would be expected to be more stable than many of the smaller EMOs. However, Edison has struggled mightily financially. An in-depth *Fortune* article (O'Reilly, 2002) profiled Edison's fast growth and lack of profits since going public in 1999. The article highlighted that while Edison had grown in enrollment as its public offering promised, its administrative costs had *not* shrunk as a percentage of revenue with that growth, as also promised. Without those administrative savings, Edison could not deliver lower-cost education, or even equivalent-cost education, since it had the uniquely for-profit burdens of generating investor return and advertising expenses. In a nutshell, the whole business model disintegrated with that reality. Edison responded by promising slower growth to allow more favorable contractual and termination arrangements to be negotiated on future contracts. By May 2003, the company was able to report a third-quarter profit (before interest, taxes, depreciation, and amortization) of $5.8 million. The company heralded the announcement as proof of a successful turnaround, and reaffirmed projections of a profitable fourth quarter. One day later, Edison filed a Securities and Exchange Commission–required report that revealed the company was in default on loans totaling $59.5 million. In fact, the third-quarter report was the *sole* example of Edison making a quarterly profit. In late 2003, the company was taken private. While, as a private company, Edison no longer reports profits publicly, the company has not indicated it was able to generate a profitable quarter again. Since going private in 2003, the primary shareholder, Liberty Partners, has removed two CEOs presumably because of continuing profitability problems.

But it is not just the for-profit firms that bear the pain of the unsustainable cost to the revenue profile of for-profit schools. The Dallas Independent School District learned in 2001 that it would cost an additional $5 million above the contracted amount to "fill in" services that the for-profit firms billed separately, or had failed to provide. In Las Vegas in 2004, seven for-profit schools cost the school board $1 million more than they did as district schools, for the same reasons. And, as noted earlier, in Sherman, Texas, the school board reported that it had incurred $4 million in hidden costs for just two schools. Many school boards have reported that the per-pupil cost at their for-profit schools far exceeds the per-pupil cost at their district schools.

Higher Student Performance

The data suggest that for-profit EMOs have not raised student performance. Cynthia D. Hill and David M. Welsch (2009) performed a four-year review of charter schools in Michigan, comparing for-profit with other charter schools, and found *no* difference in student performance at for-profit organizations. In fact, the less experienced teachers, more part-time faculty/staff, and larger class sizes adopted by EMOs as cost-containment measures portend negative student performance comparisons. Essentially all peer-reviewed literature correlates these changes with declining student performance.

Similarly, the EMO practice of reliance on canned instructional models may compensate somewhat for a lack of teacher experience and may be superficially "efficient," but the impact on overall student learning can be negative. David R. Garcia and colleagues (2009) analyzed Arizona for-profit student test scores, in comparison with other student test scores, but unlike previous studies they went beyond summary test scores to analyze subset test scores that distinguish between basic and complex skill sets. The research showed that the more prevalent "drill and practice" teaching pedagogies used to support typically less experienced teaching staff at the for-profit schools may be associated with higher levels of academic achievement on the more basic skills sets but with a resulting offsetting decrease in student performance in more complex learning activities.

In San Francisco, between 1999 and 2002, the sole for-profit charter scored last among 70 to 75 elementary schools on California's Academic Performance Index (API), in spite of costing the district the most per pupil to run, ultimately leading the city to cancel the for-profit contract (Bracey, 2002).

Even studies commissioned by for-profit EMOs suggest no clear comparative student performance advantage. The RAND Corporation (2005), in a study commissioned by EdisonLearning, reported that "most public schools operated for at least 4 to 5 years by the for-profit company Edison Schools have shown student achievement gains that match or exceed gains in schools with similar student populations." The same report also noted "while most Edison schools have shown gains in student achievement in the first 3 years of operation by the company, their average gains for this period did not exceed those of comparable public schools." In a related matter, in 2002, RAND denied an oft-repeated Edison claim that RAND had found 84% of Edison schools making "positive gains" in the 2000–2001 school year. RAND had not made such a claim and had just begun to analyze its data. RAND has not, as of this writing, confirmed such a finding (Parents Advocating School Accountability, 2009).

In fact, there appears to be numerous examples of misleading claims being advanced by the for-profit K–12 industry. For instance, in its First Annual Report, Edison compared trend data for its schools using a formula that was self-developed and not represented in the statistical literature (Bracey, 2002). Even more alarmingly, it compared its results to "Average Percentage Point gain, National Assessment of Educational Progress, US, 9- and 13-year-olds, 1994–1996." Gerald Bracey (2002) reports, "Besides the fact that the report only vaguely specifies what the numbers refer to, there is another fundamental problem with these data: They do not exist, there was no NAEP reading assessment in 1996 and no NAEP mathematics assessment in 1994."

At for-profit Dayton Leadership Academies in Ohio in 2002, the for-profit firm reported Ohio Department of Education (ODE) statistics that were highly favorable when in fact actual ODE data were far more negative. At for-profit Edison Hernandez Academy in Dallas in 2001, a news reporter interviewed students who said teachers changed their answers during standardized state testing. At for-profit Edison Charter Academy in San Francisco during 2001, many of the students were excluded from standardized state testing, hence raising the reported averages. In 2003, at for-profit Ingalls Edison Academy in Wichita, Kansas, the school's top two administrators were released after district officials documented consistent irregularities in how the school's standardized tests were reported and graded, all with the effect of dramatically if falsely raising test results.

Greater Access

The data suggest that for-profit EMOs have not raised access for minorities and disadvantaged student populations to higher quality educational opportunities. A survey of for-profit schools and corresponding district schools, conducted by the National Education Policy Center at the University of Colorado (Miron, Urschel, Mathis, & Tornquist, 2010), showed the following:

- For-profit schools operated by EMOs tended to be strongly segregated as compared to the district schools.

- For-profit schools were far more socioeconomically segregated than were the district schools. Most for-profits were divided into either high concentration of high income students or high concentration of low income students, with between 70% and 73% of the schools falling into one of these extremes.

- For-profit schools consistently enrolled a lower proportion of special needs students than did the district schools. Special needs students who were serviced by for-profit schools were in special-needs-only schools, hence highly segregated.

- English language learners (ELLs) were also consistently underrepresented in for-profit schools in all comparisons.

Why? In many cases, the for-profit schools do not offer the specialized services that normal district schools offer, so students in those categories self-select out of those choices. In other cases, since for-profit schools enroll on a choice basis, parents may be selecting based on neighborhood accessibility, hence preserving any neighborhood segregation into the schools.

Another factor could simply be that for-profit schools seek out less expensive students to educate. They can do so by the menu of services they offer, and by their neighborhood placements. A geospatial analysis of charter schools, done by researchers from the University of Illinois and Brown University (Lubienski & Gulosing, 2007), find a pattern of for-profit ringing around disadvantaged areas that would support this hypothesis.

Better Public, Nonprofit, School Performance

The data suggest that for-profit EMOs have not improved public school performance, due to increased competition. Instead for-profit schools have imposed greater burdens, financial and otherwise, on public schools. For instance, if for-profit schools (as discussed above) have lower-percentile enrollments of special education students, English language learners, and students from lower socioeconomic backgrounds, this means the district schools must pick up a disproportionately higher percentage of these "more expensive to educate" students.

Additionally, for-profit schools use the district administration programs essentially without cost, thus increasing the per-pupil cost of those programs at district schools. Similarly, the district now, without the per-pupil subsidies being passed on to the for-profit provider, must provide a host of services free to the for-profit students such as busing, medical support, theater programs, nutritional support, band programs, sports supports, and so on. Bracey (2002) reports that in San Francisco in 2001, for-profit management delayed maintenance and groundskeeping functions to such a degree that the district had to step in and provide the services although they were the responsibility of the for-profit firms (the district made this move since "it was our buildings" that were being left to deteriorate).

In the Michigan comparison of for-profit and district schools discussed previously, not only was there no difference in student performance between the for-profit and district schools, but there also was no evidence of any improvement in district performance due to the new competition from for-profits.

Positive Returns for For-Profit Shareholders

The data suggest that for-profit EMOs have not encouraged continuing or increased levels of private investment in education. The case of Edison, one of the first large and still largest EMOs, is instructive. Edison went public in November 1999 at $18 per share. It rose to a high of $34 per share in the latter half of 2000, based on Edison-generated success statistics that later proved to be highly questionable. By 2002, numerous school boards had cancelled contracts with Edison for various reasons, including performance and cost. Combined with mounting evidence of apparent data manipulation to show improvements in student performance that did not exist, these cancellations shook the stock value of Edison shares. By the end of September 2002, Edison shares had lost 98% of their value and dropped below $1.

In July 2003, Edison was taken private by its president Christopher Whittle, supported by Liberty Partners, a private equity group. Liberty let Whittle go in 2004 when profits failed to materialize, replacing him with Terry Stecz. Liberty let Stecz go in 2008, again when profits failed to materialize. Edison is not unique; other for-profit K–12 providers have had the same type of problems becoming profitable, with many now moving more into educational consulting work.

Wall Street investors were hit hard, and have shown little interest in for-profit K–12 schools since. Perhaps, for this reason, we are starting to see a definite trend of for-profit EMOs attempting to convert to nonprofit status where charitable contributions can be solicited to help finance operations. Even the second largest K–12 for-profit provider, Imagine Schools, which in the 2008–2009 school year operated 76 schools, educating 32,316 students in 10 states, applied for nonprofit status with the Internal Revenue Service in 2006 (although that status has not yet been granted).

CONCLUSION

It is both logically indefensible and now experientially proven that it is a myth that "efficiencies" can be magically extracted by for-profit EMOs to more than compensate for the additional costs implicit in K–12 for-profit schools. It is also clear that there is no documented support for claims of improved student performance at for-profit schools, as well as that there is no evidence that for-profit EMOs have eager investors willing to invest further in education, or that competition with for-profit schools makes district schools better. It is equally clear that for-profit schools impose additional burdens on school boards and encourage segregation (racial, socioeconomic, special needs, and language) within the schools.

In terms of avoiding bureaucracy, who is to say that the profit-driven bureaucracy of a for-profit corporation is preferable to the more altruistic bureaucracy of a democratically elected and accountable school board? As to innovation, why would profit-driven forces be more creative than educators who gave up more profitable fields of endeavor in order to serve?

The latest trend in for-profit K–12 education is virtual schools where the for-profit school has no brick-and-mortar costs, and standardized teaching plans are the only way to go. Historically, virtual schools have been used by pupils who cannot attend school perhaps because of a serious illness, but for-profit schools are marketing the concept to any student. Certainly this is a low-cost model and hence attractive to for-profit firms, but what a tragedy if a child who could attend school with all the socialization opportunities implied was instead lured into staying at home, staring at a computer screen.

Elementary and secondary education is a prerequisite for the informed citizenry that makes democracy functional. It is a national trust that should not be left to firms whose first loyalty must be to profit.

FURTHER READINGS AND RESOURCES

Bracey, G. (2002, February). *The market in theory meets the market in practice: The case of Edison schools.* Retrieved from http://www.epicpolicy.org/files/EPSL-0202-107-EPRU.pdf

Buckley, J., & Sattin-Baja, C. (2010). *Are ELL students underrepresented in charter schools? Demographic trends in New York City 2006–2008.* Retrieved from http://www.ncspe.org/publications_files/OP188.pdf

Deal, T. E., Hentschke, G. C., Kecker, K., Lund, C., Oschman, S., & Shore, R. (2004). *Adventures of charter school creators: Leading from the ground up.* Lanham, MD: Scarecrow Education.

Garcia, D. R., Barber, R., & Molnar, A. (2009). Profiting from public education: Education management organizations and student achievement. *Teachers College Record, 111*(5), 1352–1379. doi: 0161-4681

Gill, B., Hamilton, L. S., Lockwood, J. R., Marsh, J. A., Zimmer, R. W., Hill, D., et al. (2005). *Inspiration, perspiration, and time: Operations and achievement in Edison schools.* Santa Monica, CA: RAND Corporation.

Hassel, B. C. (1999). *The charter school challenge: Avoiding the pitfalls, fulfilling the promise.* Washington, DC: Brookings Institution Press.

Hill, C. D., & Welsch, D. M. (2009). For-profit versus not-for-profit charter schools: An examination of Michigan student test scores. *Education Economics, 17*(2), 147–166. doi: 10.1080/09645290801977017

Hill, P. T. (Ed.). (2006). *Charter schools against the odds: An assessment by the Hoover Institutions Koret Task Force on K–12 education.* Stanford, CA: Education Next Books.

Levin, M. (2006). Why is educational entrepreneurship so difficult? In F. Hess (Ed.), *Educational entrepreneurship.* Cambridge, MA: Harvard Education Press.

Lubienski, C., & Gulosing, C. (2007). *Choice, competition, and organizational orientation: A geo-spatial analysis of charter schools and the distribution of educational opportunities.* New York: National Center for the Study of Privatization in Education, Columbia University.

Miron, G., Urschel, J. L., Mathis, W. J., & Tornquist, E. (2010). *Schools without diversity: Education management organizations, charter schools, and the demographic stratification of the American school system.* Retrieved September 23, 2011, from http://nepc.colorado.edu/publication/schools-without-diversity

Molnar, A. (2006). The commercial transformation of public education. *Journal of Education Policy, 21*(5), 621–640. doi: 10.1080/02680930600866231

Molnar, A., Miron, G., & Urschel, J. (2009). *Profiles of for-profit educational management organizations: Twelfth annual report—2009–2010.* Boulder, CO: National Education Policy Center.

National Center for Education Statistics. (2010). *Number of operating public elementary and secondary local education agencies and number of students in membership by agency type and state or jurisdiction; school year 2008–09* (No. NCES 2010-346). Washington, DC: U.S. Department of Education. Retrieved from http://nces.ed.gov/pubs2010/pesagencies08/tables/table_02.asp

O'Reilly, B. (2002, December 9). Why Edison doesn't work. *Fortune.* Retrieved September 23, 2011, from http://money.cnn.com/magazines/fortune/fortune_archive/2002/12/09/333467/index.htm

Osborne, A. G., & Russo, C. J. (2011). *The legal rights and responsibilities of teachers: Issues of employment and instruction.* Thousand Oaks, CA: Corwin.

Parents Advocating School Accountability. (2009). *Edison schools.* Retrieved September 1, 2010, from http://www.pasasf.org/edison/edison.html

Plank, D. N., Arsen, D., & Sykes, G. (2000, May). Charter schools and private profits—educational management organizations. *School Administrator.* Retrieved from http://findarticles.com/p/articles/mi_m0JSD/is_5_57/ai_77382336

RAND Corporation. (2005). *RAND says most public schools managed by Edison schools match or exceed gains of comparable public schools in 4 to 5 years.* Retrieved from http://www.rand.org/news/press/2005/10/11.html

Sarason, S. B. (1998). *Charter schools: Another flawed educational reform?* New York: Teachers College Press.

U.S. Department of Education. (n.d.). Table 86. Number of public school districts and public and private elementary and secondary schools: Selected years, 1869–70 through 2007–08. *Digest of Education Statistics.* Retrieved July 18, 2011, from http://nces.ed.gov/programs/digest/d09/tables/dt09_086.asp

Weil, D. (2000). *Charter schools: A reference guide.* Santa Barbara, CA: ABC-CLIO.

Woodward, T. (2000, July 19). Edison exodus: Will a teacher revolt spell an end to the school privatization experiment? *San Francisco Bay Guardian*, p. 1.

COURT CASES AND STATUTES

Farrington v. Tokushige, 273 U.S. 284 (1927).

Pierce v. Society of Sisters of the Holy Names of Jesus and Mary, 268 U.S. 510 (1925).

6

Are publicly funded programs that afford parents the option of where to educate their children the most appropriate ways to promote educational choice?

POINT: Ralph D. Mawdsley, *Cleveland State University*
COUNTERPOINT: Timothy J. Ilg, *University of Dayton*

OVERVIEW

The two predominant means of providing parents with the option of sending their children to private schools with some degree of public financial support are school vouchers and either tuition tax credits or tax deductions. Vouchers are essentially certificates issued by a government entity, such as a school board or state educational agency, which parents can apply toward the tuition of private schools. Education tax credits and deductions work the same way as other tax credits and deductions by lowering or offsetting parents' tax liability for their tuition expenditures. Advocates of such publicly funded programs point out that without this financial aid parents who send their children to private schools still must support the public schools through their taxes even though they are not reaping any direct benefit. Those on the other side of the argument contend that public education benefits society as a whole, and most taxpayers support all governmental undertakings for the common good even though individual taxpayers do not receive direct benefit from many of those programs.

Although the controversy over school vouchers has taken center stage recently as issues of school reform and accountability have intensified since the enactment of No Child Left Behind in 2001, the concept of school vouchers is not new. Economist Milton Friedman (1980) first suggested the use of school vouchers as a means of creating competition for public schools as part of his PBS television series *Free to Choose*. Friedman's proposal was to give parents a voucher equal to the amount it would cost the public schools to educate their child. Parents could then use that voucher at any school of their choice.

Parents who have the means and can afford private school tuition have many choices as to where their children are educated. Proponents of vouchers and tax credits/deductions argue that since parents in lower socioeconomic circumstances do not have the same choices because they cannot afford private school tuition costs, their children effectively are denied an equal educational opportunity. Publicly financed vouchers and tax credits/deductions, proponents contend, will help level the playing field by giving low income parents similar options as wealthier parents.

One argument that has been advanced against the use of school vouchers and tuition tax credits/deductions is that when used to support students' enrolment in private sectarian schools they have the effect of supporting religious organization in violation of the separation of church and state doctrine of the U.S. Constitution's First Amendment. However, in 2002 the U.S. Supreme Court in *Zelman v. Simmons-Harris* ruled that a school voucher law that gave parents a choice between private schools, including religious schools, and public schools did not offend the First Amendment. The Court insisted that the statute had a secular purpose in that its intent was to provide low income students in a failing school system the financial means to attend school elsewhere. Further the Court saw that the statute's effect was neutral toward religion because it provided assistance to a broad class of parents and any benefit to religion was incidental to the independent choices made by the parents. Even so, as the essays in this chapter and in other volumes in the series point out, the separation of church and state issue still plays a major role in the debate over school vouchers.

In the point essay, Ralph D. Mawdsley, a professor of education law and the Roslyn Z. Wolf Endowed Chair in Urban Educational Leadership at Cleveland State University and one of the country's leading experts in the field, takes an affirmative position. Mawdsley begins by reviewing state statutes allowing for vouchers and tax credits and the extensive litigation over state-initiated voucher plans and tax deductions for parents who send their children to private schools. After analyzing the laws and court decisions, Mawdsley notes that although there are differences from one state to another and all do result in some loss of funds available for public education, that loss is unlikely to be dramatic. Mawdsley contends, however, that the viability of educational choice, especially for the economically disadvantaged parents, depends on some form of government-assisted funding. Further, he states that as long as education is considered to be a government function, a free-market approach would require some public funds being available to the parent-consumer-taxpayer to use to select educational services.

The counterpoint essay, authored by Timothy J. Ilg, an associate professor in the School of Education and Allied Professions at the University of Dayton, maintains that public school options have undermined the educational process for millions of children and challenges the position taken by many advocates that school choice improves school quality and efficiency, encourages innovation, and enhances opportunities for disadvantaged students. Rather than looking at options that take revenues away from public schools, Ilg concludes that advocates of school choice should be looking toward restructuring the public schools to provide students and parents more options and flexibility within that structure. He suggests that alternatives such as magnet schools, charter schools, and virtual schools within the public school system (all of which are discussed elsewhere in this volume and set) will foster innovation within the public schools while allowing parents to choose among the public schools within their districts.

As this chapter clearly emphasizes, the debate over school choice in general and publicly financed choice options in particular is far from over. As the debate continues and you read the essays in this chapter, there are a number of issues to consider. Would providing vouchers to low income families give them the same school choice options as their more affluent counterparts? Do vouchers and tax credits that can be used when students attend sectarian schools create an entanglement between religion and the state? Are school choice options, particularly when supported via publicly financed programs, the best way to spur innovation and improve the overall quality of the public schools? As the authors in this chapter point out, the debate will continue, and there are no easy answers.

Allan G. Osborne, Jr.
Principal (Retired), Snug Harbor Community School,
Quincy, Massachusetts

POINT: Ralph D. Mawdsley
Cleveland State University

Ten states—Alaska, California, Hawaii, Kansas, Michigan, Mississippi, Nebraska, New Mexico, South Carolina, and Wyoming—expressly prohibit, in their state constitutions, public education funds from going to any private school (*Bush v. Holmes,* 2006, p. 416). Since 1998, four other states— Wisconsin (*Jackson v. Benson,* 1998), Arizona (*Hibbs v. Winn,* 2004; *Kotterman v. Killian,* 1999; *Winn v. Arizona Christian School Tuition Organization,* 2009); Ohio (*Zelman v. Simmons-Harris,* 2002); and Florida (*Bush v. Holmes,* 2006)— have addressed challenges to the allocation of state funds to private schools.

The Supreme Court of Wisconsin, in *Jackson v. Benson* (1998), upheld the state's voucher plan for Milwaukee, and in *Zelman v. Simmons-Harris* (2002), the U.S. Supreme Court upheld the constitutionality of the voucher plan in Cleveland, Ohio. The Supreme Court of Florida in *Bush v. Holmes* (2006) invalidated a state scholarship program that provided state funds to students whose schools had a failing rating. In *Hibbs v. Winn* (2004), the U.S. Supreme Court rejected a constitutional challenge to an Arizona statute that permitted deductible gifts to student tuition organizations, which then, in turn, made scholarship awards to students in private (mostly religious) schools. All of the cases have in common the key issue of what constitutes public funding and whether such funding, to the extent that it goes to religious schools, violates the Establishment Clause in the First Amendment of the U.S. Constitution.

Prior to these cases, the only U.S. Supreme Court precedent was *Mueller v. Allen* (1983) where the Court upheld a Minnesota statute that permitted tax deductions to parents with children in public, nonsectarian private, and sectarian private schools. The deductions, up to $500 for elementary-aged and $700 for secondary-aged students, could be applied only to actual expenses for tuition, textbooks, and transportation. The Court held that, even though 96% of the private schools in Minnesota were sectarian and even though public school parents were not likely to qualify for a tax deduction, the state statute survived an Establishment Clause challenge because it was facially neutral in its availability to parents in public and private (nonsectarian or sectarian) schools.

DISCUSSION
Cleveland's and Milwaukee's Voucher Plans

The voucher plans in Cleveland and Milwaukee have some key similarities. Both provide that state money be paid to qualifying parents to send their children to nonpublic schools, including those that are sectarian. Parent eligibility and the amount of funding are tied to family income as related to the federal poverty level. Both plans cap the amount of money that parents can receive, but in neither instance can this sum exceed the cost of tuition. The number of vouchers is fixed in both programs, in Cleveland to a number determined by the superintendent of public instruction and in Milwaukee to a maximum of 15% of student enrollment in the Milwaukee schools. In both programs, parents apply to participating schools of their choice that decide where they use their vouchers to send their children to school.

Insofar as the overwhelming percentage of parents in Milwaukee and Cleveland used their vouchers at religious schools, both cases presented challenges under the First Amendment's Establishment Clause, according to which "Congress shall make no law respecting an establishment of religion, or prohibiting the free exercise thereof." In addition, *Jackson v. Benson* (1998) generated a challenge under the Establishment Clause in Wisconsin's constitution that prevents the use of state money to benefit religious organizations and prohibits anyone from having to support a religion without his or her consent. In both cases, the salient point was that attendance by students in religious schools receiving vouchers depended not on government action, but on private parent choice.

In upholding its funding program, the Supreme Court of Wisconsin observed,

> In our assessment, the importance of our inquiry here is not to ascertain the path which public funds travel under the program, but rather to determine who ultimately chooses that path. As with [state aid programs previously upheld by the U.S. Supreme Court] in *Mueller* [*v. Allen*] and *Witters* [*v. Washington Department of Services for the Blind*], not one cent flows from the State to a sectarian private school under the [state statute] except as a result of the necessary and intervening choices of individual parents. (*Jackson v. Benson*, 1998, p. 618)

In upholding the Cleveland voucher plan, the Supreme Court used similar language:

> No reasonable observer would think a neutral program of private choice, where state aid reaches religious schools solely as a result of the numerous independent decisions of private individuals, carries with it the imprimatur of government endorsement. (*Zelman v. Simmons-Harris*, 2002, p. 655)

Referring to the Cleveland voucher plan as one of "true private choice" that was "part of a general and multifaceted undertaking by the State of Ohio to provide educational opportunities to the children of a failed school district" (*Zelman v. Simmons-Harris*, 2002, p. 653), the Court noted that children in failing schools enjoyed a range of educational choices: "They may remain in public school as before, remain in public school with publicly funded tutoring aid, obtain a scholarship and choose a religious school, obtain a scholarship and choose a nonreligious private school, enroll in a community school, or enroll in a magnet school" (*Zelman v. Simmons-Harris*, 2002, p. 655). However, the Court also observed that the program actually created "financial *dis*incentives for religious schools" (*Zelman v. Simmons-Harris*, 2002, p. 654). Private schools received "only half the government assistance given to community schools and one-third the assistance given to magnet schools" while parents enrolling their children in private schools were required to "copay a portion of the school's tuition" (*Zelman v. Simmons-Harris*, 2002, p. 654).

Florida's Scholarship Plan

In 2006, the Supreme Court of Florida, in *Bush v. Holmes* (2006), invalidated a state scholarship program whereby the parents of a student from a public school that failed to meet certain minimum state standards could receive funds from the public treasury, which otherwise would have gone to the student's school district, to pay the student's tuition at a private school. By "divert[ing] public dollars into separate private systems parallel to and in competition with the free public schools that are the sole means set out in the Constitution for the state to provide for the education of Florida's children," the Supreme Court held that the statute violated state constitutional provisions whereby "it is . . . a paramount duty of the state to make adequate provision for the education of all children residing within its borders" and "adequate provision shall be made by law for a uniform, efficient, safe, secure, and high quality system of free public schools" (*Bush v. Holmes*, 2006, p. 398). The Florida Supreme Court reasoned that the diversion not only reduced money available to the free schools, but also diverted funds to private schools that are not "uniform" when compared with each other or the public system because many standards imposed by law on the public schools are inapplicable to the private schools receiving public monies. In sum, "the state is fostering plural, nonuniform systems of education in direct violation of the constitutional mandate for a uniform system of free public schools" (*Bush v. Holmes*, 2006, p. 398). To emphasize that private schools in Florida are not uniform, the Supreme Court observed that a number of requirements applicable to public schools are not applicable to private schools: Private school students are not required to participate in state assessments; private school teachers are not required to be certificated; private school teachers are not required to submit to background screening; and private schools are not required to teach diverse subjects, "the contents of the Declaration of Independence, the essentials of the United States Constitution, the elements of civil government, Florida state history, African-American history, the history of the Holocaust, and the study of Hispanic and women's contributions to the United States" (*Bush v. Holmes*, 2006, p. 410).

Arizona's Tax-Exempt Plan

In 1997, Arizona's legislature enacted a different statutory approach to support nonpublic school attendance. This statute permitted taxpayers to donate at least $500 to student tuition organizations (STOs) and claim a $500 tax credit (taxpayers filing jointly can claim up to $625) against their state tax obligations. STOs are tax-exempt organizations created under Section 501(c)(3) of the Internal Revenue Code that are required to allocate at least 90% of their annual revenue for scholarship and tuition grants to children to use to attend qualifying nonpublic schools of their parents' choice. STOs must provide scholarships or grants for students at more than one qualifying school. In order to qualify for money, a school cannot discriminate on the basis of race, color, sex, handicap, familial status, or national origin. The $500 can be carried forward by taxpayers but would be in lieu of a tax deduction pursuant to Section 170 of the Internal Revenue Code and taken for state tax purposes. In addition, the credit is disallowed if a taxpayer designates that the STO contribution will be used for a dependent.

STOs must contribute to more than one school. Even so, STOs can limit their donations to schools of the same religion. Thus, an STO may distribute grants only to students attending Catholic, Protestant, Muslim, or Jewish schools, or schools maintained by a single religious sect. STOs may also limit their grants to children of families who belong to a particular faith. In calendar year 1998, the first full year that the tax credit was in effect, STOs reported to the Arizona Department of Revenue that they received $1.8 million in contributions. At least 94% of that amount was donated to STOs that restricted their scholarships or grants to students attending religious schools. Further, three religious STOs received 85% of the donations made that year. The largest single recipient in 1998 was the Catholic Tuition Organization of the Diocese of Phoenix with $837,140 of the $1.8 million in diverted funds. Educational officials then provided tuition assistance to students who attended Catholic schools that the diocese operated. The second largest single recipient was an STO that restricted its grants to students attending evangelical Christian schools. The third was an STO that limited grants to Brophy College

Preparatory, a Catholic all-boys high school, and its sister school, Xavier College Preparatory for girls.

In addition to these STOs, the Arizona legislature enacted a maximum $200 tax credit for taxpayers for contributions made directly to a public school to support extracurricular activities. This public school credit has the same limit regarding Section 170 of the Internal Revenue Code and the same carry-forward provision as the tax credit statute for private schools. Although the public tax credit cannot be used for tuition, the Arizona attorney general has ruled that the credit can be used for fees.

Against this factual background, the Supreme Court of Arizona, in *Kotterman v. Killian* (1999), upheld the constitutionality of its tax credit system under both the Arizona and federal Constitution Establishment Clauses in applying a rationale that was similar to that of the Supreme Court of Wisconsin in *Jackson v. Benson* (1998). In addition, the Court found that the Arizona tax credits were similar to the ones that the Supreme Court upheld in *Mueller v. Allen* (1983).

Subsequent to *Kotterman,* the U.S. Supreme Court, in *Hibbs v. Winn* (2004), held in a jurisdictional issue that the federal Tax Injunction Act (TIA) did not prohibit federal Establishment Clause challenges to the constitutionality of the Arizona tax credit plan. On remand, the Arizona district court, in *Winn v. Arizona Christian School Tuition Organization* (2009), allowed two STOs, the Arizona Christian School Tuition Organization (ACSTO) and Arizona School Choice Trust (ASCT), and two parents of ASCT scholarship recipients to intervene as defendants. ACSTO provided scholarships only to religious schools, and ASCT provided scholarships to any private school of the parents' choice. Following the district court's dismissal of the action, the Ninth Circuit reversed the district court.

The ACSTO appealed the Ninth Circuit's decision to the U.S. Supreme Court, which, in a 5–4 decision in *Arizona Christian School Tuition Organization v. Winn* (2011), reversed the Ninth Circuit's decision. The Supreme Court held that the taxpayers, who were the plaintiffs challenging the constitutionality of the STO donations, lacked standing. The Court reasoned that when "Arizona taxpayers chose to contribute their own money to STOs, they spent their own money not the money the state had collected from . . . other taxpayers" (Arizona Christian School Tuition Organization v. Winn, 2011, p. 1447). In terms of the plaintiffs' Establishment Clause challenge, while the Arizona state government afforded the opportunity for taxpayers to create and contribute to an STO fund, "it was the private citizen who made the decision to contribute to a[n] STO and, in fact, made the contribution" (Arizona Christian School Tuition Organization v. Winn, 2011, p. 1448). The Supreme

Court, reflecting on the role of the judiciary, opined that "in an era of frequent litigation, class actions, sweeping injunctions with prospective effect and continuing jurisdiction to enforce judicial remedies, courts must be more careful to insist on the formal rules of standing, not less" (p. 1449).

CONCLUSION

The Arizona tax credit plan presents a different approach than the voucher programs upheld in Cleveland and Milwaukee. However, the political and economic debate as to whether state funds should be used to support non-public, including religious, schools is the same for all of the plans. All three represent some loss of revenues for public education. Clearly, the plans from Milwaukee and Cleveland present the greatest direct loss of funds for public schools because state monies that would otherwise go to them are used to pay for vouchers. On the other hand, Arizona's tax credit plan, as reflected in the Supreme Court's decision, has less direct effect on public school revenues since it only reduces general tax revenues, which may not necessarily be translated into reduced funds for public schools, depending on state legislative allocations.

At the heart of the voucher–tax credit debate is the political/philosophical issue as to whether all education should be subject to a free-market competitive model. A free-market model that would make public money available to parents as consumers free to "spend" their money with public and private vendors has its advocates (see Lieberman, 1993; McGroaty, 1996). Yet, such a model flies in the face of the historical pattern in the United States that public education was established as a common school system to ensure basic knowledge and literacy (see Doerr, Menendez, & Swomley, 1996; Smith & Meier, 1995) for all children. Whichever approach one takes, without up-front money, economically disadvantaged parents are unlikely to have the means to choose private education. Consequently, issues arise about providing equal educational opportunities for poor children, especially in inner city and economically disadvantaged locations.

The viability of educational choice, especially for the economically disadvantaged, depends on some form of government-assisted funding for two reasons. First, private sources of funding would never be adequate to meet the need (Moe, 1995). Second, as long as education is considered a government function, a free-market approach would depend on some measure of public funds being available to the parent-consumer-taxpayer to use to select educational services. However, this approach is not without its detractions, not the least of which is the survival of public education. To date, the limited voucher–tax credit plans in Cleveland, Milwaukee, and Arizona have not resulted in either public school insolvency or restructuring. The lack of a groundswell of post–*Zelman v. Simmons-Harris* (2002) state legislative voucher–tax credit plans suggests that the interest in state funding for nonpublic school choice may have run its course, at least for the present. Thus, while school business officials and other educational leaders need to be aware of developments with regard to vouchers and tax credits, perhaps the biggest news is that such changes are unlikely to have an immediate, or dramatic, impact on the funds that they have available for their school systems.

COUNTERPOINT: Timothy J. Ilg
University of Dayton

In the past few decades, educators and policymakers have debated the appropriateness of publicly funded programs that provide options for parents to choose the schools their children will attend. School choice does not give preference to a particular type of schooling, but rather manifests itself when a student attends school outside of his or her required attendance zone. The term *school choice* covers a wide variety of policy alternatives that expand parents' opportunities to select their children's schools. These "school choice" programs include tuition tax credits, school vouchers, open enrollment, and charter schools. With school choice becoming more prevalent throughout the country, is it time to ask some fundamental questions about this popular and powerful movement within education? How has school choice become so prevalent in so many states? Are students' interests best served with educational options? Is it wise to hand over educational policy decisions to private interests (e.g., foundations)? Will public education survive? If it does survive, what will the new structure look like, and will its fundamental goals change significantly? Will we still have a public school system that is bound by law to accept all children? Will school choice improve student outcomes or strengthen accountability?

This essay maintains that public school options have undermined the educational process for millions of children. Further, this essay challenges the widely held beliefs of education choice advocates that choice, by itself, improves school quality and efficiency, enhances opportunity for disadvantaged students, and encourages innovation through greater administrative autonomy. Schools of choice are in themselves no solution to the problems experienced within our schools. Like public schools, they vary widely in quality and as a whole have not outperformed public schools. Partisans of school choice tend to overpromise, implying that their policies will make every school and student above average. Overpromising leads inevitably to disappointment in many school districts. When it comes to raising test scores, the jury is still out on whether school choice consistently raises academic performance. This does not mean that school choice does not work, but the modest and incremental benefits of school choice call into question the ultimate value of this reform initiative. The value is particularly in question when one considers the damage done to public schools without clear benefits for the students and the community.

THE SCHOOL CHOICE DEBATE

Several early advocates of school choice have openly expressed their concerns about the movement in recent years. Sol Stern (2008) from the Manhattan Institute is no longer an ardent supporter of choice programs. Although he continues to support school choice, he thinks education reformers should refocus their energies on curriculum and pedagogy, and spend less time on market reform in education. Howard Fuller, an architect of Milwaukee's school voucher program, admitted that the program did not create the wholesale improvement in the schools that he had expected. He had hoped that vouchers would create a catalyst for public schools to create innovative programs and expand educational options for children within the schools (Hess, 2010). More recently, Diane Ravitch (2010), an early advocate for school choice, provided a passionate defense of public schools in her book, *The Death and Life of the Great American School System.* She challenges the heavy-handed approach of the federal government and private foundations to encourage the expansion of school choice programs (i.e., charter schools and voucher policies) at the expense of public schools. Ravitch critiques the continued reliance on a corporate model for school reform, and its failure to emphasize curriculum and instructional improvements. Although not opposed to charter schools, Ravitch feels that the structure itself does not guarantee success. A school with a first-rate curriculum and effective pedagogy will produce superior educational results whether it is a choice school or not. She also argues that charter schools should not be funded if they are able to cream off the best students and avoid the children who are harder to educate. Ravitch does not see a silver bullet to fix the public schools. She is convinced that public schools can be greatly improved, without the heavy hand of government or the influence of the powerful foundations. The largely structural and managerial efforts of the government, such as charter schools, voucher programs, testing, and accountability efforts, have largely proven unsuccessful in fundamentally improving public education. She insists that true reform efforts must be rooted in high standards, strong educational values, a rigorous curriculum, and the revival of strong neighborhood public schools. Foundations and think tanks have made school reform their pet projects, heavily investing in charter schools. They have been unwilling to support the local public school efforts to improve the operations of the schools.

Historically, critics of publicly funded school choice programs have focused on two issues—accountability and representation of at-risk students. They argue that optional or choice programs are often not held accountable to the federal and state educational rules and regulations. Since many of these schools are deregulated schools, they do not compete with traditional public schools on a level playing field. Without state and federal regulations, the advantages of standardization of curriculum, teacher preparation, and management that accrue when schooling systems are designed to deliver a common educational experience across numerous schools will be lost. In addition, critics are concerned with the underrepresentation of students with special needs, low income, and low English proficiency in school choice programs. Some scholars fear that choice stratifies students by ability and family background. Competition for students can actually spur disparity and restrict educational opportunities for students, rather than provide more productive schools (Ladd, 2002). More specifically, school choice opponents charge that students who are unable to leave their local schools because of their parents' educational level or lack of transportation will be hurt as additional funding is cut from their schools' budgets (Betts & Loveless, 2005). They further argue against school choice programs because they fear that they will increase segregation by race and social class and make the public schools dumping grounds for the children who are hard to educate (Fowler, 2002). They, in effect, will stratify students by family background, create niche schools that do not convey the nation's common heritage, provide taxpayer support for religious instruction, and nullify the advantages of standardization in curriculum designed to deliver a common educational experience for all children. Henry Levin (2001) notes that competition for students can result in what he calls "cream skimming," or the tendency of schools to choose students from more desirable backgrounds (less poor, higher prior achievement, etc.). Opponents of school choice have argued that it would weaken democracy. These opponents further argue that private schools and choice schools cannot provide an environment in which children meet people from different social, racial, and religious backgrounds and learn to respect them. Ultimately we must ask the question: Will school choice programs further fragment an already badly fragmented society, thereby encouraging even worse conflicts along the lines of race, poverty, class, and religion than those that currently run through American society?

In addition, opponents argue that education tax dollars belong to the state and should not be spent at the discretion of parents. In a recent case the Supreme Court ruled against four Arizona taxpayers who challenged an Arizona law that gives tax breaks for voluntary donations benefiting private schools. Under the law, Arizona citizens could receive up to $1,000 off their state income taxes for contributions to school tuition organizations. The lawsuit contended that the state had effectively been funneling taxpayer money to religious schools through a third-party "front" group. Thus, a key issue for the court was whether the tax credit meant the donated money was the government's money or the individual taxpayer's money. Of course, there was also the church and state question since the majority of scholarships were awarded to students attending religious schools. During oral arguments, the Justices appeared divided on whether the program was funded by money from the government or private contributors (*Arizona Christian School Tuition Organization v. Winn*, 2011). School choice opponents argued that the money given to the school tuition organizations funnels additional government resources to private schools and away from public schools. They further argued that most advocates of school choice are not interested in public education per se, but are simply working to fund the private sector with public monies. In a divided decision, the Supreme Court ruled in favor of the state law, and gave the educational choice advocates a significant advantage in the school choice debate. This case reversed a long series of subsequent cases that established the principle that tax money could not be used to support religious schools because the First Amendment of the U.S. Constitution requires the separation of church and state.

CRITICAL ISSUES IN SCHOOL CHOICE

An International Conference on School Choice and Educational Change, convened at Michigan State University in 2000, addressed five issues that were critical in evaluating school choice policies—student outcomes, innovation, governance, equity and access, and accountability (Plank & Sykes, 2000). On the theme of student outcomes, presenters advocating for school choice argued that increasing choice and competition in the education system would lead to improved outcomes for students, including higher test scores. Opponents of school choice policies, on the other hand, questioned the evidence on which these claims were based, and further argued that gains in student achievement could be achieved within the traditional public school structure. The opponents further argued that many traditional public schools perform superbly and those that do not can be improved with better resource allocation and management. Although school choice policies and charter programs have been studied intensively since this conference, the assessment of their effects on student achievement remains provisional at best. Research studies suggest that school choice has not had the positive effects on student achievement as predicted by its advocates but, at the same time, has not had the devastating negative impact on public schools as feared by the critics. Henry Levin, director of the National Center for the Study of Privatization in Education, questioned why education policymakers would prefer school choice over other school improvement strategies when larger achievement gains could be made by more familiar strategies, such as decreasing class size and adopting best practices in curriculum and instruction. He believes that choice and privatization have had very small educational impacts, both positive and negative. There are individual cases of both great success and great failure, but small differences on average. At this point we have no evidence that suggests that choice will lead to revolutionary improvements in the education of young people (Levin, 2001).

GOVERNANCE ISSUES

On the theme of governance, participants in support of school choice claimed that school choice policies empowered parents and teachers and reduced political interference in the educational system. They saw school choice programs as a way to work around the current dysfunctional governance structure in public schools. They argued that because schools are legislated as a basic monopoly, they had no external incentives to be competitive or consumer friendly. They further recommended a system of governance whereby states and local boards would create basic standards and individual schools would devise their own ways to meet those standards. They would let the schools set their own goals, standards, curricula, and character. Schools that failed to meet the standards would be subject to increased supervision and possible closure. Critics of school choice at the conference asserted that such policies undermine the democratic control of the schooling process. They feared the loss of public accountability that is built into the public school structure if the school choice movement dominated the educational system. Taxpayers might not be able to vote on budgetary issues, elect members of a community's board of education, or even attend public board meetings to voice their concerns. Many schools of choice operate more like private schools with a board of directors who may or may not have any direct responsibility to the parents. There are numerous examples of schools with outrageous executive salaries and high administrative costs but little or no opportunity for community input or feedback.

ACCOUNTABILITY

On the theme of accountability, school choice advocates argued that giving parents choices about the schools their children attend made schools more accountable to parents and students. Schools would be more responsive to the concerns of parents and students. Charter school teachers often cite freedom from procedural rules and related constraints as what they value the most. Ultimately, schools of choice that consistently fail to meet institutional goals are closed. In fact, most of these schools must be approved by a state agency before the application is accepted. They would question whether public schools can make the same claim. Although schools of choice would not eliminate the need for state regulations and rules, opponents questioned whether the market-based education system foreseen by choice advocates would hold schools accountable for achieving public purposes of schooling. Since many of these schools of choice can be operated by just about anyone, including private corporations, nonprofits, and individuals who may or may not have experience with operating an educational institution, they may or may not be committed to serving the needs of all of their constituents.

INNOVATION

On the theme of innovation, speakers in favor of school choice believed that market-based initiatives would spur innovation and improvement in public schools. Historically, proponents of school choice would often claim that choice would force the public schools to either compete or go out of business. Opponents, on the other hand, challenged this assertion, and suggested that traditional public schools had the capacity to foster educational improvements and innovation on their own. They also asserted that there is scant evidence that the school choice movement actually improved the public education system.

EQUITY AND ACCESS

Finally, on the theme of equity and access, Howard Fuller (2011), a professor at Marquette University, argued that choice opened up new opportunities for poor families who are trapped in poor schools. School choice empowers these families by offering a wide range of learning environments they feel are best for their children. Amy Stuart Wells (2002), an associate professor at the University of California at Los Angeles, challenged the assertion that school choice programs benefited poor and minority children. All too often choice schools operating in urban environments provide minimal services for low income students. The focus of free-market reforms is to increase the quantity of choice schools with little attention paid to their quality and to financial support. With limited resources, most choice schools hire younger, less experienced teachers, and have high rates of turnover and burnout.

CONCLUSION

School choice is going to continue to expand whether opponents like it or not. Parents like the idea of selecting a school for their children, and public support for choice has grown dramatically in the past decade. The debate over whether to enact school choice is behind us, but the question of how to achieve desired public objectives must still be considered. How will policymakers and educators structure choice policies and programs to minimize the risks of increased segregation? How can disadvantaged children be better served within schools of choice? How can we maximize the real opportunities that increased choice could offer our children while, at the same time, we restructure the traditional public school system so public schools can be more effective institutions? It is not in the best interest of our society to have winners and losers in the education system. There is no question that the school choice movement in education has undermined traditional public schools. Advocates of public schools, however, cannot advocate for returning to the "good old" days before the school choice movement began. They must recognize the public support for choice, and restructure public school education to provide students and parents more options and more flexibility within the public school structure. Alternatives such as magnet schools, charter schools, and virtual schools within public school systems will foster innovation and will allow parents to choose public schools within their districts.

FURTHER READINGS AND RESOURCES

Betts, J. R., & Loveless, T. (2005). *Getting choice right.* Washington, DC: Brookings Institution Press.

Doerr, E., Menendez, A., & Swomley, J. (1996). *The case against school vouchers.* Amherst, NY: Prometheus Books.

Fowler, F. C. (2002). The great school choice debate. *The Clearing House, 76*(1), 4–7.

Friedman, M. (1980). *Free to choose: Vol. 6. What's wrong with our schools* [Television series episode]. Video Arts TV Production.

Friedman, M., & Friedman, R. (1990). *Free to choose: A personal statement.* New York: Mariner Books.

Fuller, H. (2011). Keep intact the mission of choice program. *Milwaukee-Wisconsin Journal Sentinel.* Retrieved from http://www.jsonline.com/news/opinion/120515559 .html

Hess, F. (2010). Does school choice work? *National Affairs, 5.* Retrieved from http:// www.nationalaffairs.com/publications/detail/does-school-choice-work

Ladd, H. L. (2002). *Market-based reforms in urban education.* Washington, DC: Economic Policy Institute.

Levin, H. M. (2001). *Privatizing education: Can the marketplace deliver choice, efficiency, equity, and social cohesion?* Boulder, CO: Westview Press.

Lieberman, L. (1993). *Public education: An autopsy.* Cambridge, MA: Harvard University Press.

McGroaty, D. E. (1996). *Break those chains: The battle for school choice.* Roseville, CA: Prima.

Moe, T. (Ed.). (1995). *Private vouchers.* Stanford, CA: Hoover Institution Press.

Plank, D. N., & Sykes, G. (2000). *The school choice debate: Framing the issues.* East Lansing: The Education Policy Center, Michigan State University.

Ravitch, D. (2010). *The death and life of the great American school system: How testing and choice are undermining education.* New York: Basic Books.

Smith, K., & Meier, K. (1995). *The case against school choice: Politics, markets, and school choice.* Armonk, NY: M. E. Sharpe.

Stern, S. (2008, Winter). School choice isn't enough. *City Journal, 18*(1). Retrieved from http://www.city-journal.org/2008/18_1_instructional_reform.html

Wells, A. S. (2002). *Where charter school policy fails: The problems of accountability and equity.* New York: Teachers College Press.

Court Cases and Statutes

Arizona Christian School Tuition Organization v. Winn, 131 S. Ct. 1436 (2011).

Bush v. Holmes, 919 So.2d 392 (Fla. 2006).

Hibbs v. Winn, 542 U.S. 88 (2004).

Jackson v. Benson, 578 N.W.2d 602 (Wis. 1998).

Kotterman v. Killian, 972 P.2d 606 (Ariz. 1999), *cert. denied,* 528 U.S. 921 (1999).

Mueller v. Allen, 463 U.S. 388 (1983).

No Child Left Behind Act, 20 U.S.C. §§ 6301–7941 (2006).

United States Constitution, Amendment I.

Winn v. Arizona Christian School Tuition Organization, 562 F.3d 1002 (9th Cir. 2009).

Winn v. Killian, 307 F.3d 1011 (9th Cir. 2002).

Zelman v. Simmons-Harris, 536 U.S. 639 (2002).

7

Should homeschooling be subject to greater state regulation in such areas as teacher qualifications and curricular content?

POINT: James L. Mawdsley, *Stark State College*
COUNTERPOINT: Ralph D. Mawdsley, *Cleveland State University*

OVERVIEW

Homeschooling, as the name implies, involves educating one's children at home. Generally, homeschooled students are taught by their parents, but they may also be instructed by paid tutors or, in the age of technology, by taking virtual courses through the Internet. Although teaching children at home was the norm in Colonial times, the practice went out of fashion as states passed compulsory attendance laws to the extent that as recently as the 1980s homeschooling was legal in only two states. Even so, following a period of increased interest in homeschooling, it is now legal in all 50 states, whether by means of explicit statutes, regulations, or court decisions or implicit interpretations of regulations permitting alternative educational arrangements. The most recent federal data on homeschooling indicate that the percentage of students who are homeschooled grew from 1.7% in 1999 to 2.2% in 2003 and 2.9% (or about 1.5 million children) in 2007 (National Center for Education Statistics, 2009).

Even though homeschooling is legal in all 50 states, disagreements exist over many aspects of how instruction is provided. On the one hand, parents who homeschool their children normally are not required to be certificated or licensed as teachers or even meet minimal qualifications such as having a college degree. On the other hand, courts have reached mixed results in disputes regarding a variety of issues such as curricular content for homeschooling, state oversight in terms of whether children must take standardized tests, and whether students can participate in extracurricular activities or attend public schools on a part-time basis.

Parents homeschool their children for a multiplicity of reasons including the desire to provide them with better educational services, objections to many topics taught or methods used in both public and private schools, religious beliefs, a desire to better shape the character and moral development of their offspring, and, in some cases, family convenience. As would be expected, the curriculum and pedagogy in home school situations varies greatly. In many cases, particularly those where the parents have no formal training in education, parents procure a prepackaged curriculum that includes all necessary materials and detailed lesson plans. Many commercial outfits produce curriculum packages specifically for the home school market. Such prepackaged units tend to be expensive but generally follow a state's curricular guidelines and thus meet most requirements. In other situations, such as when parents object to the state's mandated curricular content, they may devise lessons and instructional units on their own. As indicated above, many options exist using technology, ranging from obtaining specific lessons or curricular content from the Internet to enrolling children full-time in virtual schools. (See the *Technology in Schools* volume in this series for more information on virtual schools.)

When parents choose to not send their children to the public schools, they must provide them with an equivalent education elsewhere, either at a private school or at home (Russo, 2009). In the current era of educational accountability, courts are often asked to determine whether homeschooled students are, in fact, receiving an equivalent education. Courts have considered a broad array of issues involving states' rights to regulate and oversee home schools in areas such as teacher qualifications and curricular requirements.

There is much variance in the degree to which states regulate home schools in matters of instruction. Among the most contentious issues is the topic of this chapter's debate: whether states should impose greater regulation over teacher qualifications and curricular content in home schools. James L. Mawdsley, an adjunct professor of education law at Cleveland State University and an instructor of English composition at Stark State College of Technology, takes the point position arguing that states have an interest in ensuring that children are properly educated. Ralph D. Mawdsley, a professor of educational administration and the Roslyn Z. Wolf Endowed Chair in Urban Educational Leadership at Cleveland State University, takes the opposite position stating that in an era where it has taken the federal government to prod states into establishing meaningful assessments of student performance and higher standards of teacher qualification, states should not point a finger toward home schools.

James L. Mawdsley insists that the issue should not be seen as one of parental rights. Since advocates of homeschooling claim that it provides an education equivalent to or better than that provided by the public schools, he posits that parents cannot be allowed to ignore state guidelines while claiming to have educated their children to state standards. He concludes by stating that although parents are free to direct the education of their children, they are not free to create their own standards of what constitutes an adequate education and oblige the rest of society to accept it.

Ralph D. Mawdsley, an author who has written extensively on the rights of parents to direct the upbringing of their children, feels that state regulators and courts have not been particularly sympathetic toward homeschooling. After reviewing the body of court decisions involving state attempts to regulate homeschooling, he concludes that the casé law reflects a mistrust of parents and an unduly inflated assessment of the performance of the public schools. Noting that sincerely held religious beliefs are at the core of much homeschooling, he insists that we cannot assume that private schools are available that are compatible with the parents' religious beliefs. He finds it ironic that private schools are able to exempt themselves from much state legislation but that home school parents, who lack the same clout, cannot.

The issue of how much states can regulate homeschooling will continue as parents increasingly find homeschooling to be a preferred option to sending their children to public schools. As you read the debate in this chapter, you may wish to think about the following: To what degree is the issue of state regulation one that involves families' free exercise of religion rights? Should parents' rights to direct the education and upbringing of their children trump the states' interests in developing an educated citizenry? Can the states establish minimum standards for homeschooling and create mechanisms for oversight without being overly intrusive into matters of family privacy?

Allan G. Osborne, Jr.
Principal (Retired), Snug Harbor Community School,
Quincy, Massachusetts

Charles J. Russo
University of Dayton

POINT: James L. Mawdsley
Stark State College

Homeschooling is an increasingly popular option for parents frustrated with public education. In 2007, the National Household Education Surveys Program (NHES), conducted by the Department of Education, found that 1.5 million students were being homeschooled in the United States. While this represented only 2.9% of the school-age population, this was a marked increase from 2.2% in 2003, which was in turn an increase from the 1.7% who were homeschooled in 1999 (National Center for Education Statistics, 2008, p. 1). The reason for the growing popularity of homeschooling is not difficult to discern. Generally speaking, many homeschooling parents have very specific, religiously based objections to public school. The 2007 NHES also found that 83% of homeschooling parents cited the ability "to provide religious or moral instruction" to their children as one reason why they homeschooled, an increase from 72% in 2003 (p. 2). When asked to choose the primary reason for homeschooling, "religious or moral instruction" was still the most popular answer, with 36% (p. 3). But 21% of parents chose "concern about the school environment," and a further 17% cited their "dissatisfaction with the academic instruction available at other schools" as their primary reason (p. 3).

As a matter of public policy, states have an interest in ensuring that children are educated. However, the proposition that some U.S. public schools are appalling failures at providing children with a basic education is not, in this author's opinion, seriously in doubt. The central question regarding homeschooling, however, is whether it represents any real improvement for an individual child. Surely the parent-teachers will believe that their children are improving. Only systematic regulation and testing will reveal whether students are learning what they need to learn in order to become productive members of society. The regulation of homeschooling is not the same as forcing students into public or private schools. Regulation need not be burdensome if it serves only to ensure that children are actually learning.

DISCUSSION

One of the more important cases in the history of parental rights over their children's education was *Wisconsin v. Yoder* (1972). This was an appeal by two Old Order Amish fathers and one father from the Conservative Amish Mennonite Church, each of whom had been convicted of violating Wisconsin's state compulsory attendance policy and fined $5. On the basis of their sincere beliefs, which required them to live apart from the world, they had refused to send their children to school until the age of 16, preferring instead to withdraw them after the completion of the eighth grade. Among their other arguments, the fathers asserted that the Amish had a long history of inculcating children with the values of the community through hard work. The children were being prepared for life in that community. The state-mandated 2 years of high school would have negligible educational value while damaging the ability of the parents to prepare their children for life in that world. For our purposes, the salient point in *Yoder* is that, whatever educational benefits the Amish children may have been gaining in working on their family farms, neither they nor their parents made any claim that they were receiving the functional equivalent of a high school degree. At trial, an expert witness appearing for the Amish fathers expressed the opinion that "their system of learning through doing the skills directly relevant to their adult roles in the Amish community [was] 'ideal,' and perhaps superior to ordinary high school education" (*Wisconsin v. Yoder,* 1972, p. 212). It may have been, and still may be, superior to high school, but no one claimed that it was, in fact, high school.

An important initial inquiry when examining homeschooling regulation is whether teaching children at home is functionally equivalent to a state-mandated public school education. Certainly, parents who teach their children at home would like to believe that their efforts are not inferior to those of the local schools. And they would likely assert that their children should be treated as educated individuals who have completed the equivalent of a K–12 education.

In many states, statutory authority lends weight to this assertion. For example, in Massachusetts, one of the states most restrictive of parents' rights to homeschool their children, local school officials are obligated to approve a homeschooling plan if "instruction in all the studies required by law equals in thoroughness and efficiency, and in the progress made therein, that in the public schools in the same town, but shall not withhold such approval on account of religious teaching" (Massachusetts General Laws, Chapter 76, § 1). Likewise, in Idaho, a state that is much more permissive, the relevant statute requires homeschooled children to be "instructed in subjects commonly and usually taught in the public schools" (Idaho Code, § 33-202). Texas considers "successful completion of a nontraditional secondary education to be equivalent to graduation from a public high school," and on that basis prohibits institutions of higher education from discriminating against homeschooled applicants (Texas Education Code Annotated, § 51.9241).

No doubt this is a comfort to college-bound teenagers in Texas, but these statutes in fact present a problem for their parents. To assert that a nontraditional home school is the equivalent of a public school is to implicitly accept the authority of the state to define what constitutes primary and secondary education. A federal court in New York, in *Blackwelder v. Safnauer* (1988), addressed claims by parents that a state law mandating that homeschooling parents "ensure that their children receive an education 'substantially equivalent' to that offered in public schools" was unconstitutionally vague (p. 126). Rather than mandating a single statewide standard, the statute allowed leeway to local officials to set their own standards. But as the court pointed out, "the guidelines supplied by the state legislature provide a basic framework within which local authorities can fashion educational standards designed to address peculiar local concerns" (*Blackwelder v. Safnauer,* 1988, p. 127).

One may note Justice White's concurring opinion in *Wisconsin v. Yoder* (1972), in which he was joined by Justices Brennan and Stewart:

> This would be a very different case for me if respondents' claim were that their religion forbade their children from attending any school at any time and from complying in any way with the educational standards set by the State. (p. 238)

And yet in the counterpoint essay my colleague seems to urge precisely what Justice White rejected. In the absence of comprehensive state regulation, a parent would be allowed to withdraw his or her children from public or traditional private schools, and the state would be obligated to regard those children as being enrolled in classes on little more evidence than the attestation of the parent.

It is far more important to enforce standards in homeschooling precisely because supervision is so difficult. If a teacher neglects his job in a public school, there will be multiple student witnesses and many parents who can complain. The school can then take action to rectify the situation and give the teacher appropriate guidance. If a homeschooling parent neglects his or her work, however, or simply does a poor job of teaching, the only people who could know that are the parent and his or her child/student. Therefore there must be a rigorous system of qualifications, curricular standards, and tests to ensure that the parent is competent to teach and the child is being taught correctly. The state obviously cannot be present to observe homeschooling, but by creating and enforcing standards, the state can minimize the chance of students being left without a proper instructor.

The issue of teacher qualifications is, again, one of definition. A homeschooling parent purports to be providing his or her children with the equivalent of a public education, and thus, it is appropriate to compare the home school to government schools. Such a comparison is obviously not appropriate in every aspect of the learning environment. Classroom facilities will be different, and there will be no marching band or school play, for example. In these cases, we could say that the differences are not truly central to the child's education. But arguably a qualified teacher is far more central to education than a marching band or a school play.

Requiring state licensure is by no means a negligible burden from the point of view of parents, who presumably will have to complete the requirements while at the same time teaching their children at home. But mere licensure is a minor burden compared to, for example, Highly Qualified Teacher standards. The state is not requiring that parents be more qualified than the average teacher, or that parents demonstrate mastery of each core academic subject, but merely is requiring that they meet the minimum requirements. Unfortunately, in *People v. DeJonge* (1993), the Michigan Supreme Court overturned a teacher certification requirement for homeschooling parents, on the grounds that the requirement was not the "least restrictive means" by which the state could achieve its goal of a well-educated citizenry. To the contrary, however, teacher certification is far less restrictive than inspections of home schools or constant supervision and testing. Indeed, in at least one sense a licensure requirement is minimally restrictive, insofar as it does not restrict what the parent-teacher does in the classroom at all.

The court in *People v. DeJonge* (1993) also asserted that the requirements imposed a "loathsome dilemma" upon parents. That is to say that the parents were being obligated to choose between obeying the government and obeying God. The father in the case, Mark DeJonge, testified that

> scripture is the complete and inherit [sic] word of God. That it specifically teaches that parents are the ones that are responsible to God for the education of their children. And for us to allow the State to insert [sic] God's authority, for us to submit to that would be a sin. (p. 130 n. 4)

But as long as the requirement is neutral, it should pass constitutional muster. What if a parent were to decide, on the basis of deep religious convictions, that a certain religious text, such as the Bible or the Koran, would be the only textbook in his or her home school? The state, presumably, would have to explain to the parent that, whatever his or her spiritual and literary merits, those works are not appropriate textbooks for math and science. That, too, might well be a "loathsome dilemma," and the parent would be forced to choose between God and man. But such a school would clearly not be dispensing an education that met state requirements. Should a state and its citizens be forced to recognize a student completing such a school as the equivalent of a high school graduate, merely to prevent the parent from facing that dilemma?

A more reasonable approach was taken by the North Dakota Supreme Court in *State v. Patzer* (1986). The case involved a consolidated appeal of four sets of parents, two of the Seventh Day Adventist Church, and two of the Lutheran Brethren Church, who had been convicted of violating the state's compulsory attendance laws. All four couples claimed that they had educated their children at home because of their sincerely held religious beliefs. At issue in Patzer was whether a state requirement that homeschooling parents be certified teachers was justified by the state's compelling interest in the education of children.

Another "loathsome dilemma" can arise in the area of curriculum content. Parents may find themselves obliged to teach material that they do not believe and do not wish their children to believe, either. Curriculum requirements only cover what must be presented, not the manner or context of its presentation. The state will not (and cannot) control the manner in which information is presented. For example, rather than teaching evolution as fact, the religious homeschooling parent could tell his or her child, "This is not true, but the state thinks it's important you know it, anyway." This is no different from the way in which evolution is presented at many evangelical religious schools. And this being the case, there can be no reasonable objection to a state curricular standard. If a parent wishes not simply to control the presentation of a subject, but actually to maintain her child in complete ignorance of vast swathes of human knowledge, then once again, the parent is inventing her own definition of a primary or secondary "education," which the state is not obligated to recognize.

Some would argue that giving local school administrators the power of supervision and oversight of homeschooling parents amounts to the fox guarding the henhouse. Does not the state, they might argue, have an incentive to eliminate competition? Perhaps that is true, but there is no need to begin with the proposition that school officials are acting in bad faith in trying to enforce state guidelines. If there are to be standards, they will have to be enforced by people with the necessary training and experience. Put simply, the people who happen to be qualified to assess a school, and are already on the payroll, will be the local school administrators.

This raises the issue of whether teacher qualifications are in fact being used as a pretext to prevent homeschooling by religious parents. Any government regulation, even speed limits, can be enforced selectively as a pretext for discrimination. But the fact that the regulations can be abused in this way is no reason to abandon them entirely. The question is whether teacher qualifications are in fact being used as a pretext. In the absence of large numbers of nonreligious home schoolers, it is impossible to say whether regulations on homeschooling have been created as a pretext to punish on the basis of antireligious animus. But again, as long as the regulations are neutral, there ought to be no constitutional violation.

CONCLUSION

Homeschooling purports to provide an education that is the equivalent of (or better than) that given in the public schools of the state. Parents are free to teach their children whatever they want, but they cannot be allowed to ignore state guidelines while still claiming to have educated their children to those standards. This should not be seen as an issue of parental rights. Rather, the issue is the instruction of a child in a curriculum that purports to be the equivalent of that which is used in state-recognized public and private schools. The fact that the instructor happens to be the child's parent in this case is immaterial. That the education is delivered in a private home is irrelevant. Parents are free to direct the education of their children, but they are not free to invent their own, radically new definition of what constitutes an education and oblige the rest of society to accept it.

COUNTERPOINT: Ralph D. Mawdsley
Cleveland State University

Homeschooling has been a basis of conflict for the past 50 years. A method of instruction that has been part of the fabric of U.S. history since its Colonial days became suspect as states created free public schools and enforced attendance by means of compulsory attendance statutes. Arguing that student attendance at public schools was important for creating a common culture, attendance at nonpublic schools was viewed as suspect. Even more suspect were home schools where not only was the quality of instruction in question, but so was the absence of socialization, which in an increasingly secular society became the mantra for producing cookie-cutter graduates.

No one seems to have an accurate number of the homeschooled students in the United States, but one estimate places the number between 1.7 million and 2.2 million children (Ray, 2004, p. 1). For a sense of perspective,

> more children are educated at home than are educated in the public schools of Wyoming, Vermont, Delaware, North Dakota, Alaska, South Dakota, Rhode Island, Montana and Hawaii—combined. In fact, the total number of children educated in home schools outnumbers the aggregate of children educated in the public schools of 41 individual states. (Colwell & Schwartz, 2003, p. 381)

Brad Colwell and Brian Schwartz (2003) have also noted the following:

1. All 50 states recognize that homeschooling can satisfy compulsory attendance requirements, but they differ significantly in the amount of regulation. Thirty-four states have statutes and/or administrative regulations directly addressing home schools.

2. Forty-one states require notification by those providing home instruction, with 33 requiring notification to local officials, 7 to state officials, and 1 to either local or state officials.

3. Forty-five states specify home schools to operate a specific number of days and/or hours each year.

4. Forty-four states set curriculum requirements.

5. Twenty-one states do not have specific qualifications for parents or nonparents as instructors; on the other hand, 2 states (Alabama and Michigan) require all instructors, including parents, to be certificated, but beyond these 2 states, qualifications vary widely as to diplomas, degrees, or certifications required for instructional purposes. (pp. 392–395)

The history of state responses to homeschooling has not been particularly sympathetic or understanding. In addition to a significant judicial record of truancy convictions for parents who choose to homeschool without satisfying state requirements (*State v. Patzer*, 1986), courts have upheld a wide range of regulatory methods applicable to home schools but not necessarily to other nonpublic schools (*Battles v. Arundel County Board of Education*, 1995; *Brunelle v. Lynn Public Schools*, 1998).

DISCUSSION
Teacher Qualifications

States that have set teacher certification or competency requirements on home school teachers (generally, the parents) have had to balance the interest of the state in educated citizens with the First and Fourteenth Amendment interest of parents in directing the education of their children. In *Jernigan v. State of Alabama* (1982), a court upheld a criminal truancy conviction of parents who used a Catholic correspondence course for homeschooling their children, but lacked a state teaching certificate. The court rejected the parents' Free Exercise Clause claim that exposing her children to the public school would jeopardize their salvation, concluding instead the parents had failed to produce evidence that exposure to public schools would, in fact, affect the children's salvation, and, in any case, the parents had not shown how their homeschooling would prepare their children for life in a modern society. In *State v. Patzer* (1986) the Supreme Court of North Dakota held that the state's compulsory attendance statute requiring that children be taught by certified teachers burdened parents' freedom of religion, but was nonetheless constitutional because it was the least intrusive method of protecting the state's interest in an educated citizenry. Worth noting is that the Supreme Court rejected the parents' claim that state testing to ensure student performance should be a satisfactory substitute, observing, "While a teaching certificate is no guarantee that the holder is a competent teacher, it does guarantee that the holder has been exposed to the knowledge that a competent teacher should have" (p. 639). However, in *People v. DeJonge* (1993), the Supreme Court of Michigan reversed criminal truancy convictions of homeschooling parents, concluding that the state had failed to produce evidence that teacher certification was the least restrictive means of achieving the state's interest in an educated citizenry. Upholding the parents' claim that their children receive a "Christ-centered education," the Supreme Court found that the state's requirement imposed on the parents "a loathsome dilemma: they must either violate the law of God to abide by the law of man, or commit a crime under the law of man to remain faithful to God" (*People v. DeJonge*, 1993, p. 137).

When a state imposes teacher requirements other than certification, the requirements must be definable. In *Jeffrey v. O'Donnell* (1988) a federal district court found unconstitutionally vague a state requirement that schooling must be provided by "a qualified private tutor" and that the instruction must also be "satisfactory to the proper district superintendent" (pp. 518–519). Noting that the state had provided no criteria for interpreting the terms *qualified* and *satisfactory,* the district court declared that every school district superintendent in the state could have different criteria for the terms, and to add insult to injury, once a superintendent rendered an interpretation, the only appeal from that decision was to the courts.

Curriculum Regulations

State efforts at regulating the curriculum of home schools have generated litigation as well. In *Blackwelder v. Safnauer* (1988) parents challenged the manner in which the state evaluated homeschooling programs by giving local school district superintendents unbridled discretion in determining whether a particular program provides the statutorily required level of instruction. Referencing broad state guidelines for the substantive content of the studies of public schoolchildren, the federal district court upheld these guidelines, which "allow[ed] flexibility in addressing unique local problems, enhance[d] responsiveness to the educational concerns of the communities within a particular school district, and respect[ed] this nation's tradition of vesting primary control over educational policy with local authorities" (p. 123).

Some states have imposed standardized test requirements on homeschooled students as a method of evaluating the quality of the home school educational program. In *Murphy v. State of Arkansas* (1988), the Eighth Circuit upheld a state statute providing that home school students were required to take an annual standardized test (that could be selected by the parents) and, if the child did not achieve a score within eight months of his or her grade level, the student had to be placed in a public, private, or parochial school. While recognizing that the state's requirements interfered with the parents' sincerely held religious beliefs, the court of appeals nonetheless upheld the state requirements as fulfilling a state's compelling interest "in educating all of its citizens" (*Murphy v. State of Arkansas*, 1988, p. 1041) and further noting that the state had "no means less restrictive than its administration of achievement tests to ensure that its citizens are being properly educated" (p. 1043). In *Null v. Board of Education of County of Jackson* (1993) the court rejected a parent's Equal Protection Clause claim that a state statute that made children ineligible for homeschooling if their standardized test scores fell below the 40th percentile and did not improve after remedial homeschooling was unconstitutional. While alleging a disparity between the assessment of test scores of students in public schools and those in home schools, the parents could produce no evidence to support their claim, and the court upheld the state's 40% cut-off score for home schools as "reasonably intended to promote above average scores" (*Null v. Board of Education of County of Jackson*, 1993, p. 940). In *Vandiver v. Hardin County Board of Education* (1991) the Sixth Circuit upheld a state statute that required a high school student with behavior problems who had been homeschooled for his sophomore year, using "a Christian course of instruction called Alpha Omega" (p. 929), to pass an equivalency test before credits could be transferred for courses taken as part of a nonaccredited program. Finding the state statute to be neutral and generally applicable, the court of appeals rejected the parents' Free Exercise Clause claim. Moreover, even if the parents had a Free Exercise Clause claim, the student had no religious objection to testing, and nothing in the state statute would have prohibited the student from continuing his education as part of home instruction. Worth noting is that the school district in *Vandiver* would have imposed the same testing requirement on a student transferred from a nonaccredited private or religious school. Such similarity in treatment between private or religious schools and home schools is sufficient to reject any free exercise or equal protection claims (*Hubbard v. Buffalo Independent School District,* 1998). However, not all states treat home schools and private schools similarly.

Home Schools as Private Schools?

While the previous discussion has considered the extent to which states can impose special requirements on home schools when compared to public schools, such does not necessarily address whether a state can impose different requirements on home schools than on nonpublic (private and religious) schools. The simplest and most direct claim of parents when facing differential requirements is to claim that a home school is a private school.

In an older case, *People of Illinois v. Levisen* (1950), the Supreme Court of Illinois determined that, since the state statute was silent as to home schools, they constituted private schools and, thus, fit within a statutory exception from the compulsory attendance law. The Supreme Court reasoned that "the law is not made to punish those who provide their children with instruction equal or superior to that obtainable in the public schools" (p. 215). However, almost 30 years later, the Supreme Court of Virginia, in *Grigg v. Commonwealth of Virginia* (1982), rejected a parental claim that home schools in the state were private schools, on which the state imposed fewer regulations, reasoning that Virginia has specific statutory provisions for homeschooling. The Supreme Court of North Carolina, in *Delconte v. State of North Carolina* (1985), held that attendance at home schools satisfied the state's compulsory attendance requirement, reasoning that there was no evidence to support the conclusion that the word *school,* when used by the legislature in statutes regarding compulsory attendance, evidenced a legislative purpose to refer to a particular kind of instructional setting.

The nature of state requirements can appear onerous where home schools may lack qualified teachers available in private schools. The Supreme Court of Washington, in *State v. Superior Court* (1960), reversed a trial court decision that parents who homeschooled their child for religious reasons should be exempt from the standards applicable to public and private schools. Where a home school lacked a qualified teacher, the Supreme Court reasoned that it failed to qualify as a private school in the state. Similarly, a Florida appeals court, in *State of Florida v. M.M.* (1981), ruled that the absence of statutory authority regulating the establishment of private schools in Florida did not mean that Florida parents, unqualified to be private tutors, could proclaim their homes to be private schools and withdraw their children from public schools. In effect, the state appeals court accepted the compulsory attendance distinction between "a private school supported in whole or in part by tuition charges or by endowments or gifts" and home instruction "with a private tutor who meets all requirements prescribed by law and regulations of the state board for private tutors" (*State of Florida v. M.M.*, 1981, p. 990). In *Murphy v. State of Arkansas* (1988), the Eighth Circuit upheld annual standardized achievement testing for homeschooled students, but not for private or parochial school students, reasoning that "the state must have a mechanism by which it can confidently and objectively be assured that its citizens are being adequately educated" (p. 1042). The court of appeals noted that, since the state did not impose teacher certification requirements on parents, did not require that parents follow a mandated curriculum, permitted the parents to select the standardized test to be used, and allowed the parents to be present for the testing, the state's interests would not be served by the parents' suggestions that the state parental testing of their children and parental affidavits would be adequate indicators of the children's progress.

CONCLUSION

The case law concerning regulation of homeschooled students reflects a mistrust of parents and an unduly inflated assessment of the performance of the public schools. In an era where it has taken the federal government's power of the purse, through the No Child Left Behind Act, to prod public schools into meaningful assessment of student performance, improvement of teacher qualifications, and annual revelation of student achievement, the notion that states should point a finger of suspicion toward home schools in ostrich-like fashion is nothing short of amazing. At the core of virtually all homeschooling are sincerely held religious beliefs that have both a centrifugal and a centripetal force. The child is both drawn to instruction in the home because of the centrality of religious beliefs and dismissive of attendance at a public school because of its indifference, if not hostility, toward religion. To attempt to coerce parents to send their children to less regulated private, sectarian schools assumes that such schools are available and, even if available, are compatible with the parents' religious beliefs. Despite the U.S. Supreme Court's *Wisconsin v. Yoder* (1972) decision where the Court created a constitutional flexibility for addressing the religious beliefs of parents, most courts have assiduously refused to look beyond the Amish religious beliefs and see that what was at stake was simply the educational choice of parents. Ironically, Justice Douglas's dissent in *Yoder* captured the full measure of that case, namely that "the parents are seeking to vindicate not only their own free exercise claims, but also those of their high-school-age children" (*Wisconsin v. Yoder,* 1972, p. 241). Since the state in *Yoder* challenged only the Amish children's nonattendance at a school past completion of eight grades of schooling (approximately ages 13–16) and not the nonstate regulation of the school, the concept that should have become future precedent was the Amish parents' home instruction following 8 years of school. While Justice Douglas opined that "I think the children should be entitled to be heard" (*Wisconsin v. Yoder,* 1972, p. 244), the constitutional protection that *Yoder* provides to parents to make instructional choices that do not involve a formal school has been ignored. However much legislative clout that private schools have in exempting themselves from state regulations, such does not apply to homeschooling parents who may be less likely to seek legislative action and bring attention to their homeschooling status.

FURTHER READINGS AND RESOURCES

Colwell, B., & Schwartz, B. (2003). Implications for public schools: Legal aspects of home schools. *West's Education Law Reporter, 173,* 381.

National Center for Education Statistics. (2008). *1.5 million homeschooled students in the United States in 2007.* Retrieved from http://nces.ed.gov/pubs2009/2009030.pdf

National Center for Education Statistics. (2009). Table 38, Number and percentage of homeschooled students ages 5 through 17 with a grade equivalent of kindergarten through 12th grade, by selected child, parent, and household characteristics: 1999, 2003, and 2007. *Digest of Education Statistics.* Retrieved from http://nces.ed.gov/programs/digest/d09/tables/dt09_038.asp

Ray, B. D. (2004). *Worldwide guide to homeschooling.* Nashville, TN: Broadman & Holman.

Russo, C. J. (2009). *Reutter's the law of public education* (7th ed.). New York: Foundation Press.

COURT CASES AND STATUTES

Battles v. Arundel County Board of Education, 904 F. Supp. 471 (D. Md. 1995), *aff'd,* 95 F.3d 41 (4th Cir. 1995).

Blackwelder v. Safnauer, 689 F.Supp. 106 (N.D.N.Y., 1988).

Brunelle v. Lynn Public Schools, 702 N.E.2d 1182 (Mass. 1998).

Delconte v. State of North Carolina, 329 S.E.2d 636 (N.C. 1985).

Grigg v. Commonwealth of Virginia, 297 S.E.2d 799 (Va. 1982).

Hubbard v. Buffalo Independent School District, 20 F.Supp.2d 1012 (W.D. Tex. 1998).

Idaho Code, § 33–202.

Jeffrey v. O'Donnell, 702 F. Supp. 516 (M.D. Pa. 1988).

Jernigan v. State of Alabama, 412 So.2d 1242 (Ala. Crim. App. 1982).

Massachusetts General Laws, Chapter 76, § 1.

Meyer v. State of Nebraska, 262 U.S. 390 (1923).

Murphy v. State of Arkansas, 852 F.2d 1039 (8th Cir. 1988).

No Child Left Behind Act, 20 U.S.C. §§ 6301-7941 (2006).

Null v. Board of Education of County of Jackson, 815 F. Supp. 937 (S.D. W. Va. 1993).

People of Illinois v. Levisen, 90 N.E.2d 213 (Ill. 1950).

People v. DeJonge, 501 N.W.2d 127 (Mich. 1993).

Pierce v. Society of Sisters, 268 U.S. 510 (1925).

State of Florida v. M.M., 407 So. 2d 987 (Fla. App. 1981).

State v. Patzer, 382 N.W.2d 631 (N.D. 1986).

State v. Superior Court, 346 P.2d 999 (Wash. 1960).

Texas Education Code Annotated, § 51.9241.

Vandiver v. Hardin County Board of Education, 925 F.2d 927 (6th Cir. 1991).

Wisconsin v. Yoder, 406 U.S. 205 (1972).

Should the Jewish community in the United States provide Jewish day schools for all Jewish children as a means of preserving their Jewish identity?

POINT: Marc N. Kramer, *RAVSAK: The Jewish Community Day School Network*

COUNTERPOINT: Bruce S. Cooper, *Fordham University*

OVERVIEW

A Jewish day school is a school that Jewish children attend on a full-time basis, which is designed to provide them with a religious, cultural, and general education at the same time. Jewish day schools vary. Some may be predominantly religious while others place more of an emphasis on secular studies. As the essays in this chapter show, although a vast majority of Jewish children attend public schools, Jewish day schools are thriving, and their enrollment has increased steadily during the past 30 years.

In this chapter, Marc N. Kramer, Executive Director of RAVSAK: The Jewish Community Day School Network, and Bruce S. Cooper, a professor at the Fordham University Graduate School of Education, go head-to-head on what is the best and most appropriate education for Jewish children in the United States.

On one side, Kramer argues for universal Jewish day schools that provide a dual program of religious, cultural, and secular studies. These day schools, which cover the spectrum from kindergarten through Grade 12, are run by local and national Jewish groups and denominations (Orthodox, Conservative, Reform, and a community day school association called RAVSAK) and number 999 schools, enrolling about 237,000 children in the United States in 2009 across the range of Jewish groups and denominations.

Kramer contends that Jewish day schools provide a breadth and depth of Jewish religious and moral instruction—for example, Torah, commentary, Jewish history and customs, ethics, and Hebrew—not available to Jewish children attending public and other types of private schools. Furthermore, according to Kramer, these schools graduate a new generation of Jews who are highly educated, Jewishly literate, and deeply engaged in communal and civic life and who serve as the energizing nucleus of the Jewish and general community. Kramer claims that other educational options for Jewish children cannot—by design or default—offer what day schools can provide. The proven success of these schools, their wide availability, and their close alignment with educational best practices and American ideals, in his view, suggest that Jewish day schools should be made available and affordable to all Jewish children.

Opposing him in the counterpoint essay, Cooper asserts that most Jewish families cannot afford or do not have easy access to full-time Jewish education. Hence, Cooper asserts that the Jewish community should support after-school programs, Sunday schools at local synagogues, and summer programs and youth groups that provide Jewish studies and teach Jewish practices for the majority of these children in the United States.

Of course, Cooper states, Jewish day school students are also welcome to attend Jewish summer camps, join Jewish youth organizations, and visit Israel. He adds that these programs are more essential for children not in Jewish day schools, allowing children to be with other Jewish children; learn Hebrew, Jewish history, prayers, and readings from the Torah (*Five Books of Moses*) and Prophets; and learn Jewish rites and rituals.

This debate covers two sides of this argument (although surely there are more) showing the qualities and advantages of the full-time day schools and part-time programs (summers, Sunday schools, youth programs), while explaining the limits and weaknesses of full-time day schools, and part-time after-school and summer programs. Hence, as the authors point out, what Jewish day schools offer in intensity and duration after-school and nonschool Jewish programs make up for in availability, variety, access, and lower costs.

This debate is not simply an academic exercise, as the contours of Jewish education and its future are very much a hot-button issue in the North American

Jewish community today. The conversation, at once contentious and community-building, reflects not only the denominational diversity of beliefs and practices within the Jewish community, but also the socioeconomic diversity, a shifting ethnic landscape, varying perspectives on the purposes of Jewish education, and a lack of consensus as to what it means to be an educated Jew in a modern postindustrial society.

Whichever side one takes, we see strong arguments for and against Jewish day schools, synagogue afternoon and Sunday schools, and Jewish summer camping, while noting that some Jewish families enroll their children in day schools during the day, summer programs, trips to Israel, and other events.

Whatever types and mixes or combinations of Jewish education and socialization that parents do select for their children, the authors in this chapter emphasize that these critical Jewish educational experiences, both in school and out, increase the likelihood of Jews marrying Jews, and resisting assimilation. The types of Jewish education that are available (and where) and that are workable and preferable have been debatable topics for most of the history of the Jewish people—and so they continue today.

As you read the essays in this chapter, you should reflect on the two distinct perspectives of the authors and think about what they see as the strengths and weaknesses of full-time day schools and part-time experiences in terms of promoting an understanding of the Jewish religion and culture. Would one option be more appropriate for some children than the other option? How can the need to promote Jewish identity be balanced with the need for Jewish children to assimilate in the larger society?

Charles J. Russo
University of Dayton

Allan G. Osborne, Jr.
Principal (Retired), Snug Harbor Community School,
Quincy, Massachusetts

POINT: Marc N. Kramer
RAVSAK: The Jewish Community Day School Network

The Jewish day school has no equal as it provides an unparalleled and unprecedented level of religious, cultural, moral, linguistic, and secular education to students from across the spectrum of Jewish life. Time after time the Jewish day school has been identified as the single most successful vehicle for the transmission of Jewish literacy and culture, Jewish peoplehood, and religious purposefulness, not to mention the most effective stopgap against rampant disaffiliation and assimilation (Schiff, 1966, 1988). Because of both its history of success and the vital role it plays in the preservation of Jewish life in North America, the Jewish community should dedicate the resources required to making a Jewish day school education an affordable reality for every Jewish child.

BACKGROUND

In synchrony of the arrival of Jews in America there have been Jewish day schools or some form of immersive, intensive Jewish education. This education was initially focused on boys from religiously observant homes, although as the Jewish community grew through waves of immigration from Central and Eastern Europe, so, too, did the varieties of and venues for Jewish learning (Sarna, 1986). The overwhelming number of Jews in America lived bifurcated lives: Jews at home and Americans on the street. Educationally, this meant that most American Jews attended public school during the day and a supplementary Jewish school in the afternoon and on weekends (known by a variety of names: heder, Talmud Torah, Hebrew school, Sunday school). Whereas once Jewish all-day school was the near-exclusive purview of the Orthodox, rapid shifts in minority group identity concurrent with an awareness of the impact of the Holocaust and the meteoric rise of the modern State of Israel on the world scene led to a shift in how many American Jews chose to express their Judaism in the public sphere, and this change in turn led to the exponential growth of Jewish day school education (Kramer, 2003).

Today, Jewish day schools are a thriving enterprise, with over a quarter-million children attending—enrollment up steadily for the last 30 years. This important school growth and community support—even in smaller towns where Jews are living away from the great urban centers—signal the mounting importance and popularity of modern Jewish day school education across the American Jewish landscape. Even in a day of more limited economic resources and static communal demographics, a day school education remains the education of choice for a significant number of American Jews, a number that would surely expand if the community were to assign to it the financial support needed to make it more widely available.

In addition to geographic reach, more than ever before Jewish day schools are poised to serve the broadest span of communal life—from those seeking single-gender yeshivas, to coeducational Reform, Conservative, and Modern Orthodox day schools, to trans-ideological and pluralistic Jewish community day schools that embrace both those who are traditionally identified with the Jewish community and children of intermarriages and, in some cases, children from outside the Jewish community altogether (Eisen, 1998).

This variety of Jewish day schools testifies to the growing importance of Jewish education and the adaptability of the American Jewish community to meet the needs of its children educationally and religiously (Rauch, 1984). What most Jewish day schools have in common is their dual functionality in providing a religious/cultural education at the same time and in the same place as a secular or general education while the specific subjects, time on task, and standards differ greatly and largely along denominational lines.

GROWTH AND DIVERSITY

As shown in Table 8.1, the largest types of Jewish day schools were mainly Orthodox in 2009, including yeshivas with 244 schools enrolling about 64,000 students; Hasidic schools numbering 105 with almost 61,000 students; and 86 Modern Orthodox schools, with nearly 30,000 students total. The newest and fastest growing national Jewish school group, called RAVSAK, represents the community Jewish day schools at 119, now with approximately 30,000 students.

Table 8.1

Jewish Schools, United States by Type: 2008–2009

	Enrollment of Students by Type	Number of Jewish Day Schools by Type
Centrist Orthodox	17,650	72
Chabad	12,296	73
Community (RAVSAK)	29,838	98
Hasidic	60,955	105
Immigrant/Outreach	3,432	24
Modern Orthodox	29,397	86

(Continued)

(Continued)

	Enrollment of Students by Type	Number of Jewish Day Schools by Type
Reform (PARDeS)	4,569	17
Conservative (Solomon Schechter)	13,223	50
Special Education	1,829	33
Yeshiva	63,985	244
Total	228,174	802

Source: Schick, M. (2009 August). *A census of Jewish day schools in the United States 2008–2009.* New York: AVI CHAI Foundation. Retrieved from http://avichai.org/wp-content/uploads/2010/06/Census-of-JDS-in-the-US-2008-09-Final.pdf.

While the range of Orthodox schools is by far the greatest in both total number and total enrollment, this comes as no surprise: The Orthodox community (really, a wide range of communities bound by their shared steadfast commitment to living according to Halacha [Jewish law]) has been unwavering in near universal enrollment of its children in Jewish day schools. That said, the nearly 50,000 children enrolled in non-Orthodox schools plus the many non-Orthodox children enrolled in Orthodox schools suggest a rising tide in the number of Jewish families from outside of traditional Orthodox circles seeking a full-time Jewish educational experience.

THE CASE FOR UNIVERSAL JEWISH DAY SCHOOL EDUCATION

The case for universal Jewish day school education must be prefaced with the caveat that it is not to be misunderstood as a critique of U.S. public schools. Public school is at the very heart of the success story that is America, at once the outcome and engine of liberal democracy. Countless Americans (this author included) owe a not-insignificant debt to their public educational experience.

Five arguments for universal Jewish day school experience will be advanced in this essay: (1) Jewish day schools stand at the apex of educational ideals; (2) Jewish day schools are unparalleled as vehicles for Jewish literacy, the transmittal of Jewish values and ethics, and the advancement of communal goals; (3) the options for Jewish day school education are unable to meet the standards and goals of Jewish day schools by design and default; (4) the critiques of Jewish day schools are weak and often fallacious; and (5) the Jewish community is teetering on the verge of a communal crisis that will be best attended through immersive, intensive Jewish education.

Apex of Educational Ideals

Jewish day schools provide the secret sauce of success, a winning combination of features and characteristics that make them unparalleled stand-outs in the educational marketplace.

Generally, they feature small class sizes and outstanding student-teacher ratios. The Institute of Education Sciences, the research arm of the U.S. Department of Education (2003), concludes that class size reduction is one of only four evidence-based reforms that have been proven to increase student achievement through rigorous, randomized experiments—the gold standard of research.

Jewish day schools provide early exposure to and constant, daily reinforcement of a second language (Hebrew). Research consistently demonstrates that second language acquisition has broad-reaching positive implications for educational achievement and workplace success (Bruck, Lambert, & Tucker, 1974). More so, Hebrew has been identified as one of the more difficult languages to acquire ("Language Learning Difficulty for English Speakers," 2011); after mastering Hebrew, many students find the acquisition of third and fourth languages to be significantly easier.

Jewish day schools are designed to promote outstanding morals and values. Jewish day school graduates are proven to be more compassionate, more communally engaged, and more civically aware than their peers from other school settings. A 2007 study demonstrated that Jewish day school graduates were more active and engaged in social action and social justice matters than their non–Jewish day school friends (Chertok et al., 2007). Whereas public schools are regularly embroiled in debates about character education, Jewish day schools are paradigms of effective transmission of (good) values.

Jewish day schools invite and celebrate active parent participation in school life, from governance to fund-raising to classroom volunteerism. To quote a 2001 Michigan Department of Education study, "Decades of research show that when parents are involved students have higher grades, test scores, and graduation rates; better school attendance . . . increased motivation, better self-esteem, lower rates of suspension, and decreased use of drugs and alcohol." The very same study quotes Cotton and Wikelund (1989), who state that the "more intensely parents are involved, the more beneficial the achievement effects" (p. 1).

Jewish day schools, while frequently networked with other schools of similar orientation, are fiercely autonomous institutions with strong local leadership. The very autonomy sought by charter schools and countless public schools within countless districts is at the core of the Jewish day school model.

As with parent involvement, school autonomy is considered essential to school success (Gottlieb, 2002).

Jewish day schools are powered by an internal culture of excellence. High student achievement is attained in nurturing environments where choice-college acceptance is both goal and norm. Jewish day schools are generally led by highly educated professionals and staffed by master teachers who model the multilingual, bicultural, character-driven outcomes desired for the students. With the notable exception of the more insular Jewish schools of the fervently Orthodox, which limit interaction with the wider community, it is de rigueur to see day school graduates matriculating into America's topmost colleges. According to the Jewish Day School Advocacy Forum (2005), "Jewish day school graduates go on to Ivy League schools at a rate higher than those from the competing private schools." This internal culture of excellence is bolstered by an external, parent, and community expectation for student achievement.

Day schools are networked with local synagogues, youth organizations, charities, and social service centers. The relation between a school and its local community is one of the most salient features of a desirable community. Livability.com, a quality of life index, features quality schools as a key element of what makes for a sought-after neighborhood. Jewish day schools top this scale.

Jewish day schools are powerful venues for the transmission of the best in civic values in environments that empower students to have pride in their own traditions and cultural heritage (Cohen & Kotler-Berkowitz, 2004). Whereas other schools have "pride" weeks or months, Judaism is always the subject of pride and joy.

Vehicle for Jewish Literacy, Values, Ethics, and Communal Goals

The Jewish people have survived—even thrived—for more than 3 millennia in large part due to their steadfast commitment to Jewish education. While the model has certainly changed, the essential formula for ensuring continuity is predicated on Jewish learning in intensive, immersive, and supportive environments at the intersection of teacher, student, family, community, and communal reality. There is universal consensus within the Jewish community that the day school is the single most effective vehicle for the transmission of Jewish knowledge and the single best safeguard for a vibrant Jewish future. No other forum allows for the time on task, academic rigor, high standards, close personal attention, and communal support for the advancement and application of Jewish knowledge.

Inability of Alternatives to Meet Standards and Goals

Naysayers are eager to suggest that Jewish day schools are one of many meaningful venues for substantive childhood Jewish education. To be sure, the summer camps, supplementary schools, youth groups, and even Hebrew language charter schools (which, if they are venues of Jewish education, represent a threat to the high wall separating church and state) are places where Jews attain some degree of Jewish knowledge and a sense of Jewishness. That said, each pales in comparison to the potential for positive Jewish impact.

Jewish summer camps, with an appropriate focus on socializing, sports, and personal growth, are well-deserving for the praise they receive. Some Jewish camps put an emphasis on ritual creativity and personal spiritual growth. But, summer camps are—by design—places for informal education, not substantive skill/knowledge acquisition, and it is unfair to ask camps to accomplish the tasks assigned to day schools.

The Jewish supplementary school (aka Hebrew school) is often cited as the least successful educational endeavor of American Jews. Many Jews, from the masters of American Jewish fiction to Jewish business leaders to Jewish communal leaders and countless disaffiliated Jews, speak of Hebrew school as a horrid experience that drove them from Jewish observance rather than toward it. Some have even posited that adult Jews today with no childhood Jewish education are more likely to live active Jewish lives than counterparts who attended a supplementary school. Coming at the end of a long day at school, in direct competition with extracurricular activities, and staffed by part-time and generally untrained teachers, with only a handful of hours per month, these supplementary schools are perhaps doomed by design and certainly are not analogous to day schools.

Jewish youth groups exist to promote healthy intracommunal socialization, encourage community service, and provide Jewish scaffolding for preadult life. Although Jewish youth groups happen in a Jewish context, little (if any) Jewish education unfolds. Again, it is not the purpose of these youth groups to substantively advance Jewish literacy, so again, comparison to day school is a red herring.

And speaking of red herrings, Hebrew language charter schools, a fast-emerging newcomer in the world of educational choice, proclaim that they will provide Hebrew language immersion and an academic/secular approach to the study of Jewish history. These schools are new, few, and relatively unstudied. They are also the subject of a great deal of (appropriate) scrutiny given the potential for them to breach the wall separating church and state—one of the cornerstones of American democracy and certainly an issue of great importance to Jews and other religious minorities (Goodnough, 2007). According to the Hebrew Charter School Center, proponents of Hebrew language charter schools claim that as publically funded institutions, they are decidedly secular in every way. Still, these schools are also privately funded by some well-known Jewish philanthropists, frequently opened in highly Jewish areas, occasionally established in Jewish communal spaces like Jewish Community Centers, and described by one of the funders as "Jewish" schools (Kahlenberg, 2009). New and unstudied, and ostensibly not designed to promote Jewish knowledge, values, literacy, traditions, ritual practice, or Jewish peoplehood, Hebrew language charter schools cannot be compared to Jewish day schools.

Weak and Fallacious Critiques

Those who suggest that Jewish day schools are for the privileged few tend to follow three lines of thinking: The schools are too expensive; the schools are only for "religious" Jews; and Jewish day schools are un-American.

Jewish day schools, like all other independent schools, require parents to pay tuition in return for education for their children. Jewish day schools tend to be priced below competing secular private schools, which, ironically, tend to have notable Jewish family enrollment. More so, Jewish day schools tend to offer significant financial aid, with many schools noting that between 50% and 75% of families receive some degree of tuition abatement. According to Gerald Bubis (2002), the average cost of Jewish day school tuition is $11,000 per child before financial aid, and the average cost of an eight-week day camp is $4,800: Simple computation demonstrates that the cost per day of day school is half the cost per day of summer camp. To be sure, independent schools require tuition fees, and not every family can attend without financial aid. That said, the unprecedented degree of tuition abatement offered suggests that "cost" may be more of a psychological barrier than a real one.

Some argue that Jewish day schools are only for the most traditionally observant. As noted in the opening remarks of this argument, one of the fastest growing submarkets within Jewish education is day school enrollment for the liberally aligned and unaffiliated. Interfaithfamily.com notes that virtually all Reform and community day schools welcome the children of Jewish-Gentile marriages, with the balance of community day schools, Conservative schools, and many Orthodox schools accepting children born to a Jewish mother regardless of the religion of the father (Jewish law assigns a child's religion to that of the mother). An earlier study on Jewish community day schools by the two authors of this debate noted that Jewish day schools are increasingly "the primary portal" to the rest of the Jewish community, further disavowing the notion that day schools are only for the religious (Cooper & Kramer, 2002).

Of course, the most tenuous argument—although certainly not the least voiced—is that Jewish day schools are un-American. That Jews and other religious groups in America can and do have independent schools of their own that are granted state approval to serve in proxy for public education is, in fact, a hallmark of American democracy. Jewish day schools not only promote the very best in civic values, but they graduate students who go on to become community, business, professional, academic, and political leaders who themselves continue to advance and safeguard American values. It should also not be forgotten that day school parents pay taxes that support public education despite the fact that their children are not participants in the public system, adding to state educational coffers fully without deducting substantively from them.

Communal Crisis

The Jewish community, shuttled from place to place and from extreme to extreme, has been famously called the "ever-dying people," yet to be certain, this lachrymose sense of Jewish history has fallen from fashion. Still, it is with increased volume that one hears a communal conversation about the impact of low Jewish birthrates, high rates of intermarriage, and rapid assimilation. Outside of the Orthodox community, we experience negative population growth. More and more Jews, unaware of their heritage and disconnected from their birthright by parents who themselves have only limited Jewish literacy, are disappearing from the community's ranks. Jewish day school alone is a proven antidote to assimilation. This author is an advocate of the corralling of communal resources—yes, at the expense of other important matters—to ensure that every Jewish child in America can and will attend a Jewish day school. The very institutions and priorities we most cherish as a community—the synagogue, philanthropy, Israel, social and economic justice, the pursuit of peace (just to name a few)—are all at great risk in the absence of Jewishly literate and engaged Jews. Jewish day schools produce the energizing nucleus of the North American Jewish community: All stops must be pulled out to ensure its vibrancy.

CONCLUSION

Jewish day schools, found in virtually every North American city with 5,000 Jews or more, have been proven to be the single best vehicles for advancing Jewish literacy, communal commitments, and interests, all while providing a top-tier general education that promotes American democratic values and civic engagement. There are Jewish day schools for all Jews, be they traditionally or liberally aligned, or not Jewishly aligned at all. They represent a fulfillment of the American dream and the greatest hope for a vibrant Jewish future. The alternatives to day school simply cannot provide what day schools can, and the arguments against universal day school enrollment are limited and rooted more in false assumptions and misgivings than in facts. The question of cost, of course, is really a distraction from the real issue at hand, which is one of values and beliefs. Let's not worry about whether or not the community can afford universal Jewish day school, but instead, let's worry about whether we can afford not to have these schools everywhere for all Jewish children in the United States.

COUNTERPOINT: Bruce S. Cooper
Fordham University

Most American Jewish schoolchildren, numbering about 1.8 million in the United States, simply will not, or cannot, attend full-time Jewish day schools—for these schools either are not available in their region or community, or are sometimes not of particular interest to this majority of American Jewish families. And many Jews simply cannot afford the tuition and fees for any private schools, particularly as some Jewish schools are very expensive (ranging between $5,000 and $32,000 per child per year depending on the school and grade level).

The majority of Jewish students, thus, will attend—as do 89% of all American schoolchildren in kindergarten to 12th grade—their local public schools, which have been a success story for many American Jews, who arrived in the United States from Eastern Europe and elsewhere, poor and often undereducated. Most Jewish families, therefore, sent their children to the local "common" public schools, which enabled their offspring to get their high school diplomas, go on to further and higher education, and often become a success in the American world—thus sharing the American dream.

While enrollments grew along with the American Jewish day schools (which rose from 803 to 999 American day schools) by 2010, serving kindergarten (*gan yeladim*) through 12th grade, totaling in 228,174 students in 2008–2009 and over 236,000 kids by 2011, these schools cannot be expected to educate all 1.3 million American Jewish children, or even the majority of children from Jewish families who want to use a day school (Wertheimer, 2009).

A BETTER OPPORTUNITY FOR ALL

Thus, the Jewish community should not, and cannot, look to the Jewish day school as the only—or even the major—source of Jewish teachings and traditions in the upbringing of children. Instead, the Jewish community, led by the Jewish parents and their community, should create and maintain a number of widely available Jewish educational programs. Four models come to mind: (1) after-school and weekend Jewish schools at local synagogues or Jewish Community Centers; (2) summer Jewish day camps and "sleep away" camps for children ages 5 to 21 where they live and work together and study Hebrew and Jewish subjects, sometimes in preparation for becoming Bar or Bat

Mitzvah (Son or Daughter of the Commandment); (3) a year or so of study abroad in Israel (birthright, etc.), to build Jewish knowledge and identity for all Jewish children, no matter where they live and what resources they might have, for Jewish day schools can be expensive; (4) Jewish service organizations and clubs operated by congregations and associations to give students an opportunity to help their communities and engage in service learning.

REASONS WHY DAY SCHOOLS WON'T ALWAYS WORK

The arguments against universal Jewish day schools for all Jewish children rest on several related points of view, as explained below.

Cost

Day schools are too costly for many Jewish families to afford. Day schools are private schools; thus, the Jewish community and each family therein cannot be expected to foot the expenses, ranging between $4,000 and $35,000 per year for the 12 or so years of schooling. Thus, the bill can be a luxury item for everyone. In a society that requires and treasures universal education for every child—regardless of religions, needs, location, and interests—Jewish families will often use their local public schools, as many parents have done since Jews immigrated to the United States. With the costs for private schools rising, many families simply cannot afford a private day school.

Commitment

Day schools require a commitment that many Jewish families don't have. Many Jewish families, apparently, are not sufficiently committed to or concerned about giving their children a full-time separate K–12 Jewish education to enroll them in a Jewish day school. It is not that they don't care. Rather, they themselves were often educated in a range of after-school programs, weekend Jewish synagogue Sunday schools, and summer Jewish camps; became Bar and Bat Mitzvah; and are active members of their Jewish communities. They themselves just couldn't and/or didn't attend a full-time Jewish day school.

Thus, pragmatically, supplemental Jewish schools are more available and numerous—and are easier to find and use. For the majority of Jewish families in the United States, an after-school and/or a summer Jewish education is preferable, and more practical than a full-time Jewish day school.

Interaction With Non-Jews

Attending public schools is more reflective of mainstream practices and allows Jewish children to interact with non-Jews and live the common American experiences. Jewish families may prefer to have their children attend their local public school, to help them to be part of their local community. Further, going to the local public school is perceived to give Jewish students a better chance to interact with non-Jews at schools, which would not occur if the Jewish community went to day schools.

Summer camps and supplementary school education are more likely to use "experiential" education; they may be able to achieve different goals that are also important, having a "sense of community," fitting into the general community and Jewish community, and building Jewish identity and pride.

Other Thoughts

Using Jewish programs, activities, and courses before and after public schools, holidays, summers, and years off will encourage and increase Jewish identity, becoming a Bar or Bat Mitzvah, and gaining knowledge and practices universally for all Jewish children. Perhaps the Jewish community is placing too much money in, and hopes on, the Jewish day school, as the reality and future of Jewish life and identity in the United States should be more available and universal. It's time to offer a much wider range of Jewish programs, built around the daily life and needs of the average Jewish child.

OPPORTUNITIES FOR OTHER PROGRAMS AND LEARNING

This section looks at what most Jewish families now do—when most are not attending their local Jewish day school. These have been effective for the last century in helping Jewish children to grow up to be productive members of their communities, while keeping a role in their Jewish life and practices.

Afternoon Jewish Schools

A direct, simple, and well-tested approach would be a "religious school" for all Jewish children, run by local synagogues or Jewish agencies that could with a little effort be made inexpensive or free to all Jewish children. Already, the majority of Jewish children get their religious education in their afternoon and Sunday schools, which can offer four to eight hours of direct instruction per week, increasing with boys and girls as they prepare them to become Bar and Bat Mitzvah.

Weekend, Sunday, and Summer Schools

The world of summer camping for Jewish children is extensive, and summer camps provide an intensive four- to eight-week (overnight) experience that builds Jewish identity, a network of lifelong friendships, and a sense of independence. While Jewish day school children also attend these camps, they are important for children attending public schools, as they are the most in-depth Jewish experience many children—in public schools—may have.

Camp Modin (2011), the oldest Jewish summer camp in New England (starting in 1922), explains its vision and program:

> Our goals are to know and understand each child individually, build a sense of community, and provide an *awareness of Jewish identity*. Our mission is to provide a safe, warm, and nurturing environment in which children can learn, grow, and develop lifelong friendships. (p. 3, emphasis added)

Lisa Katz (2011) explains the real value of Jewish camping in the lives of children, as she recognizes the importance of these programs for children not attending Jewish day schools:

> Many children, especially those who do not attend Jewish Day Schools or live in a strong Jewish community, get at Jewish summer camp their first real experience of living a fully Jewish life where there is no separation between their Jewish life and their surrounding secular life. The same activities that used to differentiate them from their friends at home become the activities that unite them with their friends at camp. Campers can wear a yarmulke, sing *birkat hamazon* (grace after meals), attend Friday night prayers, and feel completely a part of the world around them.

The Reform Jewish movement, like its Orthodox and Conservative counterparts, offers a range of programs that are important for parents who are more liberal on Jewish practices. These include the following:

Kallah is a program where Jewish children are able to identify and engage with the religion's culture. The program is taught by Jewish educators from all different backgrounds, and participants are able to choose their own classes that they believe they will benefit from most. Kallah is offered by the B'nai B'rith Youth Organization (BBYO): Jewish Community Organization & Jewish Youth Leadership Network for $2,500 per child.

Jewish summer camps are another popular youth activity. Places such as Camp Judaea, located in North Carolina's Blue Ridge Mountains, offer fun and educational programming to teach children about Jewish culture, identity, and religion. Summer camp activities include athletics, arts and crafts, theater, horseback riding, and learning how to speak conversational Hebrew.

Outdoor recreation for Jewish youth groups such as Temple Isaiah Junior Youth Group offers participants outdoor recreational opportunities such as hiking and rock climbing. These activities provide children with a chance to meet other Jewish children with similar interests outside of the synagogue. Other organized outdoor activities include ski trips and fishing.

Synagogues and Other Jewish Institutions

Supplementary schools are teaching Torah, religion, prayer, and ethics, including the following:

Curriculum of Jewish supplemental schools—A Jewish after-school curriculum is often centered around God, Torah (the sacred texts), Israel (as the land of Israel and as the Jewish people), Avodah (prayer and ritual), Kehilah (community), and Tikkun Olam (social action). In addition, the study of Hebrew is integrated into every lesson. The seven foci are as follows:

1. *God.* Students study and seek to develop a personal relationship with God and come to understand the covenant between God and the Jewish people as it has been experienced throughout history.

2. *Torah.* Curricula are built around biblical, rabbinic, and other sacred texts, and students will come to appreciate the Jewish value of lifelong study. They seek to develop critical skills for interpretation and integration of the sacred texts into their lives as Talmud Torah connects them to one another and to Jewish communities around the world and throughout time.

3. *Israel.* Jewish students bond with the land of Israel. They seek to have knowledge of, and foster a connection to, the state of Israel.

4. *Avodah.* Students find meaning in Jewish prayers and rituals, especially those incorporated in Jewish prayer service. In the younger grades, students become familiar with the rituals of Shabbat and the cycle of the Jewish year.

5. *Kehilah.* Students learn what it means to be a member of, and will develop the skills to contribute to, the global Jewish community.

6. *Tikkun Olam.* Mitzvot and Tikkun Olam are based on the centrality of social action to Reform Judaism.

7. *Hebrew Literacy.* Students read and become knowledgeable of vocabulary and prayers, translate key vocabulary words, and convey an understanding of key themes for each prayer.

Jewish Youth Groups and Associations

Children, too, can join Jewish youth groups, which are rich in activities and can involve trips to Israel, meetings regionally and nationally, and classes in Jewish subjects for Jewish life. "Teen Travel" is one example, sponsored by BBYO, that also runs local clubs for Jewish teenagers. "Summer Teen Travel" is a program that gives youth the option to choose from four continents for summer exploration. Travelers enjoy a hands-on journey that includes new experiences, allows them to make new friendships, and provides a new way of looking at the world.

Passport to the World is a global travel program sponsored by BBYO for Jewish teens of all backgrounds. Its trips are open to both BBYO members and nonmembers. Each program shares the same core elements of active touring, cross-cultural interactions, and meaningful Jewish experiences. The trips are designed for students enrolled in Grades 9 through 12. Organized in partnership with Authentic Israel, a leading educational program provider based in Israel, BBYO Passport brings together the best of BBYO along with Authentic Israel's three decades of professional travel experience.

BBYO is the leading worldwide, nondenominational Jewish youth movement, currently spanning 39 regions and over 25,000 members. For 80 years, BBYO has been providing opportunities for Jewish youth to develop their leadership potential and a positive Jewish identity. The Passport program provides Jewish teens with an unparalleled opportunity to explore Israel and the world at large from a physical, historical, cultural, and spiritual perspective.

Authentic Israel is a leading provider of Jewish teen travel programs in Israel and around the world. In addition to working with Jewish youth from North America and Europe, Authentic Israel provides educational touring programs for Israeli middle school and high school teens. Authentic Israel's operations in Israel are conveniently headquartered in central Israel. Each of Authentic Israel's guides is a licensed professional who connects and shares the Israel experience.

Interaction of Non-Jews With Jews

The interaction of non-Jews with Jews would not occur if the Jewish community went to day schools. Jews have long benefited from being part of the U.S. education system, and have excelled in K–12 and college. While those Jews who prefer a separate and separated education in a purely Jewish environment have the rights and the opportunities to operate their own schools, this model cannot be automatically applied to the entire Jewish community, where these schools may not be affordable, available, or requested. Thus for most Jewish children in the United States, they will continue to benefit from mainstream education where they can and do excel. To expect every Jewish child to want, afford, or use a Jewish-run education is hardly tenable in a free society.

While more and more families have that choice—to send their children to Orthodox, Conservative, Reform, or community Jewish day schools—this option will likely not become the choice or opportunity of a majority of Jews, as only about a quarter million choose it at the present time.

Thus, the Jewish community and the parents have a real responsibility to provide after-school programs, Sunday schools, weekend retreats, and intensive summer camps (day and overnight), not only for the children not attending Jewish day schools, but for all Jewish children—a place where children in public and private schools can come to know each other—to help form the new-generation Jewish community in the United States. The future depends on these after-school and summer programs, to educate the majority of Jewish children in the United States today.

Hence, as this debate shows, Jewish day schools are great for those who can find, gain admissions, and pay for them; but most Jewish children do not and cannot (Cohen, 1988). Thus, as the "alternative to Jewish day school" argument develops, we see the critical importance for after-school programs, Sunday and weekend programs, summer camping and trips, and Jewish youth groups.

Without these, many Jewish children would have nothing—no Jewish education, preparation, practices, or hope of growing up to be a practicing, active Jew in their lives and communities. To concentrate solely on Jewish day schools is to sacrifice the important majority of Jews, striving to educate and socialize their children in areas of the country where no or few day schools exist. These important special efforts are made to help these families get their children into a Jewish environment, to learn prayer and practices of being a modern Jew today.

This debate has two sides, which are not always so clear. But, Jewish children have extensive opportunities to learn and practice Judaism in day schools, afternoon schools, and summer camps. All these add up, whatever kind of school the children attend. But parents often struggle to find the right program and the right approach, whether a day school or an afternoon/summer program. To put it simply:

> Our children learn to live and love their Jewish heritage in a Jewish school. They form an eternal connection with their family's beautiful

Jewish traditions. They learn the importance of celebrating Jewish holidays and of participating in synagogue services. They taste the sweetness of learning Torah. Jewish subjects are taught in a manner to allow students to adapt at their own pace. . . . Now, any Jewish child can receive an education they deserve—a Jewish education. (Chetrit, 2001)

FURTHER READINGS AND RESOURCES

Authentic Israel: http://www.authenticisrael.com

B'nai B'rith Youth Organization: http://www.bbyo.org

Bruck, M., Lambert, W. E., & Tucker, R. (1974). Bilingual schooling through the elementary grades: The St. Lambert Project at Grade Seven. *Language Learning 24*(2), 183–204.

Bubis, G. (2002). *The costs of Jewish living*. New York: American Jewish Committee.

Camp Modin. (2011). *In pursuit of an ideal*. Belgrade, ME: Author.

Chertok, F., & Saxe, L. (2007). *What difference does day school make*. Waltham, MA: Brandeis University.

Chertok, F., Saxe, L., Kadushin, C., Wright, G., Klein, A., & Koren, A. (2007). *The impact of day school: A comparative analysis of Jewish college students*. Waltham, MA: Brandeis University.

Chetrit, M. (2001, January 9). *A better change in life: The ten advantages of a Jewish education*. Available from The Jewish Education Network website: http://www.torahkids.org

Cohen, J. (1969). New trends in Jewish education. In J. Pilch (Ed.), *A history of Jewish education in America* (pp. 201–223). New York: The National Curriculum Research Institute of the American Association of Jewish Education.

Cohen, S. M. (1988). *American assimilation or Jewish revival?* Bloomington: Indiana University Press.

Cohen, S. M., & Kotler-Berkowitz, L. (2004). The impact of childhood Jewish education on adults' Jewish identity: Schooling, Israel travel, camping, and youth groups. *UJC report series on the National Jewish Population Survey 2000–2001*. New York: United Jewish Communities.

Cooper, B. S. (1986). Jewish schools. In T. C. Hunt, J. C. Carper, & C. R. Kniker (Eds.), *Religious schools in America: A selected bibliography* (pp. 185–210). New York: Garland.

Cooper, B. S. (2007). Jewish schools. In J. Carper & T. Hunt (Eds.), *Praeger handbook of religion and education in the United States*. New York: Praeger.

Cooper, B. S., & Kramer, M. N. (2002). The new Jewish community, new Jewish schools: Trends and promises. *Catholic Education: Journal of Inquiry and Practice, 5*(4), 488–501.

Cotton, K., & Wikelund, K. (1989, May). *Parent involvement in education* (School Improvement Research Series). Portland, OR: Northwest Regional Educational Laboratory.

Eisen, A. M. (1998). *Rethinking modern Judaism: Ritual, commandment, community.* Chicago: University of Chicago Press.

Elazar, D. J. (1999). *Community and polity: The organizational dynamics of American Jewry.* Philadelphia: Jewish Publication Society of America.

Goodnough, A. (2007, August 24). Hebrew charter school spurs dispute in Florida. *The New York Times.* Retrieved September 23, 2011, from http://www.nytimes.com/2007/08/24/education/24charter.html?pagewanted=all

Gottlieb, A. (2002). School autonomy is not enough. *The Term Paper, 1*(1), 1, 6.

Hebrew Charter School Center: http://www.hebrewcharters.org/index.php

Himmelfarb, H. (1977). The impact of religious schooling: Comparing different types and amounts of Jewish education. *Sociology of Education, 50,* 114–129.

Jewish Day School Advocacy Forum. (2005). *Why a Jewish day school.* Retrieved from http://www.jdaf.net/story.html

Kahlenberg, R. (2009, January 15). The problem with ethnic charter schools. *Taking Note.* Retrieved from http://takingnote.tcf.org/2009/01/the-problem-with-ethnic-charter-schools.html

Katz, L. (2011). *Jewish summer camps in America.* Retrieved from http://judaism.about.com/od/jewishsummercamps/a/summercamps.htm

Kramer, D. Z. (1985). *The day schools and Torah Umesorah: The seeding of traditional Judaism in America.* New York: Yeshiva University Press.

Kramer, M. N. (2003). Teaching in a Jewish community school. In N. S. Moskowitz (Ed.), *The ultimate Jewish teachers handbook.* Springfield, NJ: A.R.E. Publishing.

Language learning difficulty for English speakers. (2011, May 8). Retrieved from http://en.wikibooks.org/wiki/Language_Learning_Difficulty_for_English_Speakers

Michigan Department of Education. (2002). *What research says about parent involvement in children's education in relation to academic achievement.* Retrieved from http://www.michigan.gov/documents/Final_Parent_Involvement_Fact_Sheet_14732_7.pdf

Rauch, E. (1984). The Jewish day school in America: A critical history and contemporary dilemmas. In J. C. Carper & T. C. Hunt (Eds.), *Religious schooling in America* (pp. 130–165). Birmingham, AL: Religious Education Press.

Sarna, J. D. (1986). *The American Jewish experience.* New York: Holmes & Meier.

Schiff, A. I. (1966). *The Jewish day school in America.* New York: Jewish Education Committee Press.

Schiff, A. I. (1988). *Contemporary Jewish education: Issachar, American style.* Dallas, TX: Rossel Books.

U.S. Department of Education, Institute of Education Sciences. (2003, December). *Identifying and implementing educational practices supported by rigorous evidence: A user friendly guide.* Retrieved September 23, 2011, from http://www2.ed.gov/rschstat/research/pubs/rigorousevid/rigorousevid.pdf

Wertheimer, J. (2009). Jewish education in the United States: Recent trends and issues. In D. Singer (Ed.), *American Jewish year book* (pp. 43–52). New York: American Jewish Committee.

Do private, nonsectarian schools enhance student achievement?

POINT: William Jeynes, *Witherspoon Institute and California State University, Long Beach*

COUNTERPOINT: Mark Littleton, *Tarleton State University*

OVERVIEW

Private schools are independent educational institutions that, unlike public schools, are not run by government entities. Private schools obtain their operating funds by charging tuition, although many receive donations or endowments from individuals, charitable foundations, or corporations. Since private schools are not operated by a government agency, they are able to establish selective admissions criteria and are exempt from many state regulations. There are two subgroups of private schools: those that are affiliated with a religious group (sectarian) and those that are not (nonsectarian). Most private schools in the United States are sectarian, and there are more elementary than secondary private schools. As of the 2007–2008 school year, the latest statistics available at this writing, there were 30,808 private schools covering elementary grades and 11,870 schools that had secondary grades (U.S. Department of Education, n.d.a).

Nonsectarian private schools, also known as independent schools, enroll a very small percentage of the total U.S. private school student population. Regular nonsectarian private schools (as opposed to those that have a special academic emphasis or serve only students with disabilities) make up one tenth of all private schools in the country (U.S. Department of Education, n.d.b). Nonsectarian private schools are often seen as an alternative to public schools for parents who have the means to pay the tuition, either feel that the public schools will not provide their children with an appropriate education or are concerned about the overall environment of public schools, and are not seeking a school with a religious orientation.

Parents clearly have the right to send their children to private schools. That right was firmly established by two U.S. Supreme Court opinions in the 1920s. In the first, *Pierce v. Society of Sisters of the Holy Names of Jesus and Mary* (1925), private school operators challenged an Oregon statute requiring all students between the ages of 8 and 16 to attend public schools. In addition to ruling that the statute, if enforced, would seriously impair or even destroy the profitability of the schools (which were viewed by the Court as businesses) and greatly diminish their property values, the Court found the law to be unconstitutional because it would "unreasonably interfere with the liberty of parents and guardians to direct the upbringing and education of children under their control" (*Pierce v. Society of Sisters of the Holy Names of Jesus and Mary,* 1925, pp. 534–535). The rights of private schools to operate and parents to send their children to those schools were reinforced two years later in *Farrington v. Tokushige* (1927) when the Court rejected attempts by Hawaiian officials to impose strict regulatory controls over private foreign language schools.

The debate over whether particular school choice options enhance student achievement is continued in this chapter. Here, however, the essays are concerned with outcomes generated from private, nonsectarian schools. William Jeynes, a Senior Fellow at the Witherspoon Institute in Princeton, New Jersey, and a professor of education at California State University, Long Beach, argues in the point essay that such schools have a positive effect on both students and education as a whole. In the counterpoint essay, Mark Littleton, a professor of educational administration, counseling, and psychology at Tarleton State University in Texas, states that empirical evidence to support the contention that private nonsectarian schools have more positive educational outcomes than public schools is modest, at best.

Jeynes contends that there is widespread evidence that private nonsectarian schools have more positive educational outcomes than public schools, even when the data are adjusted to account for factors such as the differing socioeconomic levels of each population. Further, Jeynes feels that education flourishes best when there is a fair level of competition between the private and public sectors. Citing his own research, he posits that private schools tend to focus more on the scholastic qualities that are related to academic outcomes, such as an emphasis on students taking harder courses, working harder, having self-disciplined work habits, and making concerted efforts to pay attention in class. He concludes by stating that we should be more appreciative of the contribution of private schools and should praise any group of schools that posts impressive academic and behavioral results, not merely the public schools.

In the counterpoint essay, Littleton focuses on the differences in the student populations between the public and private schools. He notes that due to the selective nature of private schools, which often results in a student population that is quite different from that in the public schools, an expectation exists that their students will exhibit greater achievement. However, contrary to Jeynes's position, Littleton claims that the data do not support that proposition. He feels that any greater achievement shown by private school students is due to greater parental involvement and private schools' ability to direct resources toward instruction. He emphasizes that student achievement is commensurate with socioeconomic level and private, nonsectarian school students come from families of higher socioeconomic status. In summary, Littleton emphatically states that nonsectarian schools do not increase student achievement over that of their public school counterparts but, rather, just maintain the achievement gap created by a selective admission system.

A major disagreement in these essays is over whether research data indicate that private school students achieve at a higher level than their public school peers. Much of the disagreement lies in how the data are interpreted, particularly when they are adjusted to allow for differences in the student populations of the two schools. In reflecting on this, one has to ask if private school students would fare as well academically if they attended public schools. A second question that could be asked is if public schools could increase the achievement of all students if they had more flexibility to direct their resources, and thus better target their own instructional needs. More research needs to be conducted to answer those questions.

Allan G. Osborne, Jr.
Principal (Retired), Snug Harbor Community School,
Quincy, Massachusetts

POINT: William Jeynes
Witherspoon Institute and California State University, Long Beach

For the last 45 years, social scientists have debated the merits of students attending private schools versus public schools. Clearly, researchers have directed much more of their attention toward examining private religious schools than they have private nonsectarian schools. There have been four primary reasons for this emphasis:

1. Religious schools, mostly Christian ones, make up the overwhelming percentage of private schools.

2. Religious schools tend to be rich in what James Coleman (1988) and others have described as "social capital," based on religious, moral, and self-disciplinary practices that glibly translate into higher levels of student achievement.

3. Religious private schools are generally much more affordable to the citizenry than are nonsectarian private schools. Teachers at these religious institutions are usually paid considerably less than their counterparts in public schools, and the expenditure per student is also significantly less than in either public or nonsectarian private schools, which makes sending their children to private religious schools a viable option for many Americans. In contrast, however, private nonsectarian schools are often, albeit not always, more expensive than their religious counterparts and beyond the scope of financial feasibility for numerous Americans.

4. Religious schools tend to emphasize the character qualities that attract myriad parents to the idea of sending their children to religious schools.

CHALLENGES IN DRAWING CONCLUSIONS ABOUT THE IMPACT OF NONSECTARIAN SCHOOLS

Three challenges make drawing definitive conclusions rather difficult, when it comes to discussing the relative impact of nonsectarian private schools. First, because social scientists have examined religious schools more closely than their nonsectarian counterparts, for the reasons mentioned above, they know less about nonsectarian schools than they do religious ones.

Second, in recent years the distinction between religious, less religious, and nonreligious schools has been blurred. This has particularly been enigmatic among various Catholic schools that have functioned as parochial schools for years, but have agreed to sacrifice some or all of their religious orientation in order to form charter schools or some similar entity in order to remain financially viable or meet the demands of a given community. Increasingly, religious schools have assumed a nonsectarian approach in that they have functioned independent of a formal denomination and instead have preferred to have a nondenominational "flavor" that appeals to a wide range of people. This is not surprising when one considers that nondenominational churches are the fastest-growing type of house of worship in the United States. Most ministerial leaders and social scientists believe that this trend is due to the fact that an increasing number of Americans want the benefits of church worship without becoming entangled in doctrinal issues that are sometimes relatively minor in scope. They would have a church focus on major doctrinal tenets that are central to the Christian faith such as the trinity, Christ's death and resurrection, and inviting Christ into one's heart. The same trend appears to be emerging in people's preference for religious schools. Many of the fastest-growing schools are nondenominational or interdenominational, which in a very real sense of the word is nonsectarian.

Third, the selectivity factor is prominent in nonsectarian private schools much more than is the case with private religious schools. Especially in recent decades religious private schools have shown little or no propensity to be selective in the admission of their students, as long as one is willing to cooperate with and honor the school's rules and daily protocol. In fact, one of the primary "dirty little secrets" is that public school principals will often ask private religious schools to accept certain seemingly incorrigible students who have been particularly pernicious and obstinate. These principals will make these contacts with religious private school leaders because they realize that the latter schools maintain a code of discipline that parents agree exceeds the structure that public schools can achieve. This practice is controversial among supporters of many religious private schools, because it is an agreement to take some of the very worst students, not only in terms of scholastic outcomes but also in terms of behavior, that the public schools have to offer. Many individuals at these predominantly Christian schools are divided in their opinions about this practice and each for meritorious reasons. The first group believes that as an act of love the schools should offer an opportunity for these youth to change their ways in the environs of a school that emphasizes the balance of love and discipline. The second group believes that when people care enough for children to spend school tuition in addition to heavy amounts of property, state, and federal income taxes to send their children to Christian school, it is only right to minimize the schoolchildren's exposure to the worst elements of adolescent and preadolescent society.

In spite of these rather formidable challenges in addressing the academic outcomes of nonsectarian private schools, resolving the extent to which schools with varying degrees of nonsectarianism ameliorate educational outcomes is important not only for its own right, but in ascertaining preferable practices of school choice that are periodically under consideration in certain locales in the United States.

RAISING STUDENT ACHIEVEMENT

The question that this particular chapter addresses is whether private nonsectarian schools raise the achievement of students. This question can be addressed at either the broad level or the school-specific level. If one examines this question broadly, then the issue is limited not merely to success of the private schools themselves, but also to how the presence of these private schools and their direct competition with the public schools can cause the public schools themselves to improve substantially. This hope of raising the scholastic outcomes of all students is based on the notion of initiating a program of school choice, which would include private schools via the federal government granting either tax breaks or vouchers. This proposition is based on the belief that tax breaks or vouchers would make the playing field more level so that private schools, even though they are more poorly funded than public schools, would be able to more evenly and fairly compete with public schools. This would be because some of the heavy tax burden would be lifted from the poor and middle class so that more people who normally would send their children to private schools but cannot afford it would be able to do so.

According to the economist Milton Friedman (2002) and political and education writers John E. Chubb and Terry M. Moe (1990), school choice including private schools in this way would substantially increase competition. Friedman, as well as Chubb and Moe, asserts that increasing the degree of competition at the elementary and secondary school level is one of the primary keys to improving American educational outcomes. Chubb and Moe specifically note that there is a general consensus throughout the world that American universities are the best in the world. This assertion is not based merely on conjecture, anecdotal evidence, or jingoistic personal preference. Rather, on a reasonably regular basis China, Great Britain, Germany, and *U.S. News and World Report* release separate rankings of the world's most prestigious universities. In each of these surveys American universities dominate the list of top 25 and 50 universities in the world. As one might expect, Harvard University ranks number 1 on all four lists. The other top slots are dominated by such universities as Princeton, Yale, the University of Chicago, Stanford, MIT, Cambridge, and Oxford. The question therefore arises: How can it be that American universities are generally regarded as the best in the world and concurrently the world's educators regard American public schools as mediocre at the very best? How can such two disparate realities exist concurrently? Chubb and Moe believe that the primary reason why the American university system thrives, while the public system of elementary and secondary schools does not, is that the government has almost a monopoly on the elementary and secondary schooling system. That is, nearly 90% of American children attend public schools at this level. That figure gives the government a near monopoly. Chubb and Moe claim that such a high percentage stifles competition and almost eliminates any incentive there is to improve. In contrast, Chubb and Moe point out that at the level of higher education, private and public universities are more able to compete with one another, largely because the government does not insist on dominating higher education.

It does seem that, on average, private elementary and secondary school educational choice will make it more likely that youth will excel in school and enhance the prospect that the children in both private and public schools will excel because of the presence of additional competition. In other words, student participation in school choice not only will increase the achievement levels of the participants themselves, but will do the same for all students. Because the United States has undertaken such a small and limited number of school choice initiatives, a rather narrow body of research is available on the effects of school choice programs on the educational outcomes of the surrounding public schools. In addition, although several European nations have widespread programs of school choice, they generally do not assess the effects on the education outcomes of the schools within the general environs of the school choice efforts. However, it should be noted that the primary reason why such assessments are not in their purview is because Europeans believe that there is no question that injecting greater competition into education will enhance overall scholastic outcomes. They believe that it is a waste of time to test what is so patent.

There is great evidence that these nonsectarian private schools have a direct positive impact on the academic outcomes of youth. It is true that, when adjusting for socioeconomic status, the effects of nonsectarian private schools fall short of the scholastic advantages associated with private religious schools. Nevertheless, it is important to note that even when adjusted for socioeconomic status, nonsectarian private schools do have a positive academic and behavioral influence. In addition, the reality is that there are many people who want their children to attend a private school, but who are not religious and therefore prefer a nonreligious school.

There is widespread additional evidence that various expressions of private schooling produce educational outcomes that are far better than what one finds in the public schools. Statistics indicate that in any given year half of the National Merit Scholarship winners that emerge after taking the PSAT (Preliminary SAT) are from private schools. In addition, homeschoolers, the product of another form of private school that is based in the home, nearly always win the National Spelling Bee competition.

The fact is that students from nonsectarian private schools outperform their counterparts from public schools, even when adjusted for socioeconomic status, but they do not do as well, on average, as children from religious private schools. This being the case, the question arises as to how much of this difference is a product of the strength of the private schools and to what extent these gaps are due to ongoing problems in the public schools, from which these institutions have been unable to extricate themselves.

CONCLUSION

Americans need to reconceptualize their idea of education. Currently, myriad Americans think of education as defending their particular sector of schooling, that is, the public or the private sector. In order for academic achievement to resume its surge in the United States, this attitude must change. Americans need to instead think more holistically and more altruistically and weigh what instruction is best for the American people as a whole. Americans ought to reach a place in which they rejoice at what both the private and public sectors can accomplish and contribute to the overall intellectual and moral welfare of the country. Americans should think in terms of what is good for all the children of this country rather than what is good merely for their sector. With each victory by the private educational sector and with every advance private schools make in improving academic outcomes, Americans should rejoice. Americans should feel the same way about the same triumphs in the public sector.

No matter how much one may have personally benefited from a public school education, nearly all fair-minded people will acknowledge that public schools suffer from certain academic and spiritual maladies that are significant enough that American families should have a viable alternative of where to send their children to school. And admittedly, a considerable part of the private school advantage is founded in the shortcomings of the public schools.

The weaknesses of the public schools are manifold and may not be surprising when one considers that only an average of 2% of the nation's public school dollars are spent on instructing the gifted, character education and an emphasis on the self-disciplined lifestyle are almost defunct, and material that used to be taught in earlier school grades is often taught in later grades. For example, in the 1840s school instructors taught algebra in the fourth grade. It is undeniable that the overwhelming number of public schools has retreated from the application of these principles that in years past were at the core of American educational practice. Although it is also true that certain private schools have not been faithful to continuing these practices, the expanse of the problem is far greater with public schools than it is with private schools. To whatever extent a person esteems these values, he should rejoice when private schools flourish. And even if one does not espouse precisely the same values, he should take pleasure in a diverse education system, in which a plenteous number of Americans can exercise their choice regarding where their children best fit in school.

The reality of the matter is that the vast majority of educational experts believe that schooling flourishes to the greatest degree where there exists an ample level of competition between the private and public sectors. Whatever weaknesses public schools possess, competition from the private sector can almost serve as a type of academic and moral elixir. In research by William Jeynes (2003a) and others, quantitative research was undertaken to determine why the students from a variety of private schools outperformed their counterparts in public schools. This research found that private schools tended to focus on the precise scholastic qualities that in quantitative analysis were most likely to be related to academic outcomes. The researchers include the fact that private schools are more likely to emphasize students taking harder courses, working harder, having self-disciplined work habits, and really making a concerted effort to pay attention in class. Given that research indicates that private schools emphasize the personal work habits that are most closely related to achieving at high levels scholastically, it only makes sense that private school students, including those from nonsectarian private schools, are going to outperform their counterparts in public schools. The body of literature supports the assertion that children who attend nonsectarian private schools, when adjusted for socioeconomic and other factors, may not achieve as well as students from religious private schools; but they do outperform students from public schools. Therefore the general public should be more appreciative of the contribution of these schools and laud the efforts of their teachers. Americans, including parents, teachers, and youth, should be quicker to praise any group of schools that posts impressive academic and behavioral results, not merely the public schools.

RESPONSE TO THE COUNTERPOINT

Mark Littleton's argument that nonsectarian private schools offer no advantage over public schools is largely based on a single study performed using European schools. It is extremely puzzling why he makes no reference to the numerous studies that have been done examining American schools, nor the meta-analyses that have been done on both types of schools. The fact that Littleton relies on European data is a major problem for his perspective because (1) the results of American studies generally control for the socioeconomic (SES) and selection factors that he asserts are so important, and yet they still show an academic advantage for nonsectarian private schools, and (2) research indicates that the private school academic advantage is considerably greater in the United States than it is in Europe (Glenn, 2000; Jeynes, 2003b). This second point is not surprising especially when one considers that most private schools in Europe are heavily state-regulated and state-funded, and therefore many educators would view private schools in Europe as resembling a semiprivate school rather than a private one.

Littleton also notes that he believes that part of the advantage of nonsectarian private schools is due to parental involvement, but for some unknown reason he ignores the fact that private schools strongly encourage parental involvement and high expectations probably more than any other parental qualities (Jeynes, 2011). Research on parental involvement indicates that probably about half of the high levels of parental involvement expressed at schools that emphasize this quality are due to this emphasis by the schools and about half to the parents themselves (Jeynes, 2011). What is even more puzzling is that after arguing that nonsectarian schools are not superior, but rather it is parental involvement that causes their students to do better, Littleton asserts that public schools should "require parental involvement" even as private schools do. Ultimately, then, he admits that private schools contribute to enhancing parental involvement.

And in the end, Littleton asserts, "Professor Jeynes offers that 'Americans need to reconceptualize their idea of education.' Indeed, that notion is an excellent one." Hence, it is apparent that this writer and Littleton agree on certain issues, including the importance of the achievement gap and the role of faith-based schools in reducing that gap. And admittedly, research indicates that the racial and socioeconomic achievement gaps are significantly reduced at religious private schools, but not at nonsectarian ones (Jeynes, 2003b). This is particularly encouraging because research indicates that families who send their young to faith-based schools have incomes only 18% higher than their counterparts in public schools. Although nonsectarian private schools do not offer the same benefits as religious ones, they should be acknowledged for the help they do provide to the American education system. Littleton's clear distaste for private sector education is too insular and limiting in a world that is moving toward more educational choice and diversity. And indeed, it may well be that the inefficiency of the near monopoly of the public schools contributes almost as much to the private school edge as the advantages of faith-based and nonsectarian private schools.

COUNTERPOINT: Mark Littleton
Tarleton State University

Formal educational systems may be classified into two basic categories. The first system, public education, consists of formal schooling provided by state government accessible by all eligible children. Although public education is not a fundamental right under the U.S. Constitution, each state has chosen to provide a system of public education. Since the U.S. Supreme Court's *Brown v. Board of Education* (1954) decision and its progeny, public education systems are predicated on the concept that all children, regardless of race, ethnicity, disability, or socioeconomic status, are entitled to receive the services of a public school.

Public schools must educate any child who legally meets the admission requirements established by the state. Although there are some modest attempts for public school choice, mainly charter schools and magnet schools, attendance at a specific school is primarily based upon attendance zones defined by district or campus boundaries. Based on state and case law, public schools are required to educate the children of eligible age living within those boundaries.

In 2007–2008, there were 13,924 public school districts and 98,916 schools educating over 49 million students. Of those students, 70.6% attended schools to which they were assigned, while the remainder attended a public school of some choice. Approximately 56% of the students were White, and almost 43% qualified for the free or reduced lunch program, suggesting that the students were from low socioeconomic backgrounds. Of the students completing high school at the end of the 2006–2007 academic year, 39.5% were enrolled in a four-year college during the ensuing academic year. The public school student-to-teacher ratio was 15.5 to 1 (Snyder & Dillow, 2010).

NONSECTARIAN SCHOOLS

The second system of formal schooling is private education. Generally, the term *private education* refers to situations where the child is educated at home, attends a formal sectarian school (a school predicated on the tenets of a religious doctrine), or attends a formal nonsectarian school. Different from home schools and sectarian schools, nonsectarian schools are typically entrepreneurial endeavors that require the infusion of resources from donors and/or tuition from the families whose children attend the school. Admission to nonsectarian schools is selective, and there is no guarantee that a student will be granted admission to the school because of his or her location of residence.

Nonsectarian schools can be classified as tuition-based academies, with no religious orientation or purpose, but may have a special emphasis, for example, Montessori curriculum, vocational or technical orientation, or early childhood emphasis. In 2007–2008, of the 33,740 private schools in the United States, 32% were nonsectarian. Of the nonsectarian schools, over half were considered "regular" schools indicating that the curriculum was elementary, secondary, or combined without special curricular emphasis. The regular nonsectarian schools educated more than 670,000 students, primarily in a coeducational environment. Most of the nonsectarian schools were located in suburban cities, but more students were actually educated in the urban nonsectarian schools (Broughman, Swaim, & Keaton, 2009).

A majority of the nonsectarian private schools were relatively small with only about 4% of the schools enrolling 500 or more students. The student population was decidedly White, non-Hispanic (72.7%). The ratio of students to teachers was 7.8 to 1 (Broughman et al., 2009). Although private nonsectarian school students do not qualify for the federal free and reduced lunch program, over half of the students pay tuition of $10,000 or more, which would indicate that few students come from low socioeconomic backgrounds (Snyder & Dillow, 2010). More than doubling that of their public school student colleagues, over 80% of the 2006–2007 seniors graduating from regular, nonsectarian schools attended a four-year college in the fall of 2007 (Broughman et al., 2009).

Due to the selective nature of private schools, the teaching environment is more attractive. Student behavioral problems are generally calculated to be fewer and less severe than those in public schools. As a consequence, more class time can be devoted to instruction in the private school environment than in public schools. In concert, the student-to-teacher ratio in private schools is less than the ratio in public schools, which should provide more individualized attention to student needs. Given that the teaching environment in private schools provides more time for instruction, the expectation of greater student achievement in the private school environment exists. However, the data simply do not support the expectation.

SELECTIVITY

As noted above, admission to nonsectarian private schools is selective. Selectivity may be overt as in the form of a test-based admission process, or more multifaceted as appealing to individuals who desire a specific curriculum orientation. One selectivity factor is student prior performance (Robert, 2010). Nonsectarian schools, often elite in nature, predicate admission on the performance of test-based ability. This selective admission process identifies higher performing students while, conversely, "weeding out" the lower performing students. In a form of ability grouping, the educators in the private schools can, in turn, have higher expectation of student performance and demand better performance of students than in mixed-ability schools.

Another selectivity factor is related to the socioeconomic status of students attending private schools. The research is conclusive—students with higher socioeconomic backgrounds show greater achievement on standardized tests than do students from low socioeconomic backgrounds. Nonsectarian private schools, often charging tuition for admission, target the students from the higher socioeconomic background.

A third factor in selectivity is the actual selection of the school. Wealthier and more educated parents, the ones with the resources, are more likely to choose the "best" schools for their children (Reay & Lucey, 2000). Predictably, Jennifer Jellison Holme (2002) discovered that parents often selected the "better" schools not on the basis of actual indicators of student performance, but on the social networks associated with the school. The identification of the better schools were those that served "Whiter, wealthier students" (Holme, 2002, p. 201).

A fourth selectivity factor directly relates to parents who are more likely to seek out nonsectarian schools for their children. These parents, because their middle-class status allows them more opportunities to do so, are more involved in their children's education, spend more time supervising their children's studies, and are more likely to attend to their children's homework (Lareau, 2000).

A final factor related to the selective nature of private nonsectarian schools is the teaching environment. As noted above, private schools have a lower student-to-teacher ratio, an environment with fewer behavioral problems, and a greater parental support environment. Although the quality of the employees is difficult to assess, the better teachers and administrators will seek, arguably, the more attractive teaching environments. The logical conclusion is that the better teachers and administrators will land the positions in private schools, leaving the public schools with the less competent staff. (An argument can be made that employment practices also support higher quality of staff members in private schools. Employment contracts in private schools generally allow for greater ease in the dismissal of incompetent personnel, where a vast majority of public school teachers are protected by tenure or sophisticated nonrenewal statutes. Public school employment practices make the dismissal of incompetent personnel difficult and time consuming.)

STUDENT ACHIEVEMENT

Given the comparisons of the two very different student populations, experienced educators could easily draw the conclusion that private nonsectarian schools have more positive educational outcomes than public schools because private schools can be selective in admission, choose only the more academically capable students and the more motivated parents, hire the more competent staff, and focus on a rigorous curriculum concomitant with high expectations for student performance. However, empirical evidence to support that contention is modest, at best. Peter Robert (2010) analyzed data from the Programme for International Student Assessment (PISA) database of the Organisation for Economic Co-operation and Development (OECD) to compare performance of students from public schools, private government-dependent (mostly religious) schools, and private government-independent (private nonsectarian) schools.

Robert (2010) selected 23 European OECD countries, which left him 113,000 cases. Eighty-six percent of the target group of the study (15-year-olds) consisted of public school students, and 4% were private nonsectarian school students.

Given the factors associated with selectivity, Robert's (2010) discoveries about the scores of students on the PISA were not remarkable. Students in the public schools had parents with the lowest level of education and the lowest socioeconomic status (as measured by the International Socio-Economic Index). Students from the private nonsectarian schools had parents with the greatest educational background and, by far, the highest socioeconomic status. Additionally, students in the private nonsectarian schools outperformed those in the public schools on tests in math, reading, and science.

However, when interpreting the students' scores in light of the interaction with the education market, the Human Development Index (including socioeconomic status, parental education, etc.), and schools' characteristics (e.g., community size, percent of certified teachers, amount of parental pressure), the gap between public school student performance and nonsectarian student performance disappears. Robert (2010) noted that

> with respect to social origin and the interrelationships between the components of the education market, the gain of students in private government-independent [nonsectarian] schools disappears. For math and science pupils in these schools perform significantly worse than their counterparts in the public schools, while there is no difference for reading. (p. 124)

THE DEBATE CONTINUES

In the point essay, William Jeynes argues that the nature of the competitive environment offered by the private schools leads to higher student achievement. I argue that any demonstration of greater student achievement by private schools (which is highly questionable, as noted by the data above) is due to (1) greater parental involvement or (2) private schools' ability to direct resources toward instruction.

Another theme in the point essay is the desire to celebrate the successes of private schools. According to Jeynes, "To whatever extent a person esteems these values, he should rejoice when private schools flourish." Certainly, all successes should be celebrated. If flourishing is defined as separating the haves from the have-nots, then I call into question a celebration.

Parents strive to locate the best schools for their children. And, parents who have access to more resources get their children into better schools. Often, schools are deemed "better" not because of their ability to improve student learning, but on the status associated with the families of the children who attend the "better" schools. As noted by Holme (2002), "status dominated every aspect of the study parents' choices: not only did they trust the opinions of other high-status parents in their social networks, they also read a great deal into those parents' own school choices for their children" (p. 201).

Nonsectarian schools do not increase student achievement over that of their public school counterparts; nonsectarian schools simply maintain an achievement gap created by a selective system of admission. As Robert (2010) contended, private schools contribute to maintaining educational and social inequalities from one generation to the next.

Jeynes offers that "Americans need to reconceptualize their idea of education." Indeed, that notion is an excellent one. Integrating some of the processes that private schools have at their disposal that public schools do not would be a fair start. First, public schools, through appropriate policy making, should require parental involvement and attentiveness inherent in private schools. Requiring and enforcing parent involvement will be difficult, at best.

Second, refocus public education from a business model to a model that is centered on the needs of the child. Current public school policy is geared toward high-stakes testing deemed to hold the teachers and other school officials accountable for student performance. The intent is laudable, but the consequence centers attention on testing, and on school operations. A redirected focus to the child will hold the child accountable for his or her performance, and redirect resources from accountability measures to instruction.

Finally, policymakers should work to eliminate the wide disparity in differing socioeconomic groups. A meek attempt has been made to reduce the gap in some federal social work programs (e.g., Head Start and the Elementary and Secondary Education Act), but programs of that nature have provided insignificant results.

To be sure, it is unfortunate that a study on the comparison of public and nonpublic schools has not been conducted in the United States, at least on the scale and sophistication of the European PISA study. Like the PISA study, I suspect the results would indicate that nonsectarian private schools are no better than public schools at enhancing student achievement. As numerous researchers have discovered, student achievement is commensurate with socioeconomic level.

FURTHER READINGS AND RESOURCES

Broughman, S. P., Swaim, N. L., & Keaton, P. W. (2009). *Characteristics of private school in the United States: Results from the 2007–08 Private School Universe Survey* (NCES 2009-313). Washington, DC: National Center for Educational Statistics, U.S. Department of Education. Retrieved from http://nces.ed.gov/pubs2009/2009313 .pdf

Chubb, J. E., & Moe, T. M. (1990). *Politics, markets, and America's schools.* Washington, DC: Brookings Institution Press.

Coleman, J.C. (1988). Social capital in the creation of human capital. *American Journal of Sociology*, Supplement 94, S95–S120.

Friedman, M. (2002). *Capitalism and freedom.* Chicago: University of Chicago Press.

Glenn, C. L. (2000). *The ambiguous embrace.* Princeton, NJ: Princeton University Press.

Holme, J. J. (2002). Buying homes, buying schools: School choice and the social construction of school quality. *Harvard Educational Review, 72,* 177–205.

Jeynes, W. (2003a). The learning habits of twelfth graders attending religious and non-religious schools. *International Journal of Education and Religion, 4*(2), 145–167.

Jeynes, W. (2003b). *Religion, education, and academic success.* Greenwich, CT: Information Age Press.

Jeynes, W. (2011). *Parental involvement & academic success.* New York: Taylor & Francis/ Routledge.

Lareau, A. (2000). *Home advantage: Social class and parental intervention in elementary education.* Lanham, MD: Rowan & Littlefield.

Reay, D., & Lucey, H. (2000). Children, school choice, and social differences. *Educational Studies, 26,* 83–100. doi: 10.1080/03055690097754

Robert, P. (2010). Social origin, school choice, and student performance. *Educational Research and Evaluation, 16,* 107–129.

Snyder, T. D., & Dillow, S. A. (2010). *Digest of Education Statistics 2009* (NCES 2010-013). Washington, DC: National Center for Education Statistics, Institute of Education Sciences, U.S. Department of Education.

U.S. Department of Education. (n.d.a). Table 86: Number of public school districts and public and private elementary and secondary schools: Selected years, 1869–70 through 2007–08. *Digest of Education Statistics.* Retrieved July 25, 2011, from http:// nces.ed.gov/programs/digest/d09/tables/dt09_086.asp

U.S. Department of Education. (n.d.b). *Private schools in the United States: A statistical profile, 1993–1994/nonsectarian regular schools.* Retrieved July 25, 2011, from http:// nces.ed.gov/pubs/ps/97459ch4.asp

COURT CASES AND STATUTES

Brown v. Board of Education, 347 U.S. 483 (1954).

Farrington v. Tokushige, 273 U.S. 284 (1927).

Pierce v. Society of Sisters of the Holy Names of Jesus and Mary, 268 U.S. 510 (1925).

10

Do magnet schools enhance student achievement?

POINT: Timothy J. Ilg, *University of Dayton*

COUNTERPOINT: David Dolph, *University of Dayton*

OVERVIEW

A magnet school is defined in the No Child Left Behind Act (NCLB) as "a public elementary school, public secondary school, public elementary education center, or public secondary education center that offers a special curriculum capable of attracting substantial numbers of students of different racial backgrounds" (20 U.S.C. § 7231a). Magnet schools essentially are public schools that focus on a particular discipline or offer specialized curricula, such as those that place an instructional emphasis on science, technology, or the arts. As NCLB's definition indicates, magnet schools exist at all levels: elementary, middle, and high school. Although most magnet schools are created by local school boards for the benefit of a district's own students, some magnet schools are created by the state and are open to all eligible students within the state. Many magnet schools have specific admission criteria, and some have a highly competitive enrollment process. Thus, magnet schools most often attract gifted or academically talented students. They are attractive to both parents and students because they offer programs of study that are more specialized than those in a traditional school.

Magnet schools are found in large urban school districts more often than in suburban districts, with many being located in low income areas. Inasmuch as students attending magnet schools come from all geographic areas of the school district, the student body typically represents a cross section of the community. Thus, magnet schools in large urban areas generally attract students from mixed racial, ethnic, and socioeconomic backgrounds. In fact, magnet schools first emerged in the 1960s and became more popular in the 1970s as one means for school districts to come into compliance with court desegregation orders. In drawing students from all school zones within the district, magnet schools emerged as a successful means of voluntary desegregation. Magnet schools in many cities helped the districts achieve better racial balance, particularly when the schools were located in low socioeconomic areas.

Magnet schools provide parents with one option for school choice since their enrollment is open to all qualifying students within a school district, regardless of where they live within the district. As part of its emphasis on school choice, Subchapter V, Part C, of NCLB provides assistance to school districts to create and maintain magnet schools. When NCLB was passed, Congress found that approximately 2 million students, of whom more than 65% were non-White, attended magnet schools. Under this part of the statute the federal government provides financial assistance to eligible school districts to develop and implement magnet school programs to assist in the desegregation of the schools while increasing school choice options. The federal government provides two-year grants to eligible school districts that are developing new programs or significantly revising existing programs for magnet schools that are part of an approved desegregation plan and are designed to attract students from different social, economic, ethnic, and racial backgrounds.

Since magnet schools cater to students who have a particular interest in the discipline or specialized area of study offered, they provide focused instruction and targeted learning opportunities specifically designed to develop the students' unique talents. Magnet schools generally set high academic standards, and even though they are more racially diverse than their traditional school counterparts, as the essays in this chapter will show, they are not without their critics. In particular, critics contend that magnet schools often take the brightest students away from their neighborhood schools. To the extent that school district budgets are limited, and magnet schools are usually more costly to operate, they also may take resources away from other schools in the district. Further, while magnet schools promote racial diversity, they often cause segregation of students by other criteria, such as academic ability. Critics also point out that students from low income and non-English-speaking families are often underrepresented in magnet schools as are students with disabilities.

The debate in this chapter focuses on whether magnet schools enhance student achievement. In the point essay, Timothy J. Ilg, an associate professor in the School of Education and Allied Professions at the University of Dayton, contends that magnet schools have improved students' academic achievement. Ilg claims that magnet schools improve motivation and have created climates conducive to academic success. While Ilg concedes that the research on magnet schools is far from conclusive, he contends that they have succeeded in raising the overall academic success of students. He concludes that rather than question the value of magnet schools in increasing student achievement, educators should promote the development of new magnet schools, and sustain and improve existing programs, as an integral strategy on the school choice agenda.

In the counterpoint essay, David Dolph, a clinical faculty member in the School of Education and Allied Professions at the University of Dayton, takes the opposing view. While he agrees that magnet schools have many positive attributes, his contention is that they also have a negative impact on students, families, and communities. Dolph argues that issues regarding selection processes, deferring resources from neighborhood schools, transportation, limiting student interest, and less parental involvement all detract from the overall benefit of magnet schools for students and their families.

School districts continue to develop and maintain magnet schools as a school choice option for parents. However, as these essays show, there are both positive and negative aspects to magnet schools. In reading these essays you may want to consider the following questions. Are magnet schools still needed to foster desegregation efforts? Do magnet schools create other forms of segregation? Do the benefits of magnet schools outweigh their disadvantages?

Allan G. Osborne, Jr.
Principal (Retired), Snug Harbor Community School,
Quincy, Massachusetts

POINT: Timothy J. Ilg
University of Dayton

For several decades, a far-reaching debate has raged over the efficacy of magnet schools, particularly high schools, to deliver quality education. Opponents have argued that magnet schools have not delivered on the promise of higher achievement and, in fact, have not delivered the educational innovation promised by magnet school advocates. Some opponents have actually stated that magnet schools have hurt the education of all children by drawing resources away from successful traditional public schools. These critics say traditional public schools should not have to compete with magnet schools for scarce funding and resources. They also contend that with per-pupil money going to magnet schools, traditional public schools work with smaller budgets and are less able to provide individualized, specialty programs such as art, music, and technology. In effect, magnet schools divert monies from the traditional school programs that could be used for systemwide improvements. They further argue that students with special needs may not be guaranteed fair treatment or adequate funding.

Proponents, on the other hand, say magnet schools can focus on a specific subgroup of students to meet their individual learning challenges or their particular interests. These magnet or "niche" schools can focus their curriculum and instructional practices, leading to more personalized and more effective instruction. Most magnet schools concentrate on a particular discipline or area of study (humanities, fine and performing arts, or natural sciences), while others (such as International Baccalaureate schools) have a more general focus. They are often structured differently than traditional public schools in purpose, curriculum, pedagogy, and standards.

Despite all these criticisms, the number of magnet schools has increased dramatically from the early 1970s. By 2005–2006, magnet schools were located in 31 states and enrolled more students (2 million) than charter schools. Educational reformers are convinced that the traditional public schools with their mission to be everything to all students cannot meet the needs of children, particularly urban children. Resoundingly, they have responded negatively to public schools and have called for alternative structures, such as charter and magnet schools.

This essay maintains that magnet schools have overcome the odds and have improved the academic achievement of children. These magnet schools/programs have succeeded in motivating young people from both advantaged and disadvantaged backgrounds, and have created school climates conducive to students' academic success. Good school ethos has been characterized by strong academic emphasis, a stress on positive rewards, consistent and shared values, and positive teacher expectations of students.

HISTORY OF MAGNET SCHOOLS

Magnet schools are separate schools or special programs within schools offering specific curricula designed to attract students from an entire district. Magnet schools are different from charter, private, and parochial schools in that they remain within the public school system. Thus, they remain part of the public school system bureaucracy unlike charter schools. Originally, magnet schools were created to attract students of different backgrounds in response to racial segregation in urban districts, such as New York, Chicago, and Philadelphia. These schools gained popularity in the 1970s when school officials were designing desegregation plans, and magnets were seen as an alternative to forced busing in many cities. They were considered attractive options for middle-class families and were used to "soften" the blow of forced busing. Magnet schools tend to be located in large, high-poverty urban districts and, as noted earlier, were opened to attract White students to schools in minority neighborhoods (Goldring & Smrekar, 2000). The U.S. Department of Education estimates that over half of all large urban school systems used magnets as a tool for desegregation. The Magnet Schools Assistance Program (MSAP) was developed by the U.S. Department of Education in the early 1980s as a way to encourage schools to address de facto racial segregation. Funds were given to districts that implemented either voluntary desegregation plans or court orders to reduce racial isolation. With the support of monies from MSAP, the number of magnet school programs more than doubled in the 1980s, from 1,000 to 2,400. Between 1985 and 1993, MSAP spent $739 million in school districts to promote magnet schools. In 1994, MSAP was reauthorized, and the structure of the program was refocused to ensure that all magnet schools were involved in systemic reform efforts with the emphasis on providing all students with opportunities to meet challenging content and performance standards.

Originally, magnet schools were used to reduce racial segregation voluntarily by developing schools that would draw students to specialized schools across their districts. Each magnet school would have a specialized curriculum that would draw students based on their interests. Magnet schools became models for school improvement plans, and provided students with opportunities to succeed academically in a diverse learning environment. As noted earlier, critics of magnet school programs assert that magnet schools have actually served to widen socioeconomic divisions in many locations. These opponents argue that middle-class families are more likely to choose magnet schools because they tend to be more informed of educational options than lower income parents. Having greater parental involvement than standard public schools should not be a reason to condemn magnet schools. In addition, magnet schools are accused of "creaming off" the more able students. Although some magnet schools have a competitive entrance process, requiring an entrance examination, interview, or audition, most schools select all students who apply or use a lottery system for admitting students, thus giving all students an equal chance for admittance. The argument about selective admissions criteria fails to adequately point out that less than one third of the magnet schools have selection criteria. Increasingly, the magnet schools that have retained competitive criteria are using interviews and essays to offset the segregating effects associated with the consideration of test scores, grade point averages, and audition performances only.

More recently, magnet schools have been created to promote academic opportunity and excellence within a district. Magnet schools are typically characterized by the following qualities: a unified curriculum built around a discipline or theme (such as arts or technology), a compelling mode of instruction (such as Montessori), admission to facilitate voluntary desegregation, and a voluntary student and parent selection process. Magnets are more likely to offer subject-matter-oriented programs, such as mathematics, science, aerospace, and language immersion, and less likely to offer programs focused on a particular instructional approach. In addition, these schools have been known for the development and design of innovative educational practices and methods and whole-school systemic reform efforts. They often provide unique sets of learning opportunities and encourage innovation in the classrooms.

PROMOTING INNOVATION

With the changing focus on academic achievement, magnet schools are now expected to perform many other duties beyond desegregation. Indeed, MSAP expects magnet programs to serve as models for school innovation, reform, and higher student achievement (Frankenberg & Le, 2008). Additional funding from MSAP is often tied to this concept of the magnet school serving as a model of educational reform. Three of the major goals for MSAP funding are the support of systemic reform, the promotion of innovative educational practices, and the improvement of student achievement. Rather than a drain on traditional, public schools, magnet schools serve as lighthouses of hope for the other public schools.

In recent years, school districts have shifted away from desegregation efforts and focused more on accountability and higher test scores. It is not surprising that magnet schools report a shift away from the original purpose of desegregation and a new emphasis on student academic achievement. Supreme Court decisions in the 1990s solidified the judicial retreat from desegregation by lessening the standard for school districts to be judged to have completely eliminated the effects of segregation. The decision, *Missouri v. Jenkins* (1995), is particularly relevant because it dealt with the establishment of magnet schools in Kansas City. The Supreme Court rejected the remedy of the establishment of interdistrict magnet schools and urged the local court to return the district to "local control."

RESEARCH

Unfortunately, most research studies, completed prior to 1994, focused on the ability of magnet schools to reduce, eliminate, or prevent minority isolation within districts. Several early studies did reveal that magnet schools were more effective than comprehensive urban high schools at raising student proficiency in the academic subjects. The key factors for the magnet schools with the highest achievement scores were a clearly defined purpose and a unique mission, the ability to focus on student outcomes, and organizational cohesion and flexibility to pursue that purpose. In addition, the highly successful magnet school structures have certain identifiable characteristics: common focus, decentralized governance structure, personalized learning environment, high expectations for staff and students, atmosphere of respect, and efforts to engage the entire community. They stand in sharp contrast to the huge comprehensive urban high school, and they are living proof that disadvantaged students can overcome their poverty and achieve in the right environment. The growth of these magnet school programs appears to be the most effective way to link disadvantaged urban students to productive adult lives.

Although some research studies have mixed reviews as to the academic effectiveness of magnet schools, magnet school programs have shown great promise in educating students, particularly in the urban centers. In general, magnet schools have been found to increase student achievement, student motivation and satisfaction, and parent satisfaction with the school. The first study commissioned by the U.S. Department of Education to examine the quality of education in magnets found that over 80% of schools surveyed had higher average achievement scores than the district average. Adam Gamoran's 1996 study comparing student achievement among Catholic, private, comprehensive, and magnet schools found some advantages in reading, science, and social studies for magnet school students. In addition, he noted that disadvantaged students are more likely to produce higher academic achievement in magnet schools than in comprehensive schools.

A study of magnet schools in the state of New York found that standardized test scores were higher in districts with magnet schools, and within districts, magnet schools exceeded traditional schools. Magnet school programs had increased attendance rates, decreased dropout rates, and improved graduation rates. Amy Heebner (1995) found there was a lower dropout rate in public career magnet high schools in New York. A 1998 study of magnet schools in Jacksonville-Duval County, Florida, found that students attending the magnet schools had higher norm-referenced achievement test scores in all grade levels than their counterparts in traditional schools (Poppell & Hague, 2001). A more recent study has found a positive magnet school effect on mathematics achievement in a midsized Southern city. In a report prepared for the U.S. Department of Education in 2003, researchers found that the overall achievement of students attending MSAP-supported magnet schools (as measured by standardized test scores) increased between 1998 and 2001. The researchers also found that the schools adopted a wide range of innovative programs. According to the data, MSAP schools had somewhat more positive school climates generally associated with effective schools (Christenson et al., 2003). Further evidence of positive academic gains in magnet schools comes from a recent analysis of the achievement of students in Connecticut's interdistrict magnet school programs. Through a comparison of magnet school lottery "winners" and "losers," the researchers found that attendance at the magnet high schools had a positive effect on students' reading and math scores. Students who attended magnet middle schools made greater gains in reading and slightly more gains in mathematics than students who attended the regular public schools. Furthermore, the traditional achievement gaps between White, middle-class students and minority, low income students were smaller in magnet schools. Magnet schools appear to provide an academic climate similar to suburban schools.

In addition to higher achievement levels, magnet students have stronger college expectations and are less likely to miss school or skip classes than students in traditional schools. Magnet school students reported more positive influences of adults in their schools on college expectations; more emphasis on high standards, self-discipline, and personal responsibility; and less social pressure against academic success. Magnet schools provided more opportunities for parental involvement and effective communication between home and schools (Goldring & Smrekar, 2000). After switching their children from a comprehensive to a magnet school, parents have reported that their children's interest in computers, mathematics, and science increased. Parents have also reported that their children were more motivated to learn and enjoyed school more because of their magnet school experience. Parents who choose magnet schools are generally highly satisfied with their children's education. Magnet schools promote personal interactions, are often committed to site-based management, and are less constrained by central bureaucracies. Ideally, magnet programs attract staff and administration that have an interest in the school's focus/program. Hence, the chance for personality matches and common interest bonds between staff and students are heightened. They also seem to afford teachers more autonomy and involvement in decision making at the classroom level (Goldring & Smrekar, 2000).

Critics of magnet schools focus on three issues: academic achievement, accountability, and representation of at-risk students. Research results on the academic achievement of students in magnet schools have been mixed. Bruce Christenson and colleagues (2003) found that academic progress in magnet schools was no greater than in a comparison set of public schools, once controls were introduced for changes in the demographic composition of schools. However, frequent changes to state testing meant that test scores for almost half of the schools were not available during the study. As noted earlier, more recent research studies have shown positive growth in student achievement in magnet schools. There is no doubt that additional research on student academic achievement in magnet schools is needed in order to settle this argument. The concerns that magnet schools are not held accountable to most federal and state educational objectives and that special needs, low income, and low-English-proficiency students in magnet schools are underrepresented simply cannot be substantiated. The critics have simply forgotten the Department of Education standards for magnet schools and the program evaluations that examine the success of MSAP projects. Specifically, MSAP projects must offer courses of instruction that will substantially strengthen the knowledge of academic subjects, must develop and design innovative educational methods and practices, must ensure that all students enrolled in the magnet school programs have equitable access to high quality education, and must prevent, reduce, and eliminate minority group isolation in the schools (Christenson et al., 2003). Funding is tied to these standards. It is hard to imagine that federal regulators are not holding magnet schools responsible for federal objectives. One wonders if traditional schools could withstand such scrutiny.

While research on magnets and academic achievement is far from conclusive and often complicated by methodological concerns, the basic consensus remains the same. Magnet school programs have been successful in both integrating students and raising overall student academic performance. Magnet schools continue to offer a popular option for parents who wish to support the local public schools, but who also wish to have additional educational opportunities for their children. Magnet schools, of course, are not the only educational choice option available to parents and students. While there are some similarities between magnet schools and charter schools, there are important differences. Charter schools were begun not with any intent to desegregate, but as a way to provide choice within public schools. The focus of magnet schools to create diverse student bodies is not included in the federal legislation authorizing charter schools. Magnet schools have been highly successful in offering school choice for parents in a manner that also fostered diverse schools. Magnet schools with unique educational offerings have provided enhanced academic outcomes for students within diverse and inclusive settings.

CONCLUSION

Rather than questioning the value of magnet schools to increase student achievement, educators should promote the development of magnet schools, along with sustaining and improving existing programs, as an integral strategy on the school choice agenda.

COUNTERPOINT: David Dolph
University of Dayton

Magnet schools, as currently organized, do not inherently promote or enhance student academic achievement. Magnet schools are public schools that typically provide a specialized program of study or instructional approach for students attending public schools. Magnet schools provide parents and students with choices for instructional services. However, the original intent of magnet schools was not to provide an instructional alternative, but rather to offer a means to increase racial desegregation, predominantly in large urban school districts where students did not necessarily attend a school in their residential neighborhood. Instead, students moved across interdistrict boundaries of regular attendance zones in order to enroll in a magnet school. Magnet schools attempted to further racial diversity, improve instructional outcomes for students, and provide programming that would meet student talents and interests (Smrekar, 2004).

Magnet schools began to surface as educational alternatives in the late 1960s and early 1970s. Magnet schools are categorized as public schools. Often they are part of large public school systems in urban communities; thus, they are not the same thing as private or parochial schools. Typically school systems that contain magnet schools have enrollments of 10,000 students or more. The U.S. Department of Education (2006) indicates that approximately 54% of larger urban school districts incorporate magnet schools as part of an approach to provide for racial desegregation in the district. This is in contrast to only 10% of large suburban districts that have magnet schools.

Going further, more than half of all magnet schools are located in school districts and communities that have a lower socioeconomic population. Over half of the magnet schools in the United States function as elementary schools while only 20% of magnet schools are geared toward high school students (U.S. Department of Education, 2006).

Thus, magnet schools have three characteristics that set them apart from regular public schools. First, they have a specialized curriculum or approach to instruction. Second, they attract students from outside formalized attendance zones in school districts. Third, magnet schools have increased student diversity as a goal.

As noted by the author of the point essay, there are many positive factors associated with magnet schools. Some of these factors include innovative curriculum focusing on particular areas of study such as the arts or sciences, an enriched educational environment for gifted students, or a selected instructional focus such as Montessori. As potentially positive as magnet schools are as a method both encouraging racial desegregation and providing innovative instruction, there are a number of negative aspects related to magnet schools that must be taken into consideration. It is important for educators, policymakers, parents, and students to be aware of potential downsides of magnet schools as well as benefits in order to make informed decisions.

This counterpoint essay argues that although magnet schools may provide alternatives to neighborhood schools, there are also negative consequences of the magnet school phenomenon that should be understood. This essay reviews and examines the outcomes of the magnet school movement that have had a negative impact on students, parents, communities, and student academic achievement.

SELECTION PROCESS

The first problem related to magnet schools is the process used for student selection. Magnet schools tend to be popular with parents and students as a site for educational opportunities. School districts that have magnet schools often advertise and promote the school through various public relations strategies. This effort may have a positive impact on parental and student attitudes toward magnet schools. Approximately 93% of school districts offering federally funded magnet schools and 61% of districts offering non–federally funded magnet schools as alternative settings for instruction have more requests for admittance for students than space available (U.S. Department of Education, 2006). This poses a challenge for parents, students, and the school district to develop a reasonable and equitable method of student selection. This is not only important in terms of fairness for students and parents, but it is also a potentially troublesome public relations issue for the school district if the selection process is viewed as unfair.

One approach to student selection to a magnet school is a "first come, first served" process, which often leads to behavior similar to Christmas shopping the day after Thanksgiving. Parents have been known to line up early in the morning or camp out overnight in order to be first in line to turn in applications for their child/children's admittance into the magnet school. This admittance process may provide impediments for families whose parents cannot take time off from work or do not have the ability to stand in line to turn in an application form. This approach to selection has the appearance of being unfair to the very families and students who might have the most to gain from a magnet school program. Programs that are perceived as unfair in the public eye do not enhance the reputation of a school district, particularly if the district is already being criticized for other issues.

A second approach that is often used for student selection to magnet schools is a lottery. Although this process may be viewed as a fairer procedure, the numerous interested students and their parents who are denied access because of the "luck of the draw" may still be quite unhappy with the school district.

A third method used for student selection to magnet schools is some form of a selective admission process. School districts using this approach typically employ test scores to screen and select, or in the case of magnet schools focusing on performing arts, an audition may be used.

A related issue to competitive admission processes is that students with poor grades or disciplinary or attendance issues are often excluded from magnet schools because of the admittance requirements. Again, this type of process may result in exclusion of students who would profit the most from magnet school programs.

Neighborhood schools may suffer as a result of a competitive selection process as they can be left with higher proportional numbers of students who exert negative peer influence on other students. There is potential that a school and its students will be influenced in a less than positive direction. For example, Victor Harbison (2009) indicates that since neighborhood schools do not have the advantage of student selection based on test scores, there is greater potential for academic deterioration.

Finally, since students attending magnet schools will not be going to school with other neighborhood children, further deterioration of the social fabric of a neighborhood may occur.

DESEGREGATION

A second negative outcome related to magnet schools is that they can result in a different, albeit unintended, type of segregation. Although an original intent of magnet schools was to serve as a vehicle to further racial desegregation in public schools, students attending magnet schools are not necessarily representative of a school district's overall population. For example, the U.S. Department of Education (2006) reported that students from low income families, students with limited English proficiency, and students with special needs tend to be underrepresented in magnet schools. On the other hand, specialized magnet schools may attract, and consequently isolate, students who have special abilities.

A secondary purpose for developing magnet schools was to improve academic quality through thematic programs or some form of specialized curriculum. By offering parents and students a choice of attending a school that provides a unique curriculum or a specialized focus, it was hoped that a rich and racially diverse learning environment would ensue.

Although magnet schools may still assist in accomplishing the goal of racial desegregation, curious trends have developed that might counteract the original intent. Magnet schools using a selective admission process may foster new forms of segregation. As discussed earlier, admissions processes for magnet schools vary considerably; however, one noted aspect of a number of admissions procedures is more competitive approaches to student selection. A selection process that utilizes test results, holds an audition of artistic skill, or takes discipline and/or attendance records into consideration will potentially eliminate some students who might be best served by a magnet school program.

This latter issue should be of major concern for school policymakers and administrators. It is possible that through magnet school selection processes, only more gifted students, or students who have more motivated parents, are selected. Magnet school selection procedures may tend to favor the best and the brightest in regard to who is accepted. Thus, in some cases, magnet school selection processes will actually pull more skilled students from neighborhood schools and send them to magnet schools. This has the potential of allowing students who are average in skills, either academically or artistically, to struggle in a neighborhood school offering an educational environment that provides less opportunity. If this is the case, the school district may be creating a new type of student segregation based on academic or artistic ability.

Although magnet schools potentially provide a more racially balanced student population than regular urban schools, there is a chance that other types of imbalances may occur. For example, magnet schools generally spend more per student than their non–magnet school counterparts. In addition, there are grant programs for magnet schools to receive either state or federal funds devoted to assisting achievement of racial desegregation. For example, the federal government's Magnet Schools Assistance Program provides grants to "assist in the desegregation of public schools by supporting the elimination, reduction, and prevention of minority group isolation in elementary and secondary schools with substantial numbers of minority group students" (U.S. Department of Education, 2010). An imbalance of financial resources such as this has the potential of creating a disparity in regard to instructional opportunities for students.

Yet another imbalance created by magnet schools deals with socioeconomic status (SES) of students in attendance. Arguably, magnet schools are more racially balanced than typical, urban schools. However, evidence suggests that some magnet school students will not have the same SES makeup as their counterparts in the district's regular schools. Depending on their location and the specialization of a particular magnet school, it may draw students from higher SES families as well as from families that have a higher rate of employment and level of education.

Finally, it is possible that teachers who are more innovative and effective might be attracted to teach at magnet schools rather than other schools within the same school districts. This latter idea makes intuitive sense in that many teachers enjoy working with skilled and motivated students. Since magnet schools may be populated by that type of student, it is logical that teachers may gravitate toward such an environment.

However, the opposite situation regarding teacher placement could also be a factor. Amy Klauke (1988) suggests some teachers may be placed to teach in magnet schools involuntarily. If so, teachers who are not predisposed to the teaching style being fostered by magnet schools may resent being forced to change. This can lead to resentment—not a good attitude for teachers to demonstrate.

NARROWING OF STUDENT INTEREST

Another negative result related to stratifying students based on academic or other related skills is narrowing student interest. One of the basic tenets of public education is to provide a wide range of learning opportunities for all students in order to develop well-rounded citizens. In essence, traditional, comprehensive schools attempt to be all things to all students. Students have a wide range of choices based on comprehensive curriculum. Magnet schools, on the other hand, tend to focus student interest in a particular direction. This may influence students to focus primarily on areas of strength rather than improving all potential areas of talent and ability. The impact of this type of specialization is hard to gauge; however, it is an issue worth considering for parents, school leaders, and lawmakers. This may especially be true in elementary magnet schools that narrow a child's interest at a young age.

A well-rounded citizenry has long been viewed as a desirable outcome of public education. Magnet schools may overly encourage specialization at the risk of more holistic approaches to instructional outcomes.

FUNDING MAGNET SCHOOLS

As noted earlier, magnet schools are part of public school systems but typically spend more per pupil on average. Spending funds in this manner slights neighborhood schools from much needed funding, thus diminishing instructional programs where funding is limited. To the extent that magnet schools divert limited funds away from other schools within a district, the resources within neighborhood schools may be less than they would be otherwise.

TRANSPORTATION ISSUES

Another question regarding magnet schools deals with student transportation. Transporting students to school sites outside of their neighborhoods will be more expensive to school districts. Costs such as additional bus driver time, more fuel consumed, and more maintenance costs all must be factored into school district budgets.

From a student perspective, being bused away from neighborhood schools means additional time on a school bus. Additional bus time obviously reduces time for play, study, and family interaction. As a side note, it would be interesting to study how many magnet school students do not participate in extracurricular activities because of logistical issues such as transportation.

ADDITIONAL CONCERNS

Mary Haywood Metz (1988) indicates that public schools have historically been viewed as institutions that serve as places where students can become aware of, and develop, abilities. Klauke (1988) suggests that public schools are considered as having potential to level the playing field and provide an arena where academic skill and aptitude (as well as other talents and abilities) will be given opportunities to flourish. Magnet schools may not provide that appearance. Klauke (1988) notes that magnet schools are sometimes viewed as elitist alternatives that contradict the notion of fairness in public schools.

Klauke (1988) also suggests that magnet schools offer only a token of opportunity regarding desegregation. She believes that since magnet schools impact only a small percentage of urban students, they are not really accomplishing the mission of racial desegregation. Instead, she indicates that school districts use magnet schools as a justification to not do any more to further desegregation.

In addition, Klauke (1988) indicates that principals in magnet schools often lead in more of a top-down approach. This occurs because principals need to be more directive in order to maintain staff focus on goals and objectives supported by magnet schools. This approach to leadership runs contrary to current trends for principals to foster greater teacher involvement in decision making in schools. Autocratic leadership has potential for negatively impacting teacher attitudes, and can influence the culture of the school.

Finally, Klauke (1988) believes that because student enrollment is often more selective in magnet schools, the input of parents and students may not be valued to the same degree that it is in regular public schools. Two-way, ongoing communication is essential for a successful school (Kowalski, 2011). Reducing this type of communication is not good for schools in the long run.

CONCLUSION

Magnet schools have many positive features to offer students, parents, and policymakers. For example, research by Bob Algozzine and colleagues (1998) suggests that magnet schools often foster better student attitudes toward instruction than traditional schools. Bruce Christenson and colleagues (2003) found that magnet schools provided a more positive school climate than typical public schools. Algozzine and colleagues (1998) also reported that student interest in math and science increased while attending magnet schools. Finally, magnet schools have assisted in movement toward racial desegregation in urban school districts.

Nevertheless, there are negative aspects of magnet schools. Issues regarding selection processes, deferring resources from neighborhood schools, transportation, narrowing the focus of student interest in regard to academic pursuits, and less parental involvement should be considered. Factors identified in this essay, viewed individually or collectively, may have a detrimental impact on overall school district student achievement. Magnet schools have the potential to limit student and staff constituency and resources to the extent that academic achievement is deterred not only in the magnet school but in other district schools as well. By increasing the need for resources at a magnet school, thus deferring those resources from other schools, the district as a whole can suffer. The goal of any public school is to provide equal opportunities for academic achievement and growth for all students. Magnet schools may actually impede this goal because of the numerous issues identified in this essay.

While these negative issues should be of importance to parents and students, they should also be of primary interest to policymakers. Regardless of the perspective, in order to make wise decisions for individual students and policy at large, the pros and cons of magnet schools cannot be ignored.

FURTHER READINGS AND RESOURCES

Algozzine, B., Yon, M., Nesbit, C., & Nesbit, J. (1998). Parent perceptions of a magnet school program. *Journal of Research and Development in Education, 32*(3), 178–183.

Archbald, D. A. (1991). *Magnet schools and issues of public school desegregation, quality and choice.* Palo Alto, CA: American Institutes for Research.

Christenson, B., Eaton, M., Garet, M., Miller, L., Hikawa, H., & DuBois, P. (2003). *Evaluation of the magnet schools assistance program, 1998 grantees.* Washington, DC: American Institutes for Research.

Cobb, C. D., Bifulco, R., & Bell, C. (2008). *Do magnet schools outperform traditional public schools and reduce the achievement gap? The case of Connecticut's interdistrict magnet school program.* Occasional Paper No. 167. New York: National Center for the Study of Privatization in Education.

Frankenberg, E., & Le, C. Q. (2008). The Post-Parents Involved Challenge: Confronting extralegal obstacles to integration. *Ohio State Law Journal, 69*(911), 1015–1072.

Gamoran, A. (1996). Student achievement in public magnet, public comprehensive, and private city high schools. *Educational Evaluation and Policy Analysis, 18*, 1–18.

Goldring, E., & Smrekar, C. (2000). Magnet schools and the pursuit of racial balance. *Education and Urban Society, 33*(1), 17–35.

Harbison, V. (2009). *Magnet schools: More harm than good?* Retrieved from http://kristof.blogs.nytimes.com/2009/02/10/magnet-schools-more-harm-than-good?

Heebner, A. (1995). The impact of career magnet high schools: Experimental and qualitative evidence. *Journal of Vocational Education Research, 20*(2), 27–55.

Klauke, A. (1988). *Magnet schools.* ERIC Digest Series Number EA 26. Retrieved from http://www.ericdigests.org/pre-928/magnet.htm

Kowalski, T. J. (2011). *Public relations in schools.* Upper Saddle River, NJ: Pearson Education.

Metz, M. H. (1988). In education, magnets attract controversy. *NEA Today, 6,* 54–60.

Poppell, J., & Hague, S. (2001, April). *Examining indicators to assess the overall effectiveness of magnet schools: A study of magnet schools in Jacksonville, Florida.* Paper presented at the Annual Meeting of the American Educational Research Association, Seattle, WA, April 10–14.

Smrekar, C. (2004). Magnet schools. In P. S. Fass (Ed.), *Encyclopedia of children and childhood in history and society.* Farmington Hills, MI: Gale. Retrieved from http://www.highbeam.com/doc/1G2-3402800277.html?key=01-42160D527E1B1069110

U.S. Department of Education. (2006). *Educational innovation in multiracial contexts: The growth of magnet schools in American education.* Retrieved from http://www2.ed.gov/rschstat/eval/choice/magnetgrowth.html

U.S. Department of Education. (2010). *Magnet schools assistance.* Retrieved from http://www2.ed.gov/programs/magnet/index.html

Court Cases and Statutes

Missouri v. Jenkins, 515, U.S. 70 (1995).

No Child Left Behind Act, Subchapter V, Part C—Magnet Schools Assistance, 20 U.S.C. §§ 7231–7231j (2006).

Do single-sex classes and/or schools better address the needs of elementary and/or secondary school students?

POINT: Vivian Hopp Gordon, *Loyola University Chicago*

COUNTERPOINT: Jyllian Rosa Guerriero, *University of Dayton School of Law*

OVERVIEW

As the name implies, students who attend single-sex schools or classes are separated by gender. They may attend classes in separate classrooms, buildings, or schools. Single-sex schools were fairly prevalent prior to the 20th century but have been regaining popularity recently. Single-sex schools are more common in other countries for both religious and cultural reasons.

Proponents of single-sex schools and classes suggest that they should be an option because males and females learn in different ways and the academic achievement of each gender can be increased in single-sex educational settings. Many feel that at least some students will thrive in environments that are free from the distractions and social pressures that can exist in coeducational settings. Although research on the academic advantages of single-sex schools is inconclusive, advocates argue that it should be an option for parents and students. Opponents, on the other hand, feel that single-sex schools and classes are discriminatory and represent a return to an era when boys went to shop classes and girls went to home economics.

According to the National Association for Single Sex Public Education (NASSPE), during the 2011–2012 school year at least 506 U.S. public schools will offer single-sex educational opportunities. Approximately 390 of those schools are coeducational facilities but will offer some single-sex classrooms. NASSPE estimates that 116 of those 506 schools are single-sex schools; 67 are for females, 44 are for boys, and 5 are dual enrollment meaning that the campus is coeducational but students are separated by gender for almost all classes.

It is fairly well settled that public single-sex schools are legal, but they still can run into some legal obstacles, particularly when equivalent programs for both males and females are not available. For example, in 1996 the U.S. Supreme Court in *United States v. Virginia* ruled that the Virginia Military Institute's (VMI) policy of admitting only males was unconstitutional. The Court ruled that VMI's exclusion of females from the educational opportunity offered by the school violated the U.S. Constitution Fourteenth Amendment's Equal Protection Clause. The case began when the federal government sued Virginia (VMI is part of the commonwealth's public higher education system) over the school's restrictive admission policies. The Court stated that VMI had not provided sufficient justification for its gender-based discrimination criteria. Further, the Court was not convinced that creating a separate institution for women would provide a proper remedy, in part because the proposed program would not offer a substantially equal alternative. Single-sex schools may pass constitutional muster if the educational opportunities for males and females are comparable. Private schools have more flexibility in the establishment of single-sex educational programs because they are not government funded and thus not subject to the equal protection requirements.

The No Child Left Behind Act (NCLB) includes provisions to facilitate the creation of public single-sex schools (20 U.S.C. §§ 7215(a)(23), 7215(c)). Under new Title IX regulations issued in response to NCLB's mandates, public school districts may create single-sex schools as long as attendance is voluntary, and comparable facilities, courses, and services are available to both sexes. Single-sex classes may be offered as long as the school board can provide a rationale for offering a single-sex class in that subject, offers a coeducational class in the same subject at a geographically accessible location, and conducts a review every two years to determine if the single-sex class is still required. Charter schools, however, are exempt from these regulations.

In the point essay in this chapter, Vivian Hopp Gordon, an associate professor in the School of Education at Loyola University in Chicago, argues that there are advantages to single-sex schools and classes. Gordon points to a growing body of research supporting gender-based education. In particular she notes that the research supports the proposition that separating the sexes creates a supportive environment that is more conducive to learning. Further, she cites research that indicates that there is evidence that both boys and girls fare better psychologically and have better social development in single-sex environments with reduced social pressures. Gordon emphasizes, however, that many experts insist that appropriate preparation is necessary for gender-separate classrooms to be successful. In this respect, the role of professional development is most important.

In the counterpoint essay, Jyllian Rosa Guerriero of the University of Dayton School of Law argues that single-sex schools and classes do not provide the best means of meeting the academic and social educational needs of students in both elementary and secondary schools. Guerriero, a former high school teacher, cites a 2005 report issued by the U.S. Department of Education that acknowledged that greater long-term academic achievement of students in single-sex schools was not readily apparent. She also contends that studies of self-esteem and attitude toward school also support coeducational schools. She concludes that the level of inclusiveness in public schools is what makes them excellent by fostering tolerance, acceptance, and understanding among a diverse community of children and youth.

As the debates in this chapter show, there is much disagreement over whether single-sex schools and classes are better than their coeducational counterparts in terms of academic achievement; psychological, emotional, and social well-being; and students' self-esteem. In reading these debates, you may want to think about a few questions. Are there some courses, such as physical education or sex education, that should always be taught in gender-specific classes? Are there reasons other than academic achievement that warrant the establishment of gender-specific classes? Should public school districts offer single-sex schools and classes when a significant number of their students come from families whose religion or culture demand segregation of the sexes at certain ages?

Allan G. Osborne, Jr.
Principal (Retired), Snug Harbor Community School,
Quincy, Massachusetts

POINT: Vivian Hopp Gordon
Loyola University Chicago

Gender-based education, where boys and girls are educated separately, remains hotly contested. Inherent in this debate is whether single-sex classes or schools better address the needs of elementary and secondary school students. Research on this issue often focuses not only on academic improvement but also on social interaction and perceptions of the nature of the influence such classes or schools have on children.

An important aspect of considering gender-based education is extant efforts at educational reform to enhance student achievement, particularly for diverse student populations. The direction of educational reform is to promote the academic and social success of students nationwide. One means considered by educators for achieving student improvement and success has been the notion of single-sex schools and single-sex classes. This is based on recent research showing natural differences in how boys and girls learn. When it pertains to educational reform, parents, schools, and school leaders are interested in all aspects of schooling, including whether and how gender-based education may influence the success of elementary and secondary school students.

LEGAL CHALLENGES

There are some legal challenges related to separating students by sex in schools. Title IX, a federal law, prohibits schools that receive federal funds to discriminate based on sex. The federal regulations specifically prohibit public schools from denying a student admission to any course on the basis of sex. Separation based on sex is only allowed in contact sports, sex education classes, and choruses. Existing single-sex schools established prior to the statute were also exempted. For example, in an agreement with the U.S. Department of Education, in a Title IX complaint, a school district settled by agreeing to admit male students to its all-girl algebra class. On a college campus, a course called College Algebra I was offered. The course emphasized the contributions of women in mathematics and highlighted career opportunities for women in math and science. When a complaint was brought, the college responded by opening its girls' math class to boys, but no boys signed up for the new class. A Michigan court stopped a plan to create three all-male academies for preschool through 5th grade. In a dramatic change of policy, in 2006, U.S. Office of Education Secretary Margaret Spellings eased federal regulations, allowing schools to offer single-sex classrooms and schools, as long as such options are completely voluntary. This change has given parents and school districts greater flexibility in offering gender-based education.

ACADEMIC IMPROVEMENT

One underlying rationale for having separate-sex schools or classes is that students may more readily improve academically if they are segregated by sex and taught in a manner most conducive to each group. The debate surrounding this issue is important because student success may be influenced by decisions related to this issue.

Since the inception of public education in the United States, there has been much debate about the type and role of schools to be used to educate children. Even before the beginning of public education in the United States, many students were being educated in single-sex environments, especially for the upper classes. Single-sex education is not a new phenomenon in American education. The first single-sex schools in the United States were for boys only, and many were developed by the upper class. Single-sex schools for women arose later, primarily as a result of the exclusionary admissions policies of all-male institutions. While single-sex education has been the preferred method of instruction in private and religious institutions, coeducation has been dominant in the public education domain since the beginning of broad-based public sector education in the United States.

FAMILY VALUES

Some researchers believe the reasoning behind the preference for single-sex education is related to individual or family values. Many cultures have clung to this sentiment. In rural areas, coeducation was successful as a simple and effective way to educate children in sparsely populated areas. However, in urban areas, where single-sex education was dominant, single-sex schools began to increase, particularly in the early 20th century.

RESEARCH

In today's educational climate, the popularity of single-sex educational facilities has burgeoned. In part this has come as a result of dissatisfaction with current practices and a desire for change involving more parental choice and school accountability. Recent studies and research have encouraged a different direction, that of gender-based education as a means of advancing student success and school improvement.

There has been a growing body of research in the field supporting gender-based education. These studies have examined a wide spectrum of issues related to gender-based education, including social benefits, academic benefits, long-term effectiveness on learning and achievement, self-esteem issues, leadership, and test scores. Research has indicated that girls and boys need rooms of their own because they have different learning styles: Girls learn cooperatively while boys learn competitively. Other research indicated that in a coed environment boys tend to be more aggressive and often taunted, teased, and intimated girls who spoke up in class. In one study, students were grouped according to sex in algebra and English classes and compared to coed students. Ultimately, the data indicated that the separated environment was conducive to learning—that it particularly provided a supportive environment for girls, inducing their greater participation and academic risk taking. Other studies indicated that girls consistently achieve better results than boys when both boys and girls have their own learning space. Further studies have highlighted that a gender-specific motivational structure is more possible in single-sex schools.

The question of whether girls receive better educations in all-girls schools has been examined. Most recent studies suggest that girls in single-sex schools are more confident in traditionally male subjects such as math and science. In a recent student-centered magazine, girls who were interviewed said they felt more open in a same-sex classroom and that the girls in their classes are like sisters. They observed that single-sex schools could make girls more confident at crucial times of their lives: the middle school and high school years. The girls indicated that when there are all girls in the classroom, the culture changes in a positive way.

There is evidence that single-sex school environments have a psychological impact on both boys and girls in secondary schools. For example, often in coeducational schools boys and girls are steered toward enrolling in classes that are "gender appropriate." These pressures can come from a variety of sources, including peer pressure. For example, even though a boy may be interested in pursuing art or drama, in a coeducational setting that boy may be more likely to elect other courses to fit in with the other boys. Girls report that in single-sex schools they were significantly more motivated toward and enjoyed science learning compared with students from coeducational schools. Another source of psychological impact is the prestige of the schools themselves. Single-sex schools are frequently considered more prestigious, and those students who attend often show more pride and confidence in their abilities.

A number of experiments have been conducted to examine the impact of gender-based education on boys and girls. Some of these experiments incorporated the notion that teachers should and do adjust their teaching styles when teaching boys' or girls' classes. When teachers do, there has been evidence of improved benefits for both boys and girls. Other more recent studies have found that single-sex schooling is especially beneficial to disadvantaged, at-risk children. This was reported by the Ford Foundation after a pilot study in California. Other school districts have recently started experimenting with single-sex classes for girls, mostly in math and science, arguing that this segregation raises girls' self-esteem and self-confidence, enhances their leadership and oral communication skills, boosts their standardized test scores, and increases their interest in advanced coursework in traditionally male subjects. Research related to boys within same-sex classes has indicated that boys in same-sex classrooms show significantly increased achievement in English studies compared to their coeducational peers. Other studies indicated boys in same-sex classrooms felt they received greater encouragement and appreciated the ability to talk about things that they were interested in, like sports, without ridicule from girls.

The National Association for Single Sex Public Education (NASSPE) reported in 2005 that several studies demonstrated the superior achievement levels of single-sex schools over coeducational schools. Even controlling for students' academic ability and other background factors, both boys and girls did significantly better in single-sex schools than in coed schools.

Some international studies in countries that have had single-sex schooling are also enlightening. In a large Australian study, in 2001, the country's Council for Educational Research compared performances of students at single-sex and coeducational schools over six years, involving over 270,000 students in 53 academic subjects (Tzolidis & Dobson, 2006). This study demonstrated that both boys and girls who were educated in single-sex classrooms scored an average of 15 to 22 percentile ranks higher than their coeducational counterparts. In another study in Jamaica, girls in single-sex schools were found to be the highest achievers, boys at single-sex schools were second in achievement, and boys and girls at coed schools were at the bottom of student achievement.

The "before and after" studies provide even more evidence for higher achievement levels of single-sex schools. The "before and after" studies are those that look at schools that were coeducational and then transitioned into single-sex schools. Data on achievement levels from before the switch, when the school was coeducational, were compared to data on achievement levels from after the switch to single-sex education. In these studies, the data reflected the same students, same teachers, and same facilities before and after switching to single-sex schools. In one of these schools, in London, the data indicated that the boys as well as the girls were better able to focus on academics. When they took a standardized test, the boys went from being in the 10th to 30th percentile to the 73rd percentile. Their reading averages went from the 20th to the 66th percentile, and their writing scores went from the 20th to the 53rd percentile. In another school, in Montreal, after switching to single-sex education, 85% of the students passed their final exams compared to 65% before the switch, while the rate of students going on to college nearly doubled.

A number of educators have proffered policy arguments in support of gender-based education. The American Association of University Women reported that often schools shortchange girls (Greenberg-Lake: The Analysis Group, 1992). The report concluded that girls in coed classes are victims of subtle gender bias and many teachers provide girls with less attention and encouragement than boys. Some theorists assert that even if teachers in coed schools observe how girls learn best and then later adapt their teaching styles to reach girls while disciplining boys who ridicule girls, efforts to change the teaching climate work best in a gender-based setting. Experts have also indicated that separate-sex schools are a good thing, especially for girls. They point to studies that show that teachers tend to call on boys more and take the work of girls less seriously. Too often, girls receive praise for how they look and behave rather than for what they accomplish and what ideas they have. Teachers generally report positive opinions about working in same-sex classrooms.

The girls and boys in studies have also reported differences in coed and same-sex classrooms that support gender-based education. Boys report that they receive more attention from teachers than girls do and initiate more interactions with teachers. Therefore, in a coeducational setting, educators have observed that boys exert a type of domination and social control of classroom culture. Studies about boys learning in single-sex institutions find that there is a better academic environment for boys, free of distractions. Grade point averages of boys and girls are often higher in single-sex math and science classes, compared to mixed-sex classes. Junior high school and high school girls have reported that boys in their classrooms harass them and dictated how the class would function. Educators interpreted that such coed classrooms decrease girls' academic risk taking and inhibit their participation in asking and answering questions. Girls have also reported that they remain quiet in a coeducational setting because of a fear of embarrassment and lack of self-confidence. Girls in same-sex science classes report the classes are more engaging, more interactive, and more methodical than mixed-sex classes. These girls report fewer disruptions, better opportunities to concentrate on their work, and diminished feelings of embarrassment for speaking up in class. The girls in same-sex classes also assert that the classes offer more support, less hassle, less ridicule, and less teasing from boys. These girls also observe that they feel more comfortable, share their thoughts more often, and feel less afraid to ask teachers questions during class or to offer answers for fear of being wrong.

Ultimately the issue of whether children achieve more academically through the attendance of same-sex classes is extremely important to examine and understand. In a recent large study concerning the effects of same-sex education compared with coeducational instruction, on the issue of academic gains, only 2% of the students favored coeducational instruction, and half the students showed improvement. This outcome supports the notion that children would certainly not be hurt by attending same-sex classrooms but may very well be helped academically by doing so. On the issue of social development, the girls reported feeling more comfortable in participating in discussion and activities leading to improved attitudes towards the subjects they were studying. Other studies indicated that gender-based classrooms provide increased confidence and higher self-esteem among girls while boys develop increased motivation and more commitment to schoolwork.

Many experts in the field assert that appropriate preparation is necessary for gender-separate classrooms to be successful. Appropriate preparation includes teachers receiving training in practical gender-specific classroom strategies. Another component of preparation is examination and review of best practices for the gender-separate classroom. Professional development for teachers on the ways girls and boys learn is also part of good planning when anticipating gender-based education.

Some current gender-based educational settings have shed some light on some possible directions for the future. For example, in a Maine high school, officials have found that, in the gender-based classroom setting, math scores for girls have skyrocketed, and their enrollment in advanced math classes has tripled. A Michigan high school offered a girls-only science and engineering class while a middle school in Virginia has a number of single-sex classes for academic subjects. A Maine school district set up a special all-girls algebra class, and a city in California established special classes for math-phobic girls. Teachers and parents noted that boys' accountability and self-discipline have improved. Teachers have adopted different strategies for boys and girls and have gained higher levels of satisfaction from teaching. All these current efforts are attempts at translating research to best practice to encourage student improvement and success through gender-based education.

COUNTERPOINT: Jyllian Rosa Guerriero
University of Dayton School of Law

To answer the question posed in this debate, the needs of elementary and secondary school students must be identified. Generally, there are two distinct needs that the school system fulfills for all students. The first is academic needs, and the second is social needs. Both needs must be met in order to educate individuals to their full potential. This essay will argue that single-sex schools and classes are not the best arrangement to meet the academic and social educational needs of students in both elementary and secondary schools.

BACKGROUND

Historically, coeducational schools came into being because of financial necessity. Areas of smaller populations simply did not have the means to build and run a number of schools to educate the boys and girls separately. Currently, those considerations are still taken into account. For example, recently three single-sex schools in Rhode Island merged into one coeducational institution. The reasons for that change were greatly economic.

In terms of ideology, it is likely that the movement toward coeducation started with the introduction of females into church membership. It became necessary for girls to learn to read in order to be educated about religious doctrine. This took place around the time of the Reformation movement in New England. The growing perception was that women played an essential role in the integration of children into the new republic. Reformers pushed the adoption of coeducation, arguing that educating boys and girls together better reflected their "natural" environment and better prepared them for the future. By 1900, coeducation was a standard practice in the United States.

After World War II, there rose a global influence of American standards. During this time, there was a gradual shift in gender roles across the world, affording women greater opportunity outside the traditional domestic realm. Women began to integrate into the workforce, and along with that came assertions that women should be afforded the same educational opportunities as men. While coeducation had already become an acceptable practice in the United States, it was during this time in history that it reached unmatched acceptance by the public. Since that time, American social norms have required that men and women be afforded the same educational opportunities, and the law reflects those norms.

Throughout history, coeducation has been linked with the idea of equality between the sexes in education. The idea of equality is widespread throughout the advancement of underprivileged sectors of society—not just men and women, but races and religions as well. In the United States, a cornerstone of our freedom rests on the idea of equality. To endorse a program that could potentially hinder that equality would be to take an ideological step in the wrong direction. The advancement of coeducation has marked the growth of women's rights and the expansion of the current educational system to serve all members of the population. Generally, resistance to coeducation has been greatest in societies where women's rights have been most rigidly opposed.

TITLE IX

Title IX is a law that was passed in 1972 that requires gender equity for boys and girls in every educational program that receives federal funding. The crux of the statute reads, "No person in the United States shall, on the basis of sex, be excluded from participation in, be denied the benefits of, or be subjected to discrimination under any education program or activity receiving federal financial assistance" (20 U.S.C. § 1681). In 2002, the statute was renamed as the Patsy T. Mink Equal Opportunity in Education Act.

In 2006, the Department of Education revised long-standing Title IX regulations to make it easier for public sector schools to adopt single-sex programs. These regulations are challenging because Title IX and the U.S. Constitution contain safeguards to ensure that single-sex programs in public schools serve only narrowly defined and nondiscriminatory purposes, do not perpetuate stereotypes about the abilities or learning styles of either gender, and do not result in unequal educational opportunities. The permissive 2006 regulations disregard these safeguards, and by all reports, many of the single-sex programs being implemented by public schools today are based on harmful stereotypes and do not provide equality of opportunity for the excluded gender.

To narrow the scope, in 2010, the American Civil Liberties Union and the ACLU of Louisiana appeared before the U.S. Court of Appeals for the Fifth Circuit challenging sex segregation in core curricular classes at a public middle school in Louisiana. The ACLU filed the appeal on behalf of two students and their mother on the grounds that the program was in violation of Title IX by discriminating against both boys and girls alike. The ACLU spokesperson in this case shared that the only evidence in this case—the students' actual report card grades—purportedly showed that academic performance declined during sex segregation. A federal trial court in Louisiana denied the mother's request for injunctive relief during the pendency of the action on the basis that there was no intentional discrimination in the program. On appeal the Fifth Circuit affirmed, but remanded, the case for further proceedings (*Doe v. Vermilion Parish School Board*, 2011).

THE EMPIRICAL EVIDENCE

In 2005, the U.S. Department of Education published a study that compared single-sex and coeducational schools. To be included in the study, students had to be enrolled in full-time school. They had to be in elementary, middle, or high school. Schools being studied had to be in English-speaking or Westernized countries somewhat comparable to American public sector schools. The single-sex school had to be one in which students were either completely segregated by sex or completely segregated for all classes, even if colocated in the same building. A danger and criticism of previous single-sex literature has been the confounding of single-sex effects with the effects of religious views, financial privilege, selective admissions, or other advantages associated with the single-sex school being studied.

Any positive effects of single-sex schooling on longer-term indicators of academic achievement were not readily apparent. No differences were found for postsecondary test scores, college graduation rates, or graduate school attendance rates. In 1998, one study of single-sex versus coeducational 12th-grade females at a public school found that the coeducational females returned higher overall SAT scores. Many measurable factors indicated that there was no difference between single-sex and coeducational schooling.

In the case of self-esteem, a third of the studies supported coeducational schooling while half found no difference. Given a recent extensive review concluding that self-esteem's relationship to school success, occupational success, leadership, and other desirable outcomes is modest, the implications of findings regarding self-esteem appear complementary. Furthermore, coeducational schooling has a positive impact on the self-esteem of males.

One study found in favor of coeducational schooling when it came to attitudes toward schooling. Attitudes toward schooling refer to any cognition by a student about school in general regardless of whether it is accompanied by a behavioral manifestation. Examples of these attitudes might include study commitment, sense of belonging, and so on.

A 2001 study by Janell Mensinger found that more students in single-sex schools have eating disorders than their coeducational counterparts. Eating disorders can be defined as syndromes where individuals develop an unhealthy view of their body and low self-esteem. This leads them to attempt to alter that body image by excessive weight change and through unhealthy means. One study examined the likelihood of developing an eating disorder and found that females in single-sex schools are more likely than females in coeducational schools to develop an eating disorder.

In 1990, a study by Valerie Lee and Helen Marks found a significant difference for women, in that those who attended single-sex high schools experienced more work-related sex-role stereotyping than did women who attended coeducational schools. Sex-role stereotyping refers to the endorsement of traditional attitudes toward the roles that men and women should take in the workplace. In general, stereotyping of this nature refers to the notion that women can take only certain roles in the workplace, whereas men can take broader, more powerful roles in the workplace.

In 1998, Carole Shmurak conducted a five-year longitudinal study of females in single-sex and coeducational schools. She found that girls in coed schools had no difference in SAT scores, took more science, got into significantly higher rated colleges, and were more interested in sports. She also found that girls from both coeducational and single-sex schools averaged the same on the Attitudes Toward Women Scale (AWS).

Historically, the most important research on single-sex and coeducational school differences is Reginald Dale's (1974) extensive research conducted in the 1960s and 1970s. He examined the single-sex and coeducational school issue from the perspectives of teachers and in relation to students' social and academic development. According to Dale, it was demonstrated that the average coeducational grammar school is a happier community for both staff and students than the average single-sex school. He also found that anxiety and neuroticism were lower for coeducational school students and that the social and affective benefits of coeducation were not at the expense of academic progress.

The realm of subjective satisfaction of students, parents, and teachers with the school environment found that coeducational schools had friendlier and more relaxed atmospheres, with more opportunities for pleasure-centered social contact. There was also found to be an overall attitude of pleasure with the academic setting. In 1982, Frank W. Schneider and Larry M. Coutts compared the environment of coeducational and single-sex schools. What they found was that there were critical differences between the social psychological environments of the two types of institutions. They found that coeducational school students were more likely to agree with the statement that the atmosphere of their school was pleasant. In characterizing the pleasantness of their school atmospheres, the coeducational students focused on the friendliness of their peers, positive student-teacher relations, and normal boy-girl relations. Undeniably, the coeducational school students provided a considerably more favorable description of the social psychological environments of their schools than did the single-sex school students. It was also found that coeducational schools were more conducive to the development of self-confidence and reflected less prejudiced and irrational thinking.

In 1998, Fred Mael conducted a study titled "Single-Sex and Coeducational Schooling: Relationships to Socioemotional and Academic Development." Within his study, he made a theoretical assertion that coeducational schooling is beneficial for male discipline. His studies found that boys in coeducational schools did better in math and were less neurotic. Generally, it was found that coeducation was supported empirically in the realm of discipline and social issues. He also found that students perceived coeducational schools as being more gregarious and friendly. Overall, it is logical to conclude that students' education is not exclusively academic, but must also include social experience that reflects an individual's natural environment.

THE NATURAL SOCIAL ENVIRONMENT

One of the underlying assumptions in evaluating the needs of students is that their futures will be spent in the presence of the opposite sex. Socially and professionally, it is inevitable that today's youth will, after their academic years (if spent in a single-sex educational institution), be exposed to the presence and influence of the opposite sex. Relying on that fact as basic knowledge, it logically follows that the elementary and secondary school experience should incorporate those exposures in order to produce a well-rounded and balanced approach to education.

Those who choose to be educated in a single-sex institution may find themselves at a disadvantage to those with a coeducational background. The formative years of children are the best time to expose them to the company of the other gender. Through that exposure, they learn and understand each other's behavior. That understanding then leads to better preparedness in adult life. It is proposed, with great support, that boys and girls are a positive influence on each other. Their intermingling encourages good behavior and maturity, particularly in the case of adolescent females and their tendency to exhibit greater responsibility and maturity than their adolescent male counterparts.

Entering into the professional realm with little to no professional or academic interaction with the opposite sex would surely be a detriment in today's working society. Success in a great number of fields is influenced by one's ability to communicate effectively. Effective communication is built and fostered by a thorough understanding of an audience. Doctors must understand their patients, lawyers their clients, teachers their students, and so on. Any educational philosophy that dismisses that necessity is surely missing something in its effort to produce well-rounded and educated individuals.

THE REAL ISSUE

The battle between single-sex and coeducational schooling is one that has been fought for many years. Likely, the arguments and studies will continue with little to no convincing evidence for either side. If the end goal in this discussion were to decide how best to educate our youth, efforts would be far more fruitful if expended on contextual, attainable goals within the public school sector.

As it stands, Title IX and the advancement of women's rights conclude that coeducation is the most fair from a policy standpoint. To argue that education should return to a single-sex environment would be to discount and retract the progress made in achieving equality for students of both sexes. It would risk returning to gender bias and segregation based on sex. Imposing sex segregation would open a floodgate of risks, as segregation of any kind carries with it a negative connotation and social distaste. As it stands now, every child, whether male or female, has the right to a free public education. Boys and girls have equal opportunity to choose their academic and career path. Individually, they must work hard to reach their goals, and it is based solely on their hard work and their choices as to whether or not they succeed. The evidence shows that segregating the boys and girls will in no way result in increased success for either gender. A coeducational environment promotes individuality, freedom of choice, and the accountability that comes along with being a member of a diverse community.

Currently, men's and women's roles in society have become far less differentiated. It is not uncommon to find a female CEO, a male caretaker, a female engineer, or a male chef. Coeducation prepares young people for an egalitarian society. It provides cross-sex role learning in two ways. First, the mixed-sex interaction gives students the opportunity to observe and develop appropriate expectations regarding the opposite sex. Second, curricula in coeducational schools expose students to nonstereotyped roles for both males and females.

All other research aside, the largest logistical argument for coeducation is the simple fact that it is economically efficient. It would be an unfeasible goal to segregate our current educational system based on gender given the current economic climate.

Reasonable goals in the public school system are being pursued currently. Smaller class sizes, broader curriculum choices, and increased individual student instruction, for example, are attainable steps that can be achieved through basic policy reform. Many states have adopted a requirement for teachers to earn their master's degree during their teaching careers. Providing incentives for teachers to achieve advanced degrees is another way to motivate the front-runners in the classroom, who in turn can motivate the minds of the students. Rather than focusing the lawmaking on the students themselves, policy to provide support, resources, and continuing education to instructors may be uncharted territory for many states. Thus far, providing the opportunity for teachers to become more educated in their subject matter has only returned positive results. More qualified and enthusiastic teachers will logically produce more educated and enthusiastic students.

Cornelius Riordan (1990) posits that in the United States, public schools are comprehensive, relatively nonselective, relatively egalitarian, and highly inclusive institutions. They accept the gifted and the handicapped, the affluent and the poor, those who are motivated and those who are simply required to attend. Riordan, an advocate for single-sex schooling, hypothesizes that that level of inclusiveness hinders an institution's ability to be excellent. Advocates for coeducation would argue that that level of inclusiveness is what makes the institution excellent—fostering tolerance, acceptance, and understanding among a diverse community of young people.

FURTHER READINGS AND RESOURCES

Brown, F., & Russo, C. J. (1999). Single-sex schools and the law. *School Business Affairs, 65*(5), 26–31.

Dale, R. (1974). *Mixed or single sex school: Attainment, and miscellaneous* (Vol. 3). Florence, KY: Routledge.

Greenberg-Lake: The Analysis Group. (1992). *How schools shortchange girls.* Washington, DC: American Association of University Women.

Hubbard, L., & Datnow, A. (2005). Do single-sex schools improve the education of low-income and minority students? An investigation of California's public single-gender academies. *Anthropology and Education Quarterly, 36*(2), 115–131.

Lee, V. E., & Marks, H. M. (1990). Sustained effects of the single-sex secondary school experience on attitudes, behaviors, and values in college. *Journal of Educational Psychology, 82*(3), 578–592.

Mael, F. A. (1998). Single-sex and coeducational schooling: Relationships to socioemotional and academic development. *Review of Educational Research, 68*(2), 101–129.

Marsh, H. W. (1989). Effects of attending single-sex and coeducational high schools on achievement, attitudes, behaviors, and sex differences. *Journal of Educational Psychology, 81*(1), 70–85.

Mensinger, J. (2001). *Gender and body concerns in adolescent females: Single sex and coeducational school environments.* Annual Conference of the American Psychological Association, San Francisco. ERIC Document 457490.

National Association for Single Sex Public Education. (n.d.). *Single-sex schools/schools with single-sex classrooms/what's the difference?* Retrieved July 18, 2011, from http://www.singlesexschools.org/schools-schools.htm

Riordan, C. (1990). *Girls and boys in school: Together or separate.* New York: Teachers College Press.

Salomone, R. C. (2003). *Same, different, equal: Rethinking single-sex schooling.* New Haven, CT: Yale University Press.

Schneider, F. W., & Coutts, L. M. (1982). The high school environment: A comparison of coeducational and single-sex schools. *Journal of Educational Psychology, 74*(6), 898–906.

Streitmatter, J. L. (1999). *For girls only.* Albany: State University of New York Press.

Tzolidis, G., & Dobson, I. R. (2006, March). Single sex schooling: Is it simply a "class act"? *Abington, 18*(2), 213–225.

U.S. Department of Education, Office of Planning, Evaluation and Policy Development, Policy and Program Studies Service. (2005). *Single-sex versus coeducational schooling: A systematic review.* Washington, DC: Author.

Court Cases and Statutes

Doe v. Vermilion Parish School Board, 421 F. App'x 366 (5th Cir. 2011).

Education Amendments of 1972, Title IX, 20 U.S.C. § 1681(a) (2006).

Mississippi University for Women v. Hogan, 458 U.S. 718 (1982).

No Child Left Behind Act, 20 U.S.C. §§ 6301–7941 (2006).

United States v. Virginia, 518 U.S. 515 (1996).

Is Head Start worth preserving?

POINT: Carolyn Talbert-Johnson, *University of Dayton*
COUNTERPOINT: Tamela J. Dixon, *Ohio University*

OVERVIEW

Head Start, a school-readiness program for preschool-aged low income children, provides comprehensive education, social, health, and nutrition services. Now administered by the federal Department of Health and Human Services (HHS), Head Start was created in 1965 as part of President Lyndon Johnson's War on Poverty and Great Society initiatives. Congress has reauthorized Head Start several times since its original enactment. Significant reauthorization amendments updated performance standards to make sure that children would have the basic skills needed to start school when they exited the program and directed HHS to provide services to homeless children. Current performance standards mandate that Head Start's curriculum focus on children's cognitive skills, language development, and emergent literacy skills.

Although Head Start programs are required to employ a curriculum that meets the mandated performance standards, local programs have the option to develop their own curriculum, use a curriculum developed locally or by the state education agency, or implement curricular materials developed by a commercial educational publisher. Head Start programs are operated under federal grants by public agencies, private nonprofit and for-profit organizations, and school systems. Grants are awarded directly to the local organizations that implement Head Start programs through the regional offices of the Administration for Children and Families division of HHS. One of the longest-running programs designed to address poverty in the United States, Head Start has enrolled more than 25 million children since 1965 (U.S. Department of Health and Human Services, n.d.).

Although the long-term academic benefits of Head Start are debatable, as the essays in this chapter illustrate, evidence indicates that at-risk children in the program make gains in terms of socialization, health care, and overall well-being. Most early childhood specialists agree that the preschool years are critical for developing the physical, emotional, social, and cognitive skills children need for later success in school. Thus, in spite of mixed evidence in terms of long-term results, Head Start has much support in the education community. Proponents contend that high quality early childhood education programs, such as Head Start, improve children's economic and social outcomes over a period of time. Further, advocates point out that unlike their more affluent counterparts, the parents of low income children, who have more of a need for such programs, do not always have the option of enrolling their children in private preschools. Head Start provides an alternative to families who cannot afford private preschools.

Head Start provides the requisite skills low income children and children with disabilities need to successfully begin school. Research shows that young children who have acquired basic readiness skills, such as letter, number, color, and shape recognition, and who have had experiences such as being read to by an adult, perform better in the early school years than children who have not acquired basic skills or had equivalent experiences. As is shown in the essays in this chapter and throughout this series, educators and policymakers are concerned about the achievement gap that exists between disadvantaged, minority children and their more affluent peers. However, there is little agreement on whether or how those gaps can be closed. Many educators and policymakers support the expansion of existing programs that are tailored to disadvantaged children on the grounds that limited public resources should be directed toward the families and children most in need. Conversely, others feel that the funds can be better spent elsewhere, especially in light of a lack of concrete evidence that the initial gains made by Head Start students do not translate into later academic gains and do not help to close the achievement gap.

During the fiscal year 2007, the latest year for which statistics are available from HHS, Head Start enrolled 908,412 children at an average cost per child of $7,326. In this chapter, the authors debate the question of whether Head Start is worth preserving. Carolyn Talbert-Johnson, a professor and the Associate Chair of Graduate Education in the Department of Teacher Education at the University of Dayton, argues that it is. Taking the opposing view, Tamela Dixon, a graduate assistant in the African American Research and Service Institute at Ohio University, contends that it is not.

In the point essay, Talbert-Johnson emphatically states that Head Start provides an excellent opportunity to intervene early in the learning process for at-risk students and will give them the necessary skills to perform appropriately and meet the challenges of kindergarten. Further, she notes that with the current focus on accountability, Head Start may be more necessary than ever. To support her views, Talbert-Johnson cites research that shows that children who have such an experience perform at or above the levels of children who do not attend any type of preschool program. In conclusion, Talbert-Johnson contends that Head Start is worth preserving because the long-term effects may increase educational attainment of young disadvantaged children and increase family involvement with developmentally appropriate practices that enhance the development of children cognitively, emotionally, socially, and behaviorally.

Dixon, on the other hand, insists in the counterpoint essay that there is no solid evidence that suggests there are any real advantages for children who attend Head Start. While she acknowledges that the program has some short-term benefits, Dixon points to research that shows that early academic gains diminish considerably after three years, with children who have participated in Head Start performing no better than those who did not have a preschool experience. Dixon concludes that while Head Start provides some advantages, it is not doing enough to improve the learning opportunities for at-risk children in the essential areas of language, pre-reading, and pre-mathematics knowledge and skills. Thus, she feels that Head Start is not fully achieving its purpose and is not worth preserving.

It is obvious from reading these essays that experts disagree on whether or not Head Start has fulfilled its purpose of leveling the playing field between low income and more affluent preschool students and helps to close the achievement gap between the groups. In reading this chapter, there are several questions you may want to consider. Should the effectiveness of Head Start be evaluated only by long-term academic benefits? If the research is correct, why do the academic gains made by Head Start students seem to disappear over the long term? In the long run, are students who were enrolled in Head Start better off overall than they would have been if they had not had such an experience?

Allan G. Osborne, Jr.
Principal (Retired), Snug Harbor Community School,
Quincy, Massachusetts

POINT: Carolyn Talbert-Johnson
University of Dayton

Preschool education is a contentious topic in education today. Proponents assert that pouring more funding into these programs will ensure the reduction of the achievement gap and provide disadvantaged children with a level playing field. In addition, it is evident that with the current thrust toward accountability and the demand for evidence-based strategies that support students' learning abilities, Head Start, which provides intervention early in the learning process, may be more necessary than ever. Equipping these young children with the necessary skills to perform appropriately will prepare them for the challenges of kindergarten and the formative years of schooling. However, critics question whether these programs have a lasting impact on student outcomes and their future educational experiences. The research supports the proposition that children who participate in Head Start programs perform at or above the levels of children who do not attend any type of preschool experience. This is consistent with the goal of preschool programs, such as Head Start, which is to ensure that these young children possess the readiness skills to begin school.

CHILDREN TARGETED BY HEAD START

It is not surprising that typically children who lack the requisite skills tend to be children from diverse backgrounds (e.g., racially, ethnically, linguistically, economically). These children have limited learning experiences and usually evolve from impoverished environments in urban areas. This is problematic because the literature suggests that socioeconomic status is one of the strongest predictors of performance differences in children at the beginning of the school experience. Because of the deplorable conditions in which these children live, it is likely there will be little, if any, learning opportunities within the home, as these families are striving to survive. It is not uncommon for there to be noticeable differences in the development of these diverse children, compared to their middle-class peers. One difference is their inability to use language appropriately. In addition, access to any books, papers, or materials to stimulate their minds may not be possible. Without a preschool experience these vulnerable children frequently lack the necessary skills to perform appropriately. These deficit skills may include the inability to identify the letters of the alphabet and the numbers 1 to 10, and to state their full name, address, or birthday. They also will be less likely to obtain a basic sight word vocabulary, be able to follow basic directions, write their first name, speak in complete sentences, and emit socially appropriate behavior. Head Start provides intensive instruction that includes remediation of these important skills. The needs of these fragile children are disconcerting and must be addressed as early as possible. It should be noted that there are severe consequences for these minority, disadvantaged students and for society, as well. Students who perform poorly in school are becoming part of a growing underclass, which will not have the opportunity for productive engagement in society.

Another point is the fact that many disadvantaged children come from families in which appropriate child-rearing skills are lacking. It is possible that some of these children are being raised by grandmothers because the biological parents are addicted to drugs or alcohol and are missing from the home. Sometimes older siblings or family members (e.g., an aunt) may be raising the children, or the parent is single and struggling with the daily issues of life. Family issues are prevalent for these young children because usually families have little or no education background and lack basic skills themselves. An intensive, individualized program such as Head Start can be quite beneficial for these young children. Not only will the children have access to learning, but it is possible that the child's parents and family members will also have access to important information that will be beneficial to the development of their child. A component of Head Start includes programs that train parents to work effectively with their children by enriching the home environment. This will assist in the establishment of family and professional partnerships to ensure the needs of their children are met.

EARLY INTERVENTION

Early intervention has proven to impact the performance and maintenance of skills for children, including children with disabilities. It is common knowledge that children with disabilities have deficit skills that impede their learning. For instance, for students diagnosed with learning disabilities, as many as 60% drop out of school before graduating high school. This is alarming when one considers the economic demands that more citizens attain higher levels of education. It is apparent that these trends cannot continue and are deeply troubling. With appropriate accommodations children with disabilities can attain the requisite skills to become independent functioning members of society. Early intervention has been an excellent strategy for children with disabilities in the acquisition and maintenance of skills. Public Law 99–457, an amendment to the Individuals with Disabilities Education Act, was passed to ensure that the needs of preschool children with disabilities were addressed by providing specific guidelines for early intervention and the rights of families. This is substantiated by research that shows that children with disabilities can improve their performance and in some instances maintain their new knowledge over an extended period of time due to early intervention. The same principle is applicable to Head Start since many of these children also have deficits and require intensive, individualized, curriculum-based instruction.

Interventions that are employed with children with disabilities focus on the individualized needs of these children. It is imperative that a teacher consider the learning profiles of children and provide instruction that is tailored to these learning styles. Therefore a teacher presents instruction using visual, oral, and kinesthetic strategies, as well as technological innovations. The ultimate goal is to provide children with optimal learning opportunities in the least restrictive environment. The least restrictive environment must be the environment in which the child can thrive and has opportunities for success. An additional goal is to assist these young children to participate in inclusionary settings with their general education peers. This is not always a reality for all children with disabilities. There are some children with disabilities for whom the general education environment may not be appropriate, as they will not be able to thrive or perform appropriately. Examples may include children with behavioral disorders and those with more severe disabilities (e.g., autism). It is not uncommon for these children to exhibit academic as well as antisocial behaviors. A child with a disability whose least restrictive environment is the general education classroom can be included with typically developing children either full-time or for a portion of the day, depending on his or her skills.

For children with disabilities interventions should occur not only in a preschool setting, but across multiple areas and settings through parent, teacher, and child training. Early intervention across contexts can counteract risk factors and strengthen proactive factors. It is essential that teachers of these children provide consistent responsive and nurturing teaching, while reinforcing prosocial behaviors. Children's social skills are strengthened to establish appropriate behaviors in the establishment of friendships. Positive home communication is employed, as collaboration with parents is essential to the process

The Carolina Abecedarian Project is another example of a positive program for early intervention. The program, developed by Frank Porter Graham and the Child Development Institute in 1972, was designed to address children's readiness for entry into elementary school. The target population was high-risk disadvantaged minority 4-month-old children. The interventions focused on quality child care for these young children, as well as the development of their cognitive, social, language, and gross motor skills through the age of 5 years.

Developmentally appropriate practices were implemented to ensure children's success. The results of the five-year study showed that children in the control group had higher IQs, greater improvements in reading and math scores, and higher rates of enrollment in college. The outcomes of the program were most impressive due to the intensive focus on quality child care and structured interventions that were developmentally appropriate. Even though these are excellent examples to support preschool programs such as Head Start, the effectiveness of the outcomes of longitudinal studies supporting preschool programs tends to be almost nonexistent. We do know, however, that the project utilized innovative interventions with the children.

CURRICULUM

The curriculum that is used in Head Start programs must employ performance standards that are relative to children's future educational success. The curriculum must meet the definition for a written curriculum in Head Start's performance standards and must be based on sound child development theories. Programs can develop their own curriculum, using a curriculum developed locally or by the state education agency. Programs also have the option of using teacher mentoring and individual child assessment to help implement the curriculum. The curriculum must address the cognitive and language development of children to ensure the acquisition of the fundamental skills needed to reason and to speak a language.

As the early childhood population becomes more diverse, there is a need to incorporate programs and practices that are reflective of multicultural education principles that support the uniqueness of each individual. It is beneficial for these young children to learn about diversity locally and globally. Children must acquire the necessary skills to interact with children different from themselves as early as possible, in environments conducive to learning. Young children must be knowledgeable of the unique differences that exist across cultures, traditions, and languages and determine how to relate to others. Preschool programs, such as Head Start, can include in their curriculum topics related to the pluralism that is evident in our society. Pluralistic perspectives should include not only differences apparent in the United States, but international differences as well. To enhance young children's knowledge about diversity, an example might be to include in the curriculum the basic steps in the study of a foreign language (e.g., Spanish). For instance, basic steps could include learning the first three numbers and greeting one another in Spanish. Learning another language is another learning tool that will benefit these children as they learn about other cultures. Guidelines can be developed relevant to international education in the school curriculum that allows children to begin the process of recognizing differences in others. Children can gradually be introduced to aspects of a selected target country, such as China, which would be a beginning stage in intercultural awareness. With the acknowledgement that international education is important, specific instruction can be provided for young children in their early school experience. Exposure to local, as well as global, people is a beginning step in the process and can easily be integrated into the curriculum.

Another merit of Head Start is that it provides teachers with the opportunity to develop a positive rapport with these young children in environments that are robust, active, and engaging. It allows students to begin their learning experience in a positive, supportive manner. Teachers not only focus on the cognitive development of these young children, but they also assist in their development socially, emotionally, behaviorally, and morally. The focus becomes the whole child, not just the cognitive development of the child. It is imperative that teachers are cognizant of the needs of the whole child if these children are to be successful in the early years of schooling. Teachers act as role models for these children and provide them with the identified skills to function appropriately within learning contexts. It is important that interventions are employed that address children's deficit skills; otherwise these children will begin their formative years lagging behind their peers. This cannot be tolerated, as the literature supports that once children are behind, it is possible that they will continue to lag behind and ultimately experience consistent failures in school. This directly relates to the achievement gap that is prevalent between these disadvantaged, minority children and their middle-class peers. Even though the No Child Left Behind Act (NCLB) was signed into law in 2002 to reduce and/or eliminate the achievement gap, it is disconcerting to note that children continue to fail daily within classroom settings. The reality is that far too often disadvantaged, minority children are indeed left behind, especially in the early years of school.

MEETING THE NEEDS OF AT-RISK CHILDREN

The question becomes, can we allow these fragile individuals to fail without providing them an "equal" start with their peers? Is it reasonable to expect these children to perform when they have not received the same type of family support, instruction, and opportunities as their peers? If we know that many of these children come from impoverished home environments, is it realistic to expect that they will be able to perform when in most cases they have not had any type of formal instruction that is expected of a child preparing to enter kindergarten? If we truly believe that indeed no child should be left behind, isn't it our moral obligation to provide these marginalized children with appropriate interventions that will enable them to acquire the skills to function in a learning environment? The individualized needs of students must be met, according to NCLB, and teachers must be qualified to intervene effectively.

It is disconcerting to note that children who have not participated in any type of formal preschool program frequently experience behavioral challenges because they are not able to comply with reasonable requests. In many cases these children are very active, resist authority figures, can be aggressive toward their peers as well as adults, and may emit recalcitrant behaviors that will impede any type of learning. Head Start teachers have the ability to intervene on these aberrant behaviors early so that these children will have the opportunity to perform in a socially acceptable manner. In Head Start they will learn that there are certain behaviors that will be tolerated and some that will not. The children will learn to follow the rules of the room and the concept of respect for themselves, their peers, and the teacher. Inappropriate behavior will not be tolerated, and consequences will be applied as needed. Children can acquire the requisite skills that will enable them to emit socially acceptable behaviors, which will eliminate the stigma of labels regarding their deviant behaviors.

Additionally, children will learn that they have a moral responsibility to treat others the way that they would like to be treated. For instance, John was a student in a Head Start program. He came in toward the end of the first semester of the year with few skills and basically did not know how to interact with his peers. He often yelled out in class and repeatedly had to be told to raise his hand before he spoke. The teacher was frustrated by John's behavior upon entering the classroom, but after two months of consistent directions and the development of behavioral plans, he finally began to change his behaviors and adjusted to the classroom environment. He realized that the teacher was not going to accept his resistant behavior and that there were consequences for his stubbornness. The teacher always intervened in a consistent manner, while ensuring that John performed appropriately.

Research also supports the benefits of Head Start. The ultimate benefit is that children who evolve from diverse cultures and environments have access to an education at the preschool level. The interventions that have been implemented have assisted these children in performing at acceptable levels. As stated previously, programs such as the Carolina Abecedarian Project have shown that intensive pre-K programs can indeed impact learning deficits. Unfortunately there are not a large number of programs that can support the findings of the Carolina Abecedarian Project. The project was unique in that it was supported by very sophisticated, multifaceted interventions with appropriate financing. Replications of the program, which took place decades ago, are sparse.

It is likely that preschool programs such as Head Start will impact the lives of young children beyond the formative years (i.e., kindergarten through fifth grade). There are possible long-term effects that will most likely reduce the chance that these children will not succeed in school. In spite of research that suggests that state funding of universal programs may not have any discernable impact on the long-term outcomes desired by policymakers, including grade retention, public assistance receipt, employment, and earnings, there were noticeable changes. In the Carolina Abecedarian Project, White children were 2.5% less likely to be high school dropouts and 22% less likely to be incarcerated or otherwise institutionalized as adults following state funding initiatives. These are the only effects that were noted. Even though the literature suggests that even large investments in universal early childhood education programs may not necessarily yield clear benefits, especially for disadvantaged children, the benefits of such programs outweigh the negatives. Unfortunately, there are a limited number of longitudinal studies that have researched the ultimate impact of Head Start. Therefore the results are inconclusive.

What is warranted is an understanding of the long-term effects of the outcomes of Head Start. What we do know is that there is merit in providing young disadvantaged children with intensive instruction at an early age. Equipping children with the basic skills can benefit their development and their participation in the learning experience. The bottom line is that a closer view of the principles of preschool programs, such as Head Start, is warranted. Perhaps what is needed is a review of the elements of previous programs that were successful, revisions that are tailored to the individualized needs of diverse children from disadvantaged environments, and ensuring that these children have access to quality instruction. Developmentally appropriate practices must be implemented to address the individualized needs of young children, as well as focused instruction supported by sound evidence-based standards, quality criteria, and readiness assessments. These criteria will ensure a quality preschool program for all children.

It is imperative that Head Start teachers be trained to work with this unique diverse population of students. Head Start teachers possess the requisite skills to intervene effectively by obtaining the requisite knowledge, skills, and dispositions. Also, teachers possess the dispositions to instruct, manage, interact, and relate to these diverse children, regardless of their race, ethnicity, language, and socioeconomic status, to assist these young children in becoming productive citizens of the future. Teachers become agents of change in this age of reform and provide these young children with the skills to compete in our globally competitive society. With the revisions to NCLB and other legislation, it is essential that reform agendas address preschool education because it is definitely worth preserving.

CONCLUSION

In summation, Head Start is a comprehensive early childhood development program designed to provide education, health, and social series to disadvantaged, minority children, ages 3 to 5, and their families. It is definitely worth preserving because the long-term effects may increase educational attainment of young disadvantaged children and increase family involvement with developmentally appropriate practices that enhance the development of children cognitively, emotionally, socially, and behaviorally in challenging, innovative environments. The programs are effective because they are based on sound child development theories about how children develop and learn, they employ developmentally appropriate practices, and they establish collaborative endeavors with parents.

COUNTERPOINT: Tamela J. Dixon
Ohio University

Head Start is being promoted as an effective program that ensures that disadvantaged, minority children will obtain the educational "boost" for narrowing the achievement gaps. Even though proponents of Head Start suggest that it improves the academic performance of students, the reality is that there is no real evidence that suggests there are any real advantages for children who attend Head Start. This is unfortunate, as disadvantaged students continue to lag behind their mainstream peers.

BENEFITS OF HEAD START

In agreement with the point arguments, few would argue the effectiveness of the federally funded Head Start program. Head Start is a comprehensive early childhood education program designed to assist economically and socially disadvantaged children and their families in the areas of child development, education, health, nutrition, and a variety of other social services. Since its inception in 1965, the Head Start program has continued to deliver the services it was originally designed to provide. As some of the recent literature suggests, in many instances the Head Start program has proven to better the lives and development of many of the individuals it is targeted to serve. However, in spite of the program's proven successes, those who oppose Head Start continue to struggle to find any real educational benefits associated with the program. As such, there is increasing skepticism over the program's true long-term effects on children and their families.

Those who support Head Start argue that in addition to the educational benefits that come with participating in the program, there are a number of other important benefits that also result. For example, the program provides access to health care services to children who might not otherwise receive these services and increased social services for both children and their families. This writer disagrees with this assessment and contends these findings are flawed and have been grossly misrepresented. Critics of Head Start argue that increasing funding without raising the level of standards for the program does a disservice to these children and their families. Continually rewarding a program—one with proven flaws—with substantial increases in funding creates a false sense of security in a program that really offers no true long-term advantages. Simply put, Head Start is not living up to its promises.

IMPORTANCE OF EARLY INTERVENTION

The literature stresses the importance of effective early childhood intervention, particularly with disadvantaged children. Undoubtedly, due to the multitude and magnitude of risk factors often associated with this population (i.e., poverty, uneducated or undereducated parents, single-parent home, substance abuse, sexual abuse, poor health, poor nutrition, domestic violence, parents who speak a language other than English, hunger), disadvantaged children are at a much greater risk for weak outcomes throughout their educational careers. There is no argument that differences in academic achievement vary due to any number of circumstances, such as achievement differences for children at the greatest disadvantage. These children are likely candidates for the Head Start program; however, the experience could be the deciding factor between success and failure.

While Head Start and similar prekindergarten programs assist disadvantaged children, many would agree the program, as it is currently being managed, has done anything but create a level playing field. In fact, it would appear the program fails these individuals on almost every level as it does little to put them any further ahead of their middle-class peers. Proponents of Head Start maintain the program makes an important and positive impact on children early in their educations. Current research says otherwise. Results have shown the benefits are short-lived and quickly fade early in children's educational experiences. Recent studies involving Head Start programs have consistently found academic benefits diminish considerably after three years, with children who participate in the program performing no better than those who were not enrolled in preschool programs.

ACADEMIC GAINS

Even though the point argument suggests that the academic gains are notewor- thy, the results illustrate that there are short-term effects. For children from disadvantaged backgrounds the general effect size ranges from one fifth to one third of a standard deviation. The most important issue is whether the gains and gap reductions last. Unfortunately, the evidence is scarce due to the limited longitudinal studies needed to validate the program's effectiveness. Consideration must be given to the costly, complex, and time-consuming effects of longitudinal studies. The reality is that the actual data are quite disap- pointing because the claimed gains that are evident upon entry into school change over time and the differences tend to decline. In fact, research supports that effects that may appear significant at the conclusion of the program itself frequently decline by the third grade. This alludes to the fact that even though there may be a "head start" in academic, behavioral, and social development of children, it is evident that the intensive instruction does not continue once they enter kindergarten. This illustrates that a universal preschool experience is not the most effective manner to achieve quality learning experiences and a lasting reduction in the achievement gap.

As was suggested, the Head Start program has received billions of dollars in increased funding over the past two decades. In 2008, then presidential candi- date Barack Obama's campaign was largely centered on the slogan "Change we can believe in." Two years after Americans voted for change, millions of dollars from the President's economic stimulus package have been dedicated to the overall improvement and "change" in the provisions of education in the United States. While programs such as Head Start received increased funding as a result of the President's stimulus package, they received these funds without any mandates or requirements to improve the effectiveness of their programs.

While advocates for the program have admirable desires for a universal pro- gram, the truth is that a closer review of the funding is warranted. For instance, a universal program, one that actually serves all 4 million 4-year-olds, could cost anywhere from $11.6 billion a year at the low-budget end to as much as $57.8

billion at the high-budget end. If 3-year-olds were included the sums would double. Therefore, a reasonable midlevel cost, for instance $9,000 per child, which is about the current cost for Head Start today, could be as expensive as $36 billion. What is disconcerting about this calculation is that since 85% of 4-year-olds already participate in some sort of pre-K program, as much as $30 billion of the $36 billion figure would replace money that is presently being spent by federal or state programs, as well as private charity, and out of pocket by parents. That leaves a meager sum of about $6 billion that would assist children who currently have no preschool experiences, *if* they decide to participate.

Education in the United States is in a state of emergency. Since the landmark 1954 decision of *Brown v. Board of Education,* the demographics of this country have changed in more ways than lawmakers had ever anticipated. Due to a surge in immigration coupled with a troubled economy, classrooms of today have become much more diverse. More often than not, children who start behind will likely stay behind, which leads to the most challenging problem we are faced with today in education: the ever-widening achievement gap. The achievement gap leaves disadvantaged children, usually minorities, well behind their peers on any number of educational measures. While the reasons for the achievement gap are complex and multidimensional, the overarching themes that repeatedly emerge can usually be attributed to an educational system founded on racism, sexism, classism, and discrimination based on culture and family history. It goes without saying that Head Start could be a very valuable service to children and families, but the program as it is currently operating will only continue to fail these children. As skepticism in the overall quality and performance of the program continues to grow, changes in key areas of the program could breathe new life into the troubled program.

Regardless of race, ethnicity, or socioeconomic status, school preparedness is one key area of concern for all children. While Head Start has experienced its share of successes, critics of the program argue it has not done enough to improve the language, reading, and mathematical skills necessary for children to be aptly prepared for a positive educational experience early in life. This is supported by research that has shown that children entering Head Start fall well below the national averages in their cognitive and social skills levels. Children who complete Head Start continue to fall behind the average student in the United States.

PROGRAM MANAGEMENT

A growing concern of early education is the decline in program integrity and poor management of taxpayer dollars. Head Start and similar prekindergarten programs are funded by the federal government with the primary goal being to improve children's educational development and to better prepare them for their later years in school. These government-funded programs receive billions of dollars in funding for child care and preschool education. To the displeasure of many, Head Start and similar programs have been allowed to be independently developed and maintained. Because of this hands-off approach, opponents maintain it has fallen short and lost sight of its original goal, serving disadvantaged children and their families. Head Start programs are frequently criticized for their questionable practices and handling of government funds. Further, the allocation of these resources is also called into question. Some have even called it fraud. These criticisms arise from program challengers because, despite the fact that money continues to be pumped into the budgets of these programs, little is required in return, and there has been little evidence to show any real improvements in the program's overall success.

The most serious charge is directed at the directors and managers of these programs. Leaders continually fail to meet important performance measures including health screenings for children, proper upkeep of facilities, proper classroom materials and supplies, building rent, and overall governance of the program itself. According to the literature, with other prekindergarten programs, states have the authority and are responsible for the type and quality of services provided. As such, states are held accountable for the delivery of high quality programs. On the other hand, funds for the Head Start program are directly allocated from the government and therefore lend no authority to states to align Head Start programs with other programs.

As a result of poor oversight and the lack of transparency within the programs, mismanagement of funds quickly becomes an issue. Improper use and mishandling of funds leads to a decline in the training and social services offered to children, parents, and family members in the program. Clearly this was not the intent of program organizers. Head Start was designed not only to assist children as they develop, but to serve as support for families by offering them opportunities to establish and advance their own goals while they nurture and become active participants in the development of their children. The need for better quality assurance has led to a call for more intensive oversight of social services being offered. It is important to note that the Head Start philosophy was largely built upon the idea that parents would be involved. The building of trusting collaborative relationships between parents and program officials provides an opportunity for both groups to learn from one another. Moreover, these services afford parents and family members the opportunity to construct family partnerships, to clearly define and identify roles and responsibilities, and to develop goals and strategies for themselves and their children. More important, these services aim to encourage parents and family members to take a more active role in the program and in their children's future.

CLOSING THE ACHIEVEMENT GAP

Some suggest that preschool programs can reduce the achievement gap; however, the truth is that these programs do little to narrow the achievement gap. With its target group being preschool-aged children from low income and socially disadvantaged families, Head Start was created to assist families in the area of school readiness to ensure that each child has the opportunity to reach his or her fullest potential. Since the reality is that the knowledge and skill levels of disadvantaged children are far below national averages upon entering the program, it is essential that effective interventions be employed. Research shows that a strong predictor of future school success leans heavily on acquiring the necessary language, reading, and social skills early in life. The achievement gaps between advantaged and disadvantaged children that are evident in kindergarten and throughout the school years begin long before children enter preschool and kindergarten. Ensuring that Head Start and other early childhood programs serve disadvantaged children is the challenge at both the federal and state levels.

Designed to offer a comprehensive set of services, the ultimate goal of the program is to level the playing field for children and their families in the areas of health, nutrition, education, and social services. Included in the plan was an emphasis on strong parental involvement. Many experts, both for and against the program, would have to agree the original planners were too ambitious in the beginning and the program had too many goals, making it difficult for those involved to easily comprehend or achieve. While organizers continue to make great strides in their efforts to narrow the program's focus, children from these demographics fall further behind. Clearly, when the school readiness of the nation's disadvantaged, minority children is assessed, it becomes quite clear that Head Start is not achieving its goal by eliminating the achievement gap in educational skills and knowledge needed for school. In spite of noticeable gains that are attained in Head Start, there is evidence that these children continue to perform significantly below their more advantaged peers, especially in the areas of reading and mathematics.

Without question the development of social skills is imperative to the lives of all children. Research supports the idea that children who lack quality social and interpersonal skills usually experience difficulties with learning. While Head Start programs have received high praise for being proficient in attending to the social and emotional well-being of these children, other areas, such as physical health and nutrition, have suffered. Follow-up studies have looked at achievement scores, grade retention, special education, and high school graduation to assess the long-term cognitive and academic effects of Head Start. The ability of these marginalized children to function is at best a challenge; as their basic needs have not been met, it is unlikely that they will be able to perform appropriately in learning contexts.

It is evident that proponents of these preschool programs have not consistently worked with key stakeholders, especially parents, in the learning experience. Establishing collaborative relationships with stakeholders is essential to the successful implementation of these programs. Participation in Head Start is not compulsory; therefore, it is likely that some parents may not be interested in participating in Head Start or any preschool experience. Reasons for parents' lack of participation may range from their lack of knowledge regarding preschool services/programs to their desire to not have their children in any type of preschool experience for personal reasons.

The likelihood of replicating programs like the premiere early education programs, such as the Carolina Abecedarian Project, on a large scale is impossible when one considers the conditions, circumstances, and cost structures of such programs. Additionally, it is absurd to think that the intensive features of these programs could be replicated in the creation of universal programs that proponents are advocating for in preschool education. Due to the prevalent conditions that currently operate in relation to standards and the quality of instruction for all students, the bottom line is that we still have not ensured equitable learning opportunities for all children. Currently the focus for K–12 educational policy equates quality with academic outcomes linked to evidence-based strategies. This is not the case with preschool education, as it appears that the focus primarily is on inputs like spending levels, staffing ratios, and college degrees.

A recent report from the National Research Council recommended that every preschool teacher have a four-year college degree with specialized education related to early childhood (Barnett, 2011). Yet, only one in three Head Start teachers has a four-year college degree. We agree with the point position that teachers should be qualified and well trained with the appropriate knowledge, skills, and dispositions to intervene effectively. Unfortunately, the chief impediment to acquiring better teachers is teacher pay. The average Head Start teacher's salary is only $21,000, less than the average secretary's salary and little more than half what the average kindergarten teacher earns. Better incentives are warranted to recruit and retain teachers in this area.

CONCLUSION

The bottom line is that while Head Start has made some progress, it is not doing enough to enhance the learning opportunities for children in the areas of language, pre-reading, and pre-mathematics knowledge and skills that are essential for school readiness. The knowledge and skill levels of young children entering Head Start are far below national averages, and this is disconcerting considering that these children remain behind their typical peers. In theory, it sounds appealing, but in reality an examination of the system is needed to ensure the intensive delivery of sound cognitive standards. In their current form, early education programs have not impacted the achievement gap, and there is no guarantee that these gaps can be reduced or eliminated by Head Start. Therefore, Head Start is not fully achieving its stated purpose of promoting school readiness by enhancing the social and cognitive development of disadvantaged, minority children.

FURTHER READINGS AND RESOURCES

Barnett, W. S. (2002). *The battle over head start: What the research shows* [Congressional Science and Public Policy Briefing on the Impact of Head Start]. Retrieved September 26, 2011, from http://nieer.org/resources/research/BattleHeadStart.pdf

Barnett, W. S. (2011, April 28). *Preparing highly effective pre-K teachers.* Presentation for the National Research Council, Washington, DC. Retrieved from http://www.bocyf.org/ecce_workshop_barnett_presentation.pdf

Barnett, W. S., & Belfield, C. (2006). Early childhood development and social mobility. *Future of Children, 16*(2), 73–98.

Besharov, D. J. (2005). Head Start's broken promise. *AEI Outlooks & On the Issues.* Retrieved September 26, 2011, from http://www.aei.org/issue/23373

Besharov, D. J., & Call, D. (2009, February 8). Head Start falls further behind. *The New York Times*, p. WK12.

Cascio, E. U. (2010). What happened when kindergarten went universal? *Education Next, 13*, 63–69.

Finn, C. (2009). The preschool picture. *Education Next, 5*(2), 13–19.

Hollins, E. (1993). Assessing teacher competence for diverse populations. *Theory Into Practice, 32*(2), 93–100.

Lutz, P. (1994, August 7). Head Start expanding despite problems. *The New York Times.* Retrieved September 26, 2011, from http://www.nytimes.com/1994/08/07/nyregion/head-start-expanding-despite-problems.html?src=pm

Owman, B., Donovan, S., & Burns, S. (2001). *Eager to learn: Educating our preschoolers.* Washington, DC: National Academy Press.

Ramey, C. T., Campbell, F. A., Burchinal, M., Skinner, M. L., Gardner, D. M., & Ramey, S. L. (2000). Persistent effects of early intervention on high-risk children and their mothers. *Applied Developmental Science, 4*(3), 2–14.

U.S. Department of Health and Human Services. (2003). *Strengthening Head Start: What the evidence shows.* Retrieved from http://aspe.hhs.gov/hsp/strengthenhead start03/ref.htm

U.S. Department of Health and Human Services. (n.d.). *Head Start program fact sheet.* Washington, DC: Author. Retrieved from http://www.acf.hhs.gov/programs/ohs/about/fy2008.html

Vadero, D. (2010). Researchers argue Head Start study delayed, ignored. *Education Week, 3*(5), 12.

COURT CASES AND STATUTES

Brown v. Board of Education, 347 U.S. 483 (1954).

Individuals with Disabilities Education Act, 20 U.S.C. §§ 1400–1482 (2006).

No Child Left Behind Act, 20 U.S.C. §§ 6301–7941 (2006).

Are vocational education and apprenticeship programs valuable?

POINT: Dan Schroer, *Greene County Career Center, Xenia, Ohio*
COUNTERPOINT: Paul J. Waller, *Oakwood High School, Oakwood City Schools, Ohio*

OVERVIEW

Vocational education began with federal legislation that dates back to the Morrill Act (1862) and its subsequent reauthorizations. The Morrill Act affected higher education land grant colleges (Scott & Sarkees-Wircenski, 2004). Secondary or high school career technical/vocational education draws its roots from federal legislation passed into law in 1917 known as the Smith-Hughes Act (Hocklander, Kaufman, Levesque, & Houser, 1992). The Smith-Hughes Act established federal and state boards for vocational education. This act also created separate funding, teacher preparation, licensure, and curriculum from that of "regular" or "classical," also known as comprehensive, high school education (Lynch, 2000).

Early in American history the need to educate the population in skills was a predominant theme in public schools. The United States began as an agriculture-based economy, transformed into an industrial economy, and seems to be headed in the direction of becoming an information/technology/service economy (Hendricks-Lee & Mooney, 1998). Throughout these changes in the American economy, vocational education has kept pace by changing its curriculum to match the current workforce needs. Vocational education maintains cooperative relationships with business and industry. Business and industry, which are driven by profit with technology providing a method to streamline a variety of processes, need employees trained in, or with at least an understanding of, the newest technologies. The partnership with career technical/vocational education allows business and industry the opportunity to help shape the curricula that enable these schools to produce productive employees with an understanding of the latest innovations in a variety of careers.

Recently, another initiative has pushed to the forefront of American education. The U.S. position in the world market regarding mathematic and science skills has declined, leading to a push toward increasing students' abilities in science, technology, engineering, and mathematics (STEM). This initiative seems analogous to the emphasis in mathematics and science created in 1957 with the launch of Sputnik by the former Soviet Union. STEM curriculum merges the four subjects into projects for students that have direct application in business and industry. School districts work with industry partners to develop curriculum that complements industry needs and prepares students for further study and training following high school.

Business and industry provided the impetus to establish career technical/vocational education at the turn of the 20th century and continue to shape career technical/vocational education. The 21st century provides new challenges for traditional high schools and career technical/vocational education. The global economy increases competition for educated and trained workers. Schools in the United States must prepare graduates with the skills, knowledge, and abilities to compete for the best careers. Some careers of the future are yet to be created. Preparing graduates for careers still to be discovered is a daunting task. Which existing system, traditional high school or vocational school, is best poised to prepare students for the global economy and the future?

The debates in this chapter present differing views of the value and need for vocational education at the high school level. The point essay, presented by Dan Schroer, a current superintendent at Greene County Career Center, a vocational high school (career center) in Xenia, Ohio, discusses partnerships with district schools, local businesses, politicians, and organizations as key to the successes achieved by vocational education in meeting the needs of industry. Further, Schroer identifies the increases in academic and vocational offerings at the career center enabling students to be prepared for follow-on training after graduation. In addition, Schroer discusses industry-prepared assessments that students complete in order to substantiate their preparedness for a career in that industry.

The counterpoint article written by Paul J. Waller, a current principal at a comprehensive high school in Ohio, is decidedly against continued separation and funding between "regular" and vocational high schools. Waller argues that the current global market renders the previous education system obsolete. He continues his attack on vocational education by reminding the reader of the old stigma about vocational high schools as recalled by parents. Waller presents the changes his school underwent in order to meet the STEM environment currently permeating through education. His district renovated an existing facility to accommodate a new program that alleviated the need for students to travel to a vocational school. He continues his description of the program and participation by revealing that these students would probably not have gone to a vocational school and their parents would have been reluctant to support this change for their children. In addition, Waller does soften his argument by conceding that a joint effort through restructuring may produce the best viable solution for students. Waller concludes by discussing data-driven decision making to implement curriculum, programs, instruction methodology, and courses to ensure our youth are capable of competing in the global economy of today and beyond.

As you read the following arguments for and against vocational education, consider whether there should be two separate systems of education; which, if either, is better poised to meet the needs of future generations; and, as education continues to change or evolve, what path must be pursued. If we agree that one size does not fit most in education, then, when considering costs, how will we create an educational environment that meets the needs of a diverse learning pool while exhibiting fiscal restraint coupled with giving our children a competitive advantage in the global economy?

Michael J. Jernigan
University of Dayton

POINT: Dan Schroer
Greene County Career Center, Xenia, Ohio

In 1917, Congress passed the Smith-Hughes Act providing for federal funding for agricultural education, trade, home economics, and industrial education. It also provided for the training of teachers of these subjects. This
legislation not only provided the basis for vocational education, but also set it
apart from the traditional academic high school curriculum in most school
districts. Most states established separate boards of vocational education, and
funding set aside for vocational education was kept separate and could only be
used for that purpose. Consequently, vocational education arose as an entity
separate from traditional schooling.

Mark Roberts (2001) reports that the Vocational Education Act of 1963
increased funding for vocational education and stipulated that vocational education was to be defined as "organized educational programs which are directly
related to the preparation of individuals for paid or unpaid employment, or for
additional preparation for a career requiring other than a baccalaureate or
advanced degree." David Burns (2007), the former Executive Director of
Secondary Education and Workforce Development for the Ohio Department
of Education, reported that every American youth will complete high school
with the skills and academic knowledge needed to make a successful transition
to postsecondary education or career placement without needing remediation.

Vocational education has transformed to career technical education with an
emphasis on academic preparation. In the 1960s and 1970s, vocational education was for students who could not handle college preparatory academics.
Students learned applied academics that related to their specific vocational
field. Now, students must take college preparatory academics while studying
vocational education.

With the increasing need for better educated employees, students need to be
academically prepared for postsecondary education. It is normal to find
courses such as physics, calculus, chemistry, and foreign languages in vocational
schools. These courses prepare students for lifelong education at postsecondary
institutions. Vocational education and apprenticeship programs are valuable!

SPECIFIC CAREER TECHNICAL INFORMATION

In order to demonstrate that vocational education and apprenticeship programs are valuable, sharing some specific career technical education at the
national and state levels may be helpful at this juncture. The information that

follows summarizes the need and successes of vocational education and apprenticeship programs throughout the United States.

Nationally, there are approximately 18,000 public high schools. Eighty-eight percent of those high schools offer at least one career technical education program. Over 900 schools are full-time career technical schools. During the 2005–2006 school year, there were 15.38 million students enrolled in secondary and postsecondary vocational education classes. Business and marketing was the most popular career technical program with 28% of students enrolling. Twenty-two percent were enrolled in health programs, and 12% were enrolled in education programs (National Center for Education Statistics, 2011).

In Ohio, schools are assessed on eight performance measures. Assessments are consistent across the United States, but the specific assessment varies by state. The following are the Ohio measures and the state results (Ohio Career Technical Education, 2011):

- Academic Attainment, Reading/Language Arts: 93.31%

- Academic Attainment, Mathematics: 91.68%

- Technical Skill Attainment: 63.63%

- Secondary School Completion: 95.40%

- Student Graduation Rate: 94.63%

- Secondary Placement: 88.49%

- Nontraditional Participation: 26.67%

- Nontraditional Completion: 22.81%

For year 2009, career technical education served 127,085 secondary students through many educational career field choices in the state of Ohio. Those Ohio career fields are as follows:

- Agricultural and Environmental Systems

- Arts and Communication

- Business and Administrative Services

- Construction Technologies

- Education and Training

- Engineering and Science Technologies

- Finance

- Government and Public Administration

- Health Science

- Hospitality and Tourism

- Human Services

- Information Technology

- Law and Public Safety

- Manufacturing Technologies

- Marketing

- Transportation Systems

Vocational education, now known as career technical education, serves a great number of students in 16 state career fields. Those students are performing at high levels and are receiving a "jump start" to their future by learning these career fields in high school. These students are able to enter postsecondary education, whether it is a two-year or four-year school, with education and practical experience through apprenticeship programs.

LITERATURE REVIEW

Many educational leaders have been outspoken as to the benefits of vocational education and apprenticeship programs. Susan Tave Zelman (2005) said that

> in today's global economy, every student must graduate from high school and be prepared to go on to higher education and the workforce. Jobs for the future require new knowledge and skills that all students must obtain by taking more challenging courses at the middle and high school levels. (p. 1)

Vocational education and apprenticeship programs meet this expectation.

Under No Child Left Behind (2006), states and school districts have been working to close the achievement gap to make sure that all students, including minorities and those who are disadvantaged, achieve academic proficiency. This is being accomplished through the provision of supplemental programs such as Title I, greater accountability for student success, and rigorous requirements for teacher qualifications. No Child Left Behind is guiding the academic development of schools throughout the United States.

Research has shown that college prep academics can be a valuable part of the career technical education of students. James Stone, Corinne Alfred, Donna Pearson, Morgan Lewis, and Susan Jenson (2005) reported that explicit enhancement of the math portion of the career technical curriculum can improve students' math skills without impairing their attainment of occupational skills and knowledge. The Governor's Commission for Student Success (Patient, 2000) reported that Ohio needs to begin with clear, rigorous, and reasonable academic standards. All career technical planning districts, in Ohio, are developing a college prep–plus curriculum. That curriculum will prepare students for careers and postsecondary education.

Willard Daggett (2005), President of the International Center for Leadership in Education, said that

> career and technical education must be seen as a primary deliverer of strong academic preparation. In today's environment, in terms of garnering state support and federal support, career technical education programs must go beyond skills only and contribute to results on state testing.

Nationwide, ACT has developed assessments that test student competency in vocational education and academic education. As a state example, the Ohio Career Technical Competency Assessment (OCTCA) has been developed with higher academic expectations. Thomas Friedman (2005) reported that "the jobs are going to go where the best educated workforce is" (p. 321). As educators, it is our responsibility to prepare students academically as well as for careers.

Nick Anderson (2005) reported that "some analysts say that states must make elementary and middle school math more rigorous and push more students to take Algebra I before ninth grade." In Butler County, Ohio, only one high school teaches Algebra I above the eighth-grade level. That district has informed its staff that this will end in two years. This trend has become a norm nationwide as Algebra I has been moved to middle schools.

APPLICATION OF CONCEPT

To apply vocational education to leadership development, it has been very important to analyze the career technical student organizations and Tech Prep education in regard to the everyday learning of each student.

There are seven career technical student organizations with the purpose of developing leadership, citizenship, and cooperation skills within the membership to better prepare students for future success in their specific career technical field. These organizations are incredibly important in partnering with business and industry.

Business Professionals of America is the leading CTSO (career technical student organization) for over 51,000 students, nationwide, pursuing careers in business management, office administration, information technology, and other related career fields. Over 220,000 students are enrolled in Family, Career and Community Leaders of America, a nonprofit national career and technical student organization for young men and women in family and consumer sciences education. The Future Educators Association is an international student organization, in 43 states, dedicated to supporting young people interested in education-related careers.

Health Occupations Students of America is a national student organization, with over 120,000 members, that promotes career opportunities in the health care industry and enhances the delivery of quality health care to all people. The National FFA Organization makes a positive difference in the lives of over 500,000 students, nationwide, by developing their potential for premier leadership, personal growth, and career success through agricultural education. Finally, SkillsUSA helps its 300,000 nationwide members become world-class workers, leaders, and responsible American citizens.

Over the past year, these career technical student organizations had a membership of over a million students nationwide. Every state had one or more of these organizations that promote leadership, citizenship, and cooperation skills. Each is a cocurricular program that applies classroom and laboratory learning to real-life examples. These organizations connect students to industry professionals and provide students with experiences with cooperating employers. Personally, I am a better professional due to my experiences in the National FFA Organization.

Tech Prep has also become an incredible opportunity for students. Local high schools and career technical schools set up articulation agreements with postsecondary schools. When students complete specific courses in career technical education, pass end-of-course assessments, and meet other attendance and grade requirements, students earn college credit and/or scholarships for postsecondary schools. These opportunities have increased students' chances of enrolling in postsecondary schools.

LOCAL PERSPECTIVE OF VALUE

The Greene County Career Center, in Xenia, Ohio, has begun working with all Greene County associate schools to develop a more rigorous entrance requirement. Career technical courses, such as welding technology, information technology, biotechnology, and automotive technology, require college preparatory academics in order for students to be successful. The OCTCA is an industry-prepared end-of-course assessment that indicates a student's preparedness for a career in the specific industry. These assessments require college preparatory academics in order to complete basic career skills in these programs. Students not only need to be able to pass these assessments, but they must also be ready to move on to a two- or four-year postsecondary institution to become better prepared for the workforce. Career positions without postsecondary education are not applicable in today's high-tech society.

Locally, the following events have occurred in order to develop career technical education and apprenticeship programs that lead to successful students. These practices have been used statewide and nationwide for several years.

Partnerships With Partner Schools

The Career Technical Superintendent meets regularly with all partner school superintendents to communicate school events as well as discuss future career technical programs and partnership opportunities. Currently, there are 12 career technical programs offered at the partner school locations in order to provide career technical choices for students who do not wish to leave their home schools. All building principals meet on a regular basis, as do all curriculum directors, so that communication about programs and career choices is maximized and current.

Superintendent Stakeholder Advisory Committee

A committee was developed that included several of the top 10 employers in the county, city mayors, city managers, chamber of commerce directors, legislators, and rotary members. These community leaders provide input on developing the school system as a leader in education and economic development in southwestern Ohio. These members also become advocates of the school and provide leadership in educational opportunities for the students.

There are some challenges. One challenge has been communicating to stakeholders who remember career centers as traditional vocational education centers attended by students who were not interested in attending college. The parents of today's students went to school when career technical education meant a "dumping ground." This stereotype has been difficult to change.

Marketing and results will be the key to this change. Career technical centers will need to invest time and money into the marketing of the educational improvement. Positive results need to be communicated to all stakeholders. A unified effort will make a positive difference for the future of career technical education.

Development of STEM Curriculum

Over the past couple of years, science, technology, engineering, and math (STEM) careers have become a buzzword in education circles. Curriculum has been developed to deliver on these careers, and schools have changed the names of many programs to indicate that they are STEM programs. However, career technical education has always been STEM.

Through integrated instruction, hands-on methodology, end-of-course assessments, up-to-date technology, and industry expert instruction, career technical education has led STEM education for over 40 years. Career centers are pleased that other facets of education have finally decided to follow the lead of career technical education through the development of STEM education.

CONCLUSION

Research indicates the need to increase the academic standards for students entering career technical education. Today's careers require a student who has strong career technical and academic knowledge. Many careers will require additional education upon hiring, and students need to be academically prepared for lifelong learning. Career education and apprenticeship programs provide these opportunities for students. Students have become better prepared for postsecondary experiences and careers by enrolling in career technical education and apprenticeship programs. This writer is a product of career technical education as a student in agriculture education. This writer was also a college preparatory student and completed four years of agricultural education and was involved in agriculture placement/apprenticeship programs. This writer attended The Ohio State University and received two majors: agriculture education and agriculture economics. Since graduation, he has earned a master of science degree from The Ohio State University, taught for six years, and has been a school administrator for 12 years.

Career technical education gave this writer the skills necessary to be successful in postsecondary school and in his career choice. Such success stories are many across the United States. Career technical education and apprenticeship programs make a positive difference for students.

Nationwide, students experience a wide array of career technical educational activities that have truly shaped them into capable leaders and employees.

Involvement in career and technical organizations offers members the opportunity to expand their leadership potential and develop skills for life, necessary in the home and workplace, through competitive events, service learning, and rigorous and relevant curriculum.

In the educational landscape, a wide variety of forces are bearing down on the schools and their instructors and students. Monetary resources are tight, many times causing funds to be diverted away from long-standing, successful career and technical programs and into trying to solve the "educational problem of the day." Those who do not understand what career technical programs offer and accomplish do not appreciate the great opportunities that might be eliminated in doing this. It is important for the future of our educational system, its students, and our country that all of our programs remain supported, strong, and viable.

Through career and technical education, students are afforded the opportunity to enhance their core academics while also engaging with those around them through service learning and community involvement. Participation in education through service and philanthropy shows a measurable change not only in the recipient, but also in the provider. Service learning integrates meaningful community engagement with instruction, issue identification, and reflection to enrich the learning experience. It also teaches civic responsibility, encourages lifelong community engagement, and strengthens communities for the common good.

Vocational education has provided and will continue to provide the *TICKET* to success.

T-Teamwork

Vocational education and apprenticeship programs develop teamwork skills among all students. Through classroom and laboratory activities, students work as a team to complete projects and learn through the scientific method. Through apprenticeship programs, students work as a team at the job site with mentors and peers in becoming better educated and competent in the area of study.

I-Involvement

Vocational education students are involved in classroom activities, laboratory projects, community service events, career technical student organizations, mentoring, and apprenticeship activities. This does not occur in any other educational setting. Vocational education truly involves students in many areas of educational competence.

C-Commitment

Students are committed to setting goals and developing a plan of action to reach the goal in all facets of vocational education and apprenticeship programs. In many cases, a student commits two or four years to be involved in the specific career technical program.

K-Knowledge

Students earn knowledge every day through vocational education and apprenticeship programs. The knowledge is gained through hands-on instruction where the students become actively involved in the learning process as they complete real-life projects. The knowledge gained propels the students to be better prepared for postsecondary education as well as career placement.

E-Enthusiasm

Career technical student organizations develop enthusiasm in students toward their personal success as well as the success of their classmates. No other educational entity develops leadership, citizenship, and cooperation skills as vocational education.

T-Tomorrow

When a student has developed teamwork, becomes involved and committed to success, gains vocational and apprenticeship knowledge, and is enthusiastic about the future, tomorrow will become a whole lot brighter! Vocational education and apprenticeship programs develop the future of competent workers and leaders in the United States.

COUNTERPOINT: Paul J. Waller
Oakwood High School, Oakwood City Schools, Ohio

Career education, or career technical education as it is now called, is no longer valuable to the learners of today and tomorrow. At one time industry, and having a career in manufacturing, was viable in the United States. This is no longer the case in our global society so that vocational education and apprenticeship programs are no longer valuable.

The benefits of career technical education are diminished because traditional college preparatory high schools are now taking the best aspects of career technical education and the traditional college preparatory high school and are blending them together to meet the needs of the 21st-century learner. Students in today's schools need to develop 21st-century skills, which include collaboration, critical thinking, creativity, and communication. These skills are developed in classrooms that no longer have walls. This can be accomplished online in the virtual world, through internships, multidisciplinary projects, simulations, and so on. At one time vocational education programs provided these very same learning opportunities to our students, but this now happens in STEM (science, technology, engineering, and math) programs in a traditional high school. The point is the old paradigm of a high school no longer exists.

CHALLENGES FOR 21ST-CENTURY STUDENTS

The National Assessment of Vocational Education study mentioned that the academic rigor in vocational programs has increased yet gaps still remain (U.S. Department of Education, 2004). This study suggested that more work is needed to raise the achievement levels of all students. The National Assessment of Educational Progress (NAEP) shows that students who participate in vocational programs are far less likely to score proficient in reading or math as defined by the NAEP scores.

States that choose to fund vocational programs are eligible to apply for federal grants. According to the U.S. Department of Education, the Carl D. Perkins Vocational and Technical Education Act of 2006 is the principal source of federal funding to states for the improvement of postsecondary career and technical education. Schools also receive local dollars based on state funding formulas that are different from traditional public school funding. Data from the Department of Education (2004) show some states choose not to participate in vocational education while other states choose to focus only on postsecondary vocational education. Many states, however, including Ohio, fund two parallel systems with similar goals and objectives.

During a time of economic recovery from the worst recession since the Great Depression, it seems ridiculous that we would be funding two systems. This requires using federal and local tax dollars to pay for teachers and administrators in each system. Parallel systems should be joined into one system combining resources and reducing the amount of overhead required to educate our students in the 21st century.

Twenty-first-century skills are essential for today's learners. Career technical and traditional high schools working side by side focusing on these essential skills is a waste of resources and requires students to make a choice that is not viable in today's global society. These two parallel systems need to be combined into one system that focuses on the needs of our students in a rapidly changing 21st-century global society.

Ian Jukes, a respected author and speaker and the director of the InfoSavvy Group, a consulting group that provides development in the areas of assessment and evaluation, and Ted McCain and Lee Crockett (2010) state that our current kindergartners will have between 14 and 16 careers in their lifetime. Providing these students with a skill set under the old vocational/career technical paradigm is no longer viable or, for that matter, responsible. We can't prepare them for the technology of tomorrow because we do not know what that will be. We have to focus on the problem solving, collaboration, critical thinking skills, and creativity that our students will need to be successful. Jukes further states that we need to find a way to look at education as we never have before. We need to shift our paradigms and stop doing things just because that's the way we've always done things in the past.

It is absolutely imperative to restructure schools in the United States to meet the needs of our students. We are already losing one generation of learners, so time is essential. We need to design schools with the results of our students in mind. Before we make changes to the structure of our schools, we must first clearly understand what will be different instructionally. It is absolutely essential that the organizational structure be used as a tool to support and challenge our students to meet the current and future demands of the 21st century (Daggett, 2008).

The only way for teachers and administrators to truly develop programs for students of the 21st century is to truly know each individual student. The days of having programs set in "stone" and then fitting students into these slots are here no longer. We must develop our programs around the learning styles, interests, and talents of our students. We need to focus on our students' needs first, in order to develop instructional strategies that are effective and rigorous.

Willard R. Daggett (2008), who founded the International Center for Leadership in Education in 1991, believes that by focusing on strategies and practices, highly successful schools design safe, secure, and caring learning environments. Since the type of environment is designed around the students' interests, the curriculum becomes much more relevant to the students. Daggett says that relevance then results in a more rigorous program because the students are intrinsically motivated to dig deeper and move their learning from the knowledge level of Bloom's taxonomy (1956) to the synthesis or application level.

A good example of this exists at Fairfield High School in Cincinnati, Ohio. During the period of 2003–2009, Fairfield High School had more students taking vocational classes in the high school than students attending the vocational school off-site. School administrators used current buildings and teachers to educate more students than the vocational school, which had a principal, two assistant principals, and three guidance counselors. At the same time the vocational school also employed a superintendent, a treasurer, and many other district office personnel.

Fairfield High School had over 2,400 students enrolled in Grades 10–12. The principal found it very difficult to convince students to enroll in the Butler Tech career center for their junior and senior years. This is due mainly to the negative stigma that still exists regarding vocational schools. The author of *Shop Class as Soulcraft,* Matthew Crawford (2009) states,

> Today, in our schools, the manual trades are given little honor. The egalitarian worry that has always attended tracking students into "college prep" and "vocational ed" is overlaid with another fear that acquiring a specific skill set means that one's life is determined. (p. 19)

In the 1980s, there was a prevalent model that involved a vocational school that was part of the high school. Students who were interested in vocational school would take classes in a designated part of the building. The students enrolled in the traditional school would walk through the vocational school occasionally, but for the most part the vocational students were considered by their peers to be separate from the regular high school.

OVERCOMING THE CHALLENGES

So how do we overcome these challenges? Fairfield High School started implementing satellite programs in the school. These were courses that were funded by its career technical partner, Butler Tech, but used classrooms throughout the traditional high school. Students could take career technical classes such as engineering, work and family life, business, internship, and so on. There was nothing that physically differentiated Butler Tech teachers from Fairfield High School teachers except where they received their paycheck. When these programs were implemented in the high school, enrollment grew, and the demand for these courses became higher than the school's capacity.

This is a model that could and should be implemented across the country. The goal of increased academic rigor would be achieved while at the same time resources would be conserved in a time when finances are very limited. This also blurs the lines that parents and students see between vocational and college prep, thus dispelling the negative perceptions that many parents and students hold toward vocational education.

A high-performing high school in Dayton, Ohio, named Oakwood High School, recently made a step in the right direction. The school had a traditional wood shop as of the 2009–2010 school year. When asked why it offered wood shop courses, the answer was that it's always been that way.

During the summer of 2010, Oakwood High School implemented an engineering program. To give a little history, Oakwood is a school that is steeped in tradition. The first graduating class received its diplomas in 1924. The present building is the same building in which those students were taught. However, until 2010 the same industrial arts course (wood shop) was still in place.

The data that were collected from students through senior exit surveys indicated that 30% of Oakwood senior students were interested in becoming engineers. Yet Oakwood had no engineering opportunities for its students, except through an off-site vocational program in which two students were enrolled in 2009. The structure of the program did not fit the needs or interests of the students.

After implementing the engineering program, Oakwood had 74 students enroll in the first year. Remember, only two students were enrolled in the very same program when students had to go off-site to participate. Through a partnership with a local community college, Oakwood students have the opportunity to earn 18 college credits before they graduate from high school, and will earn a full scholarship to the community college.

Oakwood High School also formed a council of local educators from the nearby colleges, business owners, and engineers to help monitor, evaluate, and improve its model. By doing so, the school is ensuring that its students' curriculum is not only relative to their needs but also relative to what is occurring in the real world. This will ensure students enter the workforce well prepared.

In this class, students are paired into teams in which they have to develop their own rocket. They have to design, test prototypes, and then predict the performance of the rocket using their problem solving, critical thinking, creativity, and communication skills.

It is important that principals form partnerships with career technical administrators and teachers. They should think of vocational education not as a separate system, but as members of the team who have the same goals for their students.

Every year the principal at Oakwood meets with each teacher to go over his or her goals for the year. Each teacher is required to have at least two goals that are aligned with the district mission. One of these goals must center on the concept of differentiation. Differentiation is used in the classroom to meet students where they are in terms of how they learn. A differentiated classroom will feel different to each student because the instruction is being customized to meet his or her individual needs. Within the engineering program at

Oakwood High School, educators are providing students with the 21st-century skills they will need to go into the aerospace, mechanical, or biomedical field, or whatever new careers the future brings.

FOCUSING ON THE FUTURE

In today's and tomorrow's world, it is no longer acceptable to force students to choose between career technical and a traditional/college preparatory route. Educational leaders must work together to provide seamless opportunities for their students to acquire these essential 21st-century skills.

Students today can access information, facts, and knowledge almost instantly from the Internet. We need to provide our students with real problem-solving opportunities, apprenticeships, and internships that will give them the experience and confidence to be successful in this global society.

Data must be used to guide the instruction of our students on a regular basis. Two questions principals should ask their teachers are "Are the students learning?" and, if so, "How do you know?" The way the teachers know the answers to these questions is through formative and summative assessments. Formative assessments must be common among subject areas and must be deliberate and organized in such a way that teachers can easily access the assessment data so that they can adjust their instruction to meet the needs of their students. The use of formative ongoing assessments allows teachers to differentiate their instruction not only based on the student's interests but also based on the student's level of understanding at that point and time.

Here is a wonderful and exciting example of how a teacher has made learning relative to her students. She facilitates an entrepreneurship contest. A local businessman from her community partners with the school to provide scholarship money to the student who creates the most innovative entrepreneurship business idea. Students create their ideas throughout the year and develop projects that are aligned with their standards and learning outcomes while at the same time they are participating in a competition in which the winner will receive scholarship money. Many of the students create business ideas based on their interests. They are responsible for designing the business plan, including their marketing plan, and putting this in writing to be judged by local business professionals. This type of real-life learning is a perfect example of how vocational and traditional education can be combined for the maximum learning for students.

It is vital that each school adopt a mission statement that captures the purpose for the school. For example, "Doing what is best for students is our guiding principle" is a perfect example of a mission statement that can be used as a guiding principle for all decisions made by the school.

Educational leaders need to continue to find ways to focus students on the future. The days of helping students decide what they want to be is over. The college track versus the vocational track is no longer a model that works. High schools need to be reinvented on a continual basis to meet the needs of their students and the constantly changing global society. Daggett (2008) states that successful schools are focused on the future and develop future-based systems. These systems are focused on teaching students how to think, not simply on communicating to them what they should know.

We need to work with teachers to adjust their instruction to fit in today's high-tech world. We need to come together and create a new 21st-century paradigm where we meet the needs of all learners. In 1963 it was necessary to pass the Vocational Education Act. Education has come a long way since then. Now we as educators must work to move these two paradigms, vocational and college preparatory, together so that all educators are working together to provide our students with the experiences and skills they need for jobs and careers that are beyond our imagination. Creating such paradigms will conserve and maximize our limited resources as the United States recovers from these challenging economic times as we continue to focus on the changing global society.

FURTHER READINGS AND RESOURCES

Anderson, N. (2005). Maryland students aim to go from X to G (graduation). *The Washington Post.* Retrieved from http://www.washingtonpost.com/wp-dyn/content/article/2005/11/08/AR2005110801700.html

Bloom, B. S., Engelhart, M. D., Furst, E. J., Hill, W. H., & Krathwohl, D. R. (1956). *Taxonomy of educational objectives: The classification of educational goals; Handbook I: Cognitive Domain.* New York: Longman.

Burns, D. (2007). The need to bring it all together. *2007 Policy and Leadership Forum.* Columbus, OH: Ohio Department of Education.

Crawford, M. B. (2009). *Shop class as soulcraft: An inquiry into the value of work.* New York: Penguin.

Daggett, W. (2005, September). Educational leadership: Rigor & relevance. *Techniques, 80*(6). Retrieved September 26, 2011, from http://www.acteonline.org/content.aspx?id=5076

Daggett, W. R. (2008). *Rigor and relevance from concept to reality.* Rexford, NY: International Center for Leadership in Education.

Friedman, T. (2005). *The world is flat.* New York: Farrar, Straus & Giroux.

Hendricks-Lee, M. S., & Mooney, T. (1998). A teacher union's role in systemic educational reform. *Contemporary Education, 69*(4), 218–222.

Hocklander, E. G., Kaufman, P., Levesque, K., & Houser, J. (1992). *Vocational education in the United States: 1969–1990* (NCES 92-669). Washington, DC: U.S. Department of Education Office of Educational Research and Improvement.

Jukes, I., McCain, T. D., & Crockett, L. (2010). *Living on the future edge: Windows on tomorrow.* Thousand Oaks, CA: Corwin.

Lynch, R. L. (2000). *New directions for high school career and technical education in the 21st century* (ERIC Document Reproduction Service No. ED444037). Washington, DC: National Institute for Education.

National Center for Education Statistics. (2011). *Career technical education statistics.* Retrieved from http://nces.ed.gov/surveys/ctes/highlights.asp

Ohio Career Technical Education. (2011). *2009–2010 secondary statewide workforce development annual performance report.* Columbus: Ohio Department of Education.

Ohio Department of Education. (2005). *CTAE November 2005 update.* Retrieved December 28, 2010, from http://www.ode.state.oh.us/ctae/News/2005/Nov_2005/default.asp

Ohio Department of Education. (2005). *Secondary workforce development.* Retrieved from http://www.ode.state.oh.us/GD/Templates/Pages/ODE/ODEPrimary.aspx?page=2&TopicRelationID=1419

Ohio Department of Education. (2005). *2004–2005 annual report on educational progress in Ohio.* Retrieved December 28, 2010, from http://www.ode.state.oh.us/report-card/state_report_card

Patient, W. (2000). *Expecting more: Higher achievement for Ohio's students and schools.* Columbus, OH: Governor's Commission for Student Success.

Popham, W. J. (2006). *Assessment for educational leaders.* Boston: Pearson/Allyn & Bacon.

Roberts, M. (2001). *Vocational Act of 1963.* Retrieved December 28, 2010, from http://dana.ucc.nau.edu/~mr/vte591/1963.htm

Scott, J. L., & Sarkees-Wircenski, M. (2004). *Overview of career and technical education* (3rd ed.). Homewood, IL: American Technical Publishers.

Senge, P. M. (2006). *The fifth discipline: the art and practice of the learning organization.* New York: Doubleday/Currency.

Silverburg, M., Warner, E., Fong, M., & Goodwin, D. (n.d.). *National assessment of vocational education.* United States Department of Education. Available from http://www.ed.gov

Stone, J., Alfred, C., Pearson, D., Lewis, M., & Jenson, S. (2005, September). *Building academic skills in context: Testing the value of enhanced math learning in CTE.* Columbus, OH: National Dissemination Center for Career and Technical Education.

Tomlinson, C. A. (1999). *The differentiated classroom: Responding to the needs of all learners.* Alexandria, VA: Association for Supervision and Curriculum Development.

U.S. Department of Education. (2004). *National assessment of vocational education: Final report to Congress.* Retrieved from http://www2.ed.gov/rschstat/eval/sectech/nave/navefinal.pdf

U.S. Department of Education, Office of Vocational and Adult Education, Carl D. Perkins Career and Technical Education Act of 2006. (n.d.). *Report to Congress on state performance, program year 2007–2008.* Washington, DC: Author.

Zelman, S. T. (2005). *2004–2005 annual report on educational progress in Ohio.* Columbus: Ohio Department of Education.

Court Cases and Statutes

Carl D. Perkins Vocational and Technical Education Act, Pub. L. No. 109-270 (2006).
Morrill Act, Pub. L. No. 37–108 (1862).
No Child Left Behind Act, 20 U.S.C. §§ 6301-7941 (2006).
Smith-Hughes Act, Pub. L. No. 64–347 (1917).
Vocational Education Act, Pub. L. No. 88–210 (1963).

Are year-round schools an appropriate way to improve student outcomes?

POINT: Carolyn Talbert-Johnson, *University of Dayton*

COUNTERPOINT: Aaron Cooley, *New England College*

OVERVIEW

Most schools in the United States operate on a 10-month or 180-day school year regardless of whether they follow a traditional calendar or not. The traditional school calendar was established during agrarian times when children were needed to work on the farms during the warm weather months. Today, many educators and policymakers feel that the traditional school calendar is outmoded and advocate for year-round schools. A year-round school is one that operates on a 12-month basis rather than a traditional school calendar whereby classes are not held for 8 to 10 weeks over the summer. Students in schools using a year-round schedule do not necessarily attend school for more days during the year. Rather, smaller school breaks are distributed evenly throughout the year. Proponents of year-round schools claim that such a schedule results in better school achievement and better attendance on the part of both faculty and students. Further, it is claimed that a year-round schedule is more conducive to learning because it reduces fatigue and burnout for both students and faculty and eliminates the regression that normally occurs during the traditional summer vacation. Detractors, however, insist that there is no conclusive evidence that students achieve better on a year-round schedule, and that there are a number of problems with such schedules.

The National Association for Year-Round Education (NAYRE) (2007) reported that as of 2007, the last year for which statistics are available, in the

United States there were 2,764 public year-round schools operating in 387 school districts in 44 states. Slightly less than half of those schools were in California alone where 154 school districts operated schools on a year-round basis. All totaled, 2,099,633 students nationwide were enrolled in year-round schools during the 2006–2007 school year.

There are many different types of year-round education programs, but most require a reorganization of the traditional school calendar to replace the long summer vacation with several smaller breaks evenly distributed throughout the year. For example, in one arrangement students attend school for 45 days and then have 15 days off. This cycle is repeated four times a year. Students enrolled in year-round programs typically attend the same classes and receive the same type and amount of instruction as students whose schools operate under a traditional school calendar. The only distinction is that the year-round calendar is organized into instructional blocks and vacation periods that are evenly distributed across 12 months.

Although many school systems offer instructional programs during school breaks, students usually attend these programs only on a voluntary basis or to make up credits for failed courses. Students in other industrialized countries that have longer school years often score higher on international measures of achievement than U.S. students. The issue of whether the United States should follow the lead of other countries and adopt a longer school year, although not part of the discussion in this chapter, has been at the center of many recent policy debates. Even so, it is an important consideration, as some year-round schools, more commonly known as extended year schools, provide more than the traditional 180 days of instruction per year.

The debate in this chapter is whether year-round schools offer an appropriate means of improving student achievement. Carolyn Talbert-Johnson, a professor and the Associate Chair of Graduate Education in the Department of Teacher Education at the University of Dayton, takes the point position and argues that year-round calendars are well worth considering. Aaron Cooley, who teaches courses in public policy and education at New England College, takes the opposing view in the counterpoint essay and contends that there really are no concrete academic benefits to students enrolled in year-round schools.

Talbert-Johnson claims that with the increased emphasis on student outcomes and school accountability, year-round schools offer a viable means of improving the achievement of students, especially those who are educationally disadvantaged. She cites research indicating that year-round schools have particular benefits for students from lower socioeconomic levels, those at risk of school failure, and students with special needs. She further notes that year-round schools make better use of facilities, reduce discipline problems, increase the attendance of both teachers and students, and decrease the student dropout rate. Talbert-Johnson sees year-round schools as an approach that will benefit all learners in an environment conducive to learning. Rather than continue the debate over the pros and cons of year-round schooling, she feels that it is time to focus on identifying the most effective extended year programs for each school district's student population.

In the counterpoint essay, Cooley maintains that year-round schools have not demonstrated the outcomes needed to have the concept advanced as a broader strategy for school districts around the country to replicate. Since enough achievement gains have not been shown, Cooley feels that the debate only serves to distract educators and policymakers from a more substantive, comprehensive, and transformative educational reform policy. In conclusion, he acknowledges that more research needs to be done but suggests that year-round schools offer little more than a rearranging of the parts of a complex educational system without addressing more substantive and pressing reform issues.

As both of this chapter's authors point out, the debate over the benefits and feasibility of year-round schooling will continue. As you are reading this chapter, you might want to think about some of the issues related to setting up year-round school schedules. What effect will year-round schooling have on summer employment for youth? What additional expenses or cost savings will be involved by opening schools all year? What effect will a year-round schedule have on extracurricular activities? How will year-round school schedules affect family schedules, especially if children in one family are on different schedules?

Allan G. Osborne, Jr.
Principal (Retired), Snug Harbor Community School,
Quincy, Massachusetts

POINT: Carolyn Talbert-Johnson
University of Dayton

As teachers, administrators, and schools wrestle with the current demands for accountability in student outcomes, year-round education offers a viable solution to the issue of improvement in academic achievement for all students, especially low-performing students. The alternative school calendar is an attractive option for districts. The impact of year-round education at the national level is evident, as there is a dramatic increase in the number of year-round schools across the nation.

GROWTH OF YEAR-ROUND SCHOOLS

An example of growth comes from North Carolina, where the number of year-round schools has grown from 73 in 1994 to 121 in 2000 (National Association for Year-Round Education, 2000). There are two basic types of year-round models in North Carolina, schoolwide (SW) and school-within-a-school (SWS). In the SW model all children in a school attend school on a year-round or 12-month calendar, whereas in the SWS model one group of students attends on a year-round calendar while the others attend on a traditional 9-month calendar. Teachers in this model are usually divided into two groups across the two options. The SWS model has a traditional and revised schedule operating in unison with each program having its own teachers and students, but operating on the same campus with the same administrative staff.

There are other types of calendar arrangements in North Carolina's year-round schools from the most common type where students attend school for 45 days and then break for 15 days to a single-track schedule where different groups of students begin the school year at different times. Therefore, this increases the attractiveness of year-round options because schools have the luxury of determining which model is most beneficial for their population and situation. The general consensus has supported that the outcomes of year-round education are at least as positive as (or better than) those achieved under the traditional school calendar. Unfortunately, the number of quality published studies to support these findings is limited. Although research has touted the benefits of year-round education, there is no conclusive reason as to why achievement may be slightly higher in year-round schools. However, one possibility is that these schools can use intercessions to provide remediation and enrichment activities, thereby increasing students' exposure to the curriculum.

It is interesting to note that the year-round schools in North Carolina all offer some form of remediation and/or enrichment during intersessions, some of which are mandatory for students who are behind academically. This increases opportunities for success for these lower-achieving students and could possibly lower the achievement gap as well. While achievement is one benefit to year-round education, there are others including the cost savings associated with these schools and stakeholder preferences.

SCHEDULE FLEXIBILITY

Many districts are embracing the year-round option as it allows greater flexibility in the schedule and is a drastic change from the traditional schedule. Most advocates for year-round education believe that it is a valuable way to help student achievement. The balanced calendar, with a rich variety of intersession activities, provides opportunities for advancement and enrichment, as well as an opportunity for students to gain new knowledge and skills to perform at acceptable levels.

Advocates for year-round education suggest that these programs (a) make better use of school facilities, (b) increase student and teacher attendance, (c) reduce the number of discipline and behavioral problems, and (d) decrease student dropout rates. There is also the contention the year-round school reduces the possibility for students "forgetting," or maintaining less information, due to the shortened breaks between instructional sessions. This is important as it allows teachers to spend more time on new content and less time reviewing previous content at the beginning of each new session. Additionally, students have the opportunity to take remedial, advanced, and/or enrichment courses, which can be advantageous for performance outcomes.

RESEARCH

The National Association for Year-Round Education and results from Internet searches suggest that there is a growing body of research and literature focusing on year-round schools. The reality is that the number of rigorous empirical studies remains relatively limited. An even more disconcerting fact is that the research findings have been inconclusive, especially the studies that have focused on traditional indicators of academic achievement (e.g., standardized test scores). However, some program evaluation studies have reported higher levels of achievement after a year-round education program was implemented.

In this current era of education reform, the topic of extending the school year continues to be a controversial subject. A report by the National Education

Commission on Time and Learning (1994) suggests the importance of time in education, the extent to which time controls what happens in schools, and the need for efficient use of time to promote greater student achievement. It is likely that extending the school year will have a positive impact on students' learning because there is a continuum to the learning experience. The major conclusion of the report called for more time devoted to instruction and learning in core subjects. Additionally, subsequent international comparative investigations, such as the Third International Mathematics and Science Study (U.S. Department of Education, 2009), found that countries in which students spend more days in school and more time during the day on mathematics and science instruction demonstrate higher achievement in those subjects. Ultimately, this research illustrates that the quantity and the quality of instructional time that is available to students are absolutely critical in determining student outcomes. This research has impacted the debates about time and learning and the adoption of the year-round school calendar, which is a practice for many schools throughout the nation. The National Association for Year-Round Education reported in 2007 that more than 3,000 K–12 year-round schools enrolled more than 2 million students in the United States, and the number is increasing.

Schools have selected the extended school year option as an opportunity to address the negative effects of summer learning loss during the traditional two- to three-month break from school. The literature reports the effects of summer vacation on academic achievement and has found that all students lose some of their math and spelling skills, and many lose reading skills, over the period of the traditional summer break. Research supports that year-round schools provide children the advantage of not losing information over the long summer breaks and the possibility of retaining more due to the intensive, focused instruction with shorter breaks. Extending the school year with a modified schedule means that there are no breaks lasting longer than 8 weeks, which allows schools to keep students in a learning mode throughout the school year.

The schedule for year-round schools may vary based on the agenda of the school. For instance, some schools go for a period of 45 days with a 15-day break before the next 45-day session, whereas it is possible that schools may follow each 60-day session with a 20-day break. Again schools tailor their breaks or intersessions for remediation and enrichment, depending on their agendas. The reality is that year-round schooling can take many forms with ultimately the same goals. As the schools consider the schedule, it is possible for them to include extra learning opportunities during the intersessions. This is beneficial for those students who are at risk for school failure, perform below grade level, and have histories of poor performance at the end of the school year. It should be noted that schools can be single-track with students and school personnel all following the same schedule, or multitrack with students and teachers divided into two or more groups following staggered schedules (which is used to reduce overcrowding). It is not clear which is the preferred option; however, many believe it may be the multitrack schedule because the school can increase its enrollment to ease overcrowding and also benefit from cost savings.

An example of year-round schools includes the Washington area suburban schools, which implemented summer learning opportunities. To illustrate the various forms of year-round opportunities, some schools have developed a math instruction camp and a middle school technical camp. Another example is an elementary school that offered Little Authors Workshop and We Do Robotics, whereas schools in Montgomery County, Maryland, offered activities from a 4-week program, to an engineering camp, to an array of drama and arts programs. However, in most communities these activities are not for all students. A survey of 30,000 households by the Afterschool Alliance (2010) reveals that three out of four U.S. schoolchildren do not participate in summer learning programs, even though parents of 56% of those students not participating would like them to. With the increase in the number of year-round schools, it implies that parents are interested in these alternative schools and are key stakeholders in the process. Parents realize that these schools provide a better use of instructional time for their children.

Research suggests that extending the school year may be beneficial for students, especially minority economically disadvantaged students. The key issue in education continues to be the achievement gap that is evident between minority students and their middle-class peers. One study found that low income students made similar achievement gains to other students during the school year; the widening of the achievement gap between the two groups occurred during the summer. Another study found that summer learning loss is more pronounced for math facts, spelling, and other academic material that is concrete rather than conceptual. If students attend year-round schools, they may be able to reduce the achievement gap. Since it is common knowledge that children from diverse populations often have cognitive learning deficits that impede their ability to perform appropriately, gaining access to quality instruction enhances their opportunity to increase their skills.

The merit of year-round schools is well documented in research. Additionally, there is research to support the many benefits of designing an extended school year, especially for students from diverse backgrounds. Minority students from impoverished environments benefit from year-round schooling. It is not surprising that most research implies that students in year-round schools do as well as or slightly better than students in traditional schools in terms of academic achievement. It is also interesting to note that parents, teachers, and students typically have positive experiences and attitudes about the extended school year experience.

It is important to analyze the effect of year-round schooling, as it can benefit not only minority students from impoverished environments, but students with specialized learning challenges, such as children with disabilities. The extended school year provides these children with an opportunity for additional time to acquire basic skills and possibly the maintenance of these skills. The benefits are evident not only in the cognitive development of students, but there are also benefits to the social, emotional, and behavioral performance of students. The point is that the benefits outweigh the negatives regarding the development of children with disabilities in extended school year settings.

As schools consider the impact of extending the school year, it is wise to recognize the many benefits of this move. The literature supports that children with disabilities lose a certain amount of instruction during school breaks, especially during the summer. These individuals require consistent and repeated opportunities to practice during the acquisition phase of learning. It is not uncommon for some of these children (e.g., those who are cognitively delayed, those with attention deficit/hyperactivity disorder, those with autism) to require numerous instructional opportunities of previously taught information because of their cognitive deficits. An extended school year allows these children to have more opportunities to acquire a skill with a shorter period of time for breaks. The shorter breaks would allow these students less time to lose key information and would assist in their maintenance of skills.

Key stakeholders should be included in the planning for developing an extended school year; therefore, staff, parents, and community members should be invited to participate in the discussion and planning before committing to a change in the traditional schedule. Designing the school schedule may be challenging to ensure that extending the year will be beneficial for all learners. Ultimately, the main purpose for extending the school year is to address the needs of the student population.

The most conclusive research finding is that students from impoverished socioeconomic levels can benefit from a year-round schedule. Because many of these students are performing below grade level due to their lack of basic skills, a year-round schedule would provide more time for these students to improve their skills. Developing an extended school program in urban districts is an appropriate move, because of the loss that occurs during the traditional schedule. Karl L. Alexander, Doris R. Entwisle, and Linda S. Olson (2007) of Johns

Hopkins University found that by ninth grade, accumulated learning loss for impoverished minority children accounted for two thirds of the achievement gap between them and higher income children who had summer learning opportunities, which included academics, as well as the arts (e.g., visiting the library, museums).

While achievement is a major consideration in the development of the extended school year schedule, there are other benefits that should be considered. Including the arts in the experience provides these students with knowledge regarding their communities and the impact of the arts on their lives. Schools are providing remediation and enrichment for students during the breaks so that students have opportunities to relearn material, practice skills, catch up, or experience nonacademic enrichment activities consistently throughout the year.

There are other advantages to an extended school year, including greater satisfaction due to the frequent breaks during the school year. Students, as well as teachers, respond favorably to the additional scheduled breaks. The literature supports that there is also better attendance by students and teachers. The balanced schedule is enjoyable to students and teachers because it allows them to have pleasant fall and spring holidays without being a part of summer crowds. In addition, the extra weeks during the winter intersession are especially appreciated and welcomed.

Year-round schools can only be successful when stakeholders, including teachers, principals, and parents, actively participate in the process and believe in its merits. Teachers participate because they believe it will be beneficial to both their students and themselves. Therefore, it is essential that schools prepare for the change from the traditional schedule by careful planning. The staff has to determine the kind of year-round schooling that would be beneficial for its population, as well as identify any plausible problems that may evolve with a change in the schedule. Ultimately, all students should benefit from extending the school year and have access to quality educational experiences in the process. This will ensure that indeed no child is left behind. Research already illustrates the many benefits of the extended school year; however, the importance of intersession instruction cannot be overstated. The additional time can make a difference between success and failure in the lives of students, including those from impoverished backgrounds.

Extending the school year with a rich variety of intersession activities, with opportunities for advancement and enrichment, provides an effective manner to ensure that indeed all students have the opportunity to experience success in the learning environment. There are three key advantages to a year-round calendar, including (1) increased student achievement; (2) greater satisfaction among teachers, students, and parents; and (3) cost savings. The benefits related to the first two have been articulated. Cost savings is usually associated with multitrack year-round schools because it allows schools to postpone the need to build new schools in areas experiencing significant population growth, such as urban districts.

Other studies have supported the benefits of year-round education. In earlier research the effectiveness of year-round education was discovered on the basis of several studies that focused on achievement, cost, satisfaction, and other outcomes. The results indicated that (a) achievement in year-round schools is equal to or greater than achievement in traditional schools; (b) teachers and students in year-round schools have more positive attitudes; (c) most parents are satisfied with a year-round program if it is well implemented; and (d) single-track programs cost as much as or more than traditional school programs, whereas mutitrack programs can result in significant cost savings if the programs are implemented well. Ultimately, many studies supported that achievement in year-round schools appears to be slightly higher than in traditional schools. It also appears that the longer a child participates in year-round schools, the greater the opportunity for academic success.

Year-round school advocates assert that year-round education is quite attractive especially at the elementary and middle school level (K–8). This is supported by the fact that in 2005–2006, about 2,200 public elementary schools and nearly 300 public middle schools in the United States were following a modified schedule. That equates to more than 1.8 million K–8 students and illustrates that more K–8 schools are transitioning from a traditional schedule to a modified schedule. Advocates suggest that the year-round schedule provides additional opportunities to set a balanced foundation and the modified schedules are advantageous to all learners, including English language learners, low-performing students, and students with disabilities. High schools are not as eager to adopt the extended year schedule. A reason for this may be that high school officials fear the year-round schedules may impact after-school activities, especially athletics.

Even though there is limited empirical research to support the achievement gains of students, the merits of the alternative schedule are noteworthy. The author asserts that we must be cautious in the interpretation of the results regarding achievement gains because of the inconsistencies with methodologies employed. It is advisable that factors should be considered when determining the merits of year-round education. For instance, consideration must be given regarding the distinctions relevant to the alternative schedule across schools (e.g., to reduce the pressures of overcrowding versus those focused on efforts to increase academic achievement). There are also distinctions regarding whether schools will offer educational options during the intersessions (e.g., remediation, acceleration and enrichment) or select not to include any instruction during the intersessions. Research notes that schools that offer academic options during the intersessions can have a positive impact on the education of Hispanic migrant students because the flexible schedule of year-round schools is likely to be more compatible with the seasonal schedules of migrant workers. This is another validation of the impact of year-round schools on diverse populations.

Given that many year-round programs are magnet programs and may draw students from outside the school's normal attendance zone, the consideration of student performance is important. Future research should (a) investigate the length of time that a school has been operating year-round and (b) measure possible differences in pedagogical practices between traditional and year-round schools. This research could mediate the effects of year-round education on students' academic achievement and the achievement gap and could also determine whether a year-round schedule results in changes in daily instructional activities.

CONCLUSION

The debate regarding the effectiveness of year-round education will continue, as schools strive to identify an approach that will benefit all learners in environments conducive to learning. According to the research, the extended school year option benefits in particular students from lower socioeconomic levels, those at risk of school failure, and students with special needs. It is time to allay any concerns regarding the extended school year and assist school districts in identifying the most effective extended year programs for their student populations.

COUNTERPOINT: Aaron Cooley
New England College

Public debates and policy discussions about education in the United States have been in a crisis mentality at least since *A Nation at Risk* was issued in 1983. Of course, one could point to earlier crisis moments, such as the launch of Sputnik by the Soviet Union, which spurred the nation to take a look at its public educational system and make needed improvement. Regardless of the origin of this paradigm, the crisis attitude has negatively impacted public schools around the country and has been especially harmful to the marginalized populations that are consistently underserved by their options for public education. In the face of educational achievement gaps among demographic groups of students, many efforts and strategies have been promoted to meet this critical challenge. One prominent educational reform advanced in recent years suggests that to improve the learning and performance of struggling students they should attend school year-round instead of for the traditional school year with an extended summer break. However, this option does not include additional days of instruction or a longer school day, unlike other school time reforms.

It is, of course, admirable to focus on trying to improve the educational system through novel ideas and experimental new programs. This type of Deweyan educational policy that constantly seeks to meet evolving challenges and changes in the workplace that students will eventually enter should be sought at every turn. However, the promotion of year-round schools to improve student outcomes does not fall into this category and all too narrowly defines the terms of educational and life success. This is not to say that students and parents should not have year-round schools as an option for education. Simply, year-round schools fail to demonstrate the types of outcomes needed to advance as a broader strategy that districts around the country could replicate as they showcase enough achievement gains. Further, and more important, it puts a veneer of reform over deeper and more significant needs in educational and social reform for sustained progress and growth.

The following sections of this counterpoint essay have two general aims. The first is to address and rebut the points made in the point essay of the chapter, and the second is to further demonstrate how year-round schools distract from a more substantive, comprehensive, and transformative educational reform policy. Again, these efforts at reform through year-round schools are well intentioned and often born out of a desire to meet a perceived community or district need, but on balance these efforts are largely an insufficient means of improving student outcomes and fail to address the day-to-day changes required to improve public education. The spirit of this counterpoint essay is to continue the conversation about the best and most effective means for improving the public education system with particular emphasis on marginalized youth, which is a solid point of agreement from which to diverge into the means of achieving such a goal.

TIME IN SCHOOL

One of the first assertions made in the point essay is that more time in school improves outcomes. The research referred to suggests that having students in school for longer amounts of time during the day and for more days increases test scores and therefore improves student outcomes. This research offers a possibly promising reform in terms of increasing the instructional time to international norms as students in other industrialized and industrializing countries routinely spend many more days in schools and often have longer school days or additional semirequired tutoring after school. For example, countries such as China and Japan have many more school days (200-plus) than the traditional 180 days in the United States. Similarly, most European countries have more days in their school calendars. However, this point on longer school years is immaterial to the question of whether or not year-round schools would produce better outcomes as the year-round schools up for debate in this discussion do not increase the overall number of days of instruction or the amount of time teaching students each day. They only alter the spacing of breaks during the year.

Yet, even if the school year was lengthened and the day increased in time, one could not infer that students in the United States would necessarily reach the performance levels on international comparisons with peer countries. It certainly could happen, but there are too many intervening factors that complicate the equation to support such an anecdotally based assumption and related reform policy. One of the primary reasons that this improvement would not be ensured is that the level of poverty among children in the United States is far higher than that in the countries that score higher on international tests even though they have similar levels of development. Therefore, if this proposal was implemented, it could not guarantee being able to overcome the present and existing barriers to success faced by students in the United States on international performance metrics.

The fundamental issue highlighted by the point essay in drawing attention to the amount of time in school and the further discussion of it in this counterpoint essay is that the length of a school day and year is a reform canard. It sounds great as political rhetoric, but fails to be implemented because of the country's lack of interest in investing in public education in a significant way and sustainable fashion that meets the needs of its students. Hence, a longer school day and longer school year were promoted by President Barack Obama as a positive reform strategy. When he did this, he was lauded by the centrist (left and right) probusiness coalition for this support, but this idea has not come with the resources to create such a revamped system, and as previously mentioned there is reason to believe student outcomes would improve if it did come to pass.

Again, it is important to reiterate here that the argument for year-round schools should not rely upon a longer school year for support. Doing this undercuts the perceived value of a change in the school calendar. Further, it muddies the water of the issue at hand by adding in elements from a separate debate. So, taking apart this link made in the point essay shows that simply changing how the time in school is spread out does not necessarily change what happens on a day-to-day basis when the hard work of teaching and learning is done.

ASSESSING STUDENT OUTCOME

The next crucial point mentioned that needs addressing is how improvement in student outcomes is being defined and in what areas of study it is operative. The way the definition of student outcomes is used offers little room for anything not related to the standardized testing regime of the last 25 years in educational policy. By focusing on outcomes in this sense, many of the most important aspects of learning and development are left out. Indeed, the point piece is correct in asserting that more time spent on subjects can lead to better test scores. However, when districts, states, and the federal government gravitate to testing certain subjects, other subjects must be pushed out of the curriculum. Improving student comprehension of material in the extensively tested fields of math and English is positive, and if year-round schools could definitively prove improvement on this question, that would be a step in the right direction. Yet, the evidence for this claim would undoubtedly come from test scores that are often raised through extensive test prep before they are completed. This may be solid evidence for a PowerPoint presentation to an education oversight committee, but it fails to see the big picture of creating well-rounded students who can apply material to interdisciplinary fields of inquiry in the arts and sciences that require critical analysis, logic, and creativity. Unfortunately, by defining success in terms of student outcomes narrowly, the argument for year-round schools neglects that other fields will still get less of the school day and students will continue to know less and less about the country's history, civic traditions, and cultural legacies in artistic and musical forms. At the very least, the point essay's definition of a core subject could be opened to be more inclusive to subjects that are often the reasons students continue to come to school such as to be in the marching band or to paint sets in a drama class.

DIFFICULTIES ADAPTING TO SPORTS SCHEDULES

Following on this point of student retention, the point essay mentions a problem of year-round schools fitting the academic schedule with a traditional high school sports schedule. This may seem to be of little consequence as public schools are not set up and supported by the state for athletic competition. However, sports are often a way to get students to remain involved in the life of a school and its community. Athletes must remain academically eligible to play and are incentivized to aspire to do better for the possibility of a scholarship to college. These are no small concerns as these student-athletes gain esteem and social standing through their involvement with sports teams along with learning lessons of leadership, camaraderie, and self-discipline. Hence, disrupting sports schedules is not trivial and could certainly counteract the positive student outcomes that year-round schools assert that they achieve.

SUMMER LEARNING LOSS

Another major argument for year-round schools offered by the point essay and supporters of the movement more generally is that the traditional school calendar hampers students' development, because of summer learning loss. Some research discussed in the point essay indicates that this is an unfortunate possibility of the present traditional calendar, which can adversely affect marginalized populations more than other student groups. However, much of this summer learning loss could be ameliorated by reforms to the present educational system that puts more emphasis on student and parental responsibility for educational maintenance during breaks. Looking exclusively to the school and teachers as the source of motivation for success is indicative of a more substantial problem that will inhibit students from reaching their full potential long after summer has faded into fall. Certainly, students' progress during the school year would benefit from learning the skills of independent work and meeting deadlines for summer reading lists without the usual pressures of the school environment. Hence, just altering the length and timing of student breaks could allow students and parents to cede too much responsibility to the school during the rest of the year. Indeed, much research and anecdotal evidence from teachers and administrators indicates that increasing parental involvement in their children's education would improve educational achievement much more than altering the school calendar.

Another supporting point on summer learning loss is that these losses are often the result of a teaching and testing system that emphasizes short-term results over longer-term understanding and application of material. So, the continued emphasis on "drill and skill" style instruction promotes somewhat artificial results in terms of what genuine knowledge students are actually retaining beyond reciting the material they memorized one week on the end-of-year tests they take the next week. Hence, the summer learning loss critique of a traditional school year by supporters of year-round schools may be based on an inflated gap that is due to the ways in which students are presently being taught and the ways this learning is being assessed. Therefore, an alternate strategy would be to have students learn and teachers educate with regard for long-term comprehension and application of course material that engenders less loss during any breaks, be they long or short.

LEARNING OUTSIDE OF SCHOOL IN THE SUMMER

Working to assist these marginalized and struggling students is an unequivocally positive step; however, the move to year-round schools also hampers these students' opportunities to have other summer enrichment experiences that can be more valuable as they age specifically, through Upward Bound and other TRIO programs. It is certainly true, as the point essay makes clear, that students from marginalized populations have lower attendance rates for summer enrichment and camp programs. These are not experiences that should be exclusively for middle-class and upper-class students, and further philanthropic efforts should be directed toward the goal of increasing participation of marginalized youth to give them similar opportunities to other students. The opportunities for positive social growth and development in natural settings or even the team building of a day camp are outcomes that must be included in the calculus of overall student improvement. Facilitating these types of experiences for students could prove transformative to students, and year-round schools would make attending these programs more difficult.

ALTERNATIVE REFORMS NEEDED

One of the crucial assumptions of the point essay and supporters of year-round schools is that what is currently happening in schools on a day-to-day basis is presently working to educate students in a sufficient manner. As such, they assert that just changing the traditional calendar will produce better outcomes. Unfortunately, this misses the need for a much more comprehensive educational reform strategy that encompasses a far more robust perspective on changing the educational opportunities for marginalized youth. Instead, efforts directed at calendar reform could be used to revamp schools to act in more innovative ways such as allowing students greater ability to be paced through curriculum at their own speed. This would give both high-achieving and struggling students the opportunity to make progress on a schedule that meets their present learning needs and abilities. Such a reform would be dramatically beneficial to student outcomes in ways that altering the calendar would not be able to address.

Another assumption that the year-round argument is based on is that all learning must occur in school and any time away from school is detrimental to students. The point essay mentions research that alludes to this notion. However, it is not definitive and neglects to account for many institutions and organizations that provide education and positive social development for students outside of school during the traditional calendar breaks. Religious groups, civics clubs, and scouting programs all provide students a chance to learn in settings different from a traditional classroom. These organizations could be harmed due to schedule changes in a year-round format, and students who attend them would not be able to grow and succeed in new ways.

EVALUATING THE PRACTICAL ARGUMENTS

One practical upside of year-round schools is that they can create better student outcomes if schools are so highly crowded that tracking student cohorts in and out allows more students to attend the school during the year. This is, of course, a solution to a problem that should have a solution of more public investments in education, but it can provide short-term relief to overcrowding. On the practical downside, families with multiple children often face having students track in and out at different times making family schedules more difficult to construct. From the facilities perspective, having students in school in hot climates would also raise the costs of cooling the facilities during the summer months when temperatures regularly exceed 85 degrees.

CONCLUSION

The final point is perhaps the most significant. Young people today are faced with ever-increasing pressures from the moment that they start school and in some cases even before as "tiger moms" get children on waiting lists for preschool as soon as they are born. So, competition and the drive to succeed have pushed students to have increasing levels of stress as well as driving them to act out and rebel against these pressures. Giving young people a break to enjoy their childhoods must be seen as a positive rationale for the present system. People have their entire lives to work without extended breaks, and young people should get a reprieve from this for as long as they can. In short, kids should be allowed to be kids.

To sum up, the effort to reallocate school days in a year-round calendar is a well-intentioned effort and certainly should be an option for parents who feel that it best suits their child's learning needs and family schedule. However, there are too many variables and countervailing issues to definitively state that it improves student outcomes. More research must be done, and the defining terms of student outcomes must be expanded to adequately meet the present educational environment. Consequently, year-round schools offer little more than rearranging the parts of the complex educational system without addressing more substantive and pressing reform issues.

FURTHER READINGS AND RESOURCES

Afterschool Alliance. (2010). *American after 3PM.* Retrieved from http://www.after schoolalliance.org/AA3PM.cfm

Alexander, K. L., Entwisle, D. R., & Olson, L. S. (2007). Lasting consequences of the summer learning gap. *American Sociological Review, 72*(2), 167–180.

Ben-Peretz, M., & Rainer, B. (Eds.). (1990). *The nature of time in schools: Theoretical concepts, practitioner perceptions.* New York: Teachers College Press.

Callahan, R. (1962). *Education and the cult of efficiency.* Chicago: University of Chicago Press.

Cuban, L. (2008). The perennial reform: Fixing school time. *Phi Delta Kappan, 90*(4), 240–250.

Illich, I. (1971). *Deschooling society.* New York: Harper & Row.

Mathews, J. (2010). Summer school is a great tool, if only more students would use it. *The Washington Post,* pp. 1–2.

National Association for Year-Round Education: http://www.nayre.org

National Association for Year-Round Education. (2000). *Growth of year-round public education in the United States over a 15-year period.* San Diego, CA: Author.

National Association for Year-Round Education. (2007). *Statistical summaries of year-round education programs 2006–2007.* Retrieved from http://www.nayre.org/ STATISTICAL%20SUMMARIES%20OF%20YRE%202007.pdf

The National Commission on Excellence in Education. (1983). *A nation at risk: The imperative for educational reform.* Washington, DC: Author.

National Education Commission on Time and Learning. (1994). *Prisoners of time.* Washington, DC: U.S. Government Printing Office.

North Carolina Department of Public Instruction. (2000). Year-round schools and achievement in North Carolina. *Evaluation Brief, 2*(2). Retrieved September 26, 2011, from http://www.ncpublicschools.org/docs/accountability/evaluation/eval briefs/vol2n2-yr.pdf

St. Gerard, V. (2007). Year-round schools look better all the time. *Communicator, 30*(1), 56–58.

Stenvall, M. J. (2001). Balancing the calendar for year-round learning. *Principal, 3,* 19–21.

U.S. Department of Education. (2009). *Highlights from TIMSS 2007: Mathematics and science achievement of U.S. fourth- and eighth-grade students in an international context.* Retrieved from http://nces.ed.gov/pubs2009/2009001.pdf

15

Are Native American schools a viable means of enhancing student achievement?

POINT: Carolyn A. Brown, *Fordham University*
COUNTERPOINT: Rachel Trimble, *American Institutes for Research*

OVERVIEW

Native Americans are educated in a variety of settings including public schools, charter schools, and private schools. The Bureau of Indian Education (BIE) of the U.S. Department of the Interior currently educates over 48,000 students in 183 elementary and secondary schools located on 64 reservations in 23 states. Of those schools, 124 are tribally controlled under BIE contracts or grants, and 59 are operated directly by the BIE. The BIE also operates or funds off-reservation boarding schools and peripheral dormitories for students attending the public schools (Bureau of Indian Education, 2011). Approximately 70% of the BIE schools are located in four states—Arizona, Oklahoma, North Dakota, and South Dakota. Although the BIE oversees these schools, each is governed by its own school board. In 2001 the General Accounting Office reported that most teachers in BIE schools were fully certified for the subjects or grade levels they taught.

Under federal regulations the BIE is charged with providing quality educational opportunities for Native Americans from early childhood through life in harmony with a tribe's needs for cultural and economic well-being and in keeping with the wide diversity of Indian tribes and Alaska Native villages as distinctive cultural and governmental entities. Further, in doing so the BIE is required to consider the whole person by taking into account the spiritual, mental, physical, and cultural aspects of the individual within his or her family and tribal or village context (25 C.F.R. § 32.3).

Unfortunately, as reported by the General Accounting Office (2001), a significant gap exists between the achievement of students attending BIE schools and those in the public schools as measured by their performance on standardized tests and other measures. The report acknowledged that there may be a number of reasons for this. The report emphasized that academic performance is associated with the educational and income levels of students' parents and that students attending BIE schools often come from families with lower than average education, employment, and earning levels. Although most of the teachers at BIE schools are fully certified, administrators state that some schools experience difficulties recruiting and retaining qualified staff. Further, officials reported that the educational technology in BIE schools is often better than in the public schools, but the technical support to maintain computers and assist teachers with technology is limited. The report also noted that problems with school facilities exist and some are in inadequate condition. Finally, the report commented that BIE schools have a higher percentage of students with disabilities.

The two essays in this chapter examine the question of whether Native American schools provide a viable vehicle for improving the achievement of their students and thereby close the achievement gap that now exists. In the point essay, Carolyn A. Brown, an associate professor in the Graduate School of Education at Fordham University, takes the position that such culturally sensitive schools result in better student outcomes. In the counterpoint essay, Rachel Trimble, a senior consultant at the American Institutes for Research, disagrees, arguing that state-funded public schools where Native American students are integrated with non–Native American students offer the most viable solution to improving Native American education.

Brown notes that in culturally sensitive schools students are educated in caring, trusting, and respectful classroom environments. She contends that such environments increase the learning of American Indian students who achieve best in small, community-centered settings where teachers are responsive to their needs. Further, the degree of community involvement found in Native American schools, she feels, increases the graduation rates of Native Americans. Brown concludes that tribal schools, utilizing a culturally based curriculum and instruction, are uniquely positioned to raise the educational attainment of American Indian students. This is due, in part, to the fact that they are accessible to and situated within the context of and controlled by the tribal community. In being an integral part of the milieu of community services that support Native American families, these schools help maximize students' potential for achievement.

Citing the substantial achievement gap that exists, Trimble maintains that education for Native American students has long been substandard. She supports her claim by referencing research that shows that the achievement of many Native Americans is well below grade level and they are more likely to drop out of school than their White counterparts. Trimble agrees that Native American students need good quality teachers who can instruct diverse students and incorporate a multitude of culturally relevant strategies into their teaching. She contends, however, that Native American students can be included in the public schools in a way that fosters a respectful and engaging learning environment to support them in both their academic achievement and their cultural sense of self. She concludes that public schools provide the most viable means of closing the achievement gap partly because they have greater resources with which to provide the necessary culturally relevant curriculum and materials and quality professional development.

In reading the essays in this chapter, you may wish to think about two questions. First, is the achievement gap between Native American students and White students any different from the achievement gap between other minority groups and White students? Second, given that great efforts have been made throughout the United States since the 1954 U.S. Supreme Court decision in *Brown v. Board of Education* to integrate American schools, does it make sense to segregate Native Americans in their own schools?

Allan G. Osborne, Jr.
Principal (Retired), Snug Harbor Community School,
Quincy, Massachusetts

POINT: Carolyn A. Brown
Fordham University

The education of Native American children has reflected decades of misguided policies directed at changing rather than serving Native American culture. Native American education, until the 1970s, was controlled by the federal government and focused primarily on enculturation of children into Euro American society. Native American education was provided by a patchwork of remote, rural schools funded by the Bureau of Indian Affairs (BIA), or various missionary efforts.

BACKGROUND

In the late 1960s, on the heels of the civil rights movement, Native American activism broke loose across the United States. The American Indian Movement (AIM) gained attention in 1972 when it seized the BIA office in Washington, D.C., and, shortly after, organized a standoff with police on the Pine Ridge Reservation in South Dakota. AIM activities challenged treaty agreements in court, and in 1972 Congress passed the Indian Education Act (IEA), which was followed in 1975 by the Indian Self-Determination and Education Assistance Act (ISDEAA). These two laws had a substantial impact on education for Native American students, and are pivotal to a discussion of how Native American schools are uniquely positioned to enhance the academic achievement of Native American children.

IEA allocated funds to schools serving Native American children on and off reservations. The act, for the first time, recognized and provided funds to serve the approximately 600,000 (92%) Native American children who attend state public schools off reservations. Nearly half of these students (46%) attend small, rural schools where 50% or more of the students are Native American.

The remaining 8% of Native American students attend either a BIA funded and controlled school or one of a growing number of tribally controlled schools. These BIA/tribal schools are small (under 300 students), geographically remote, and often run down or in temporary buildings and have limited access to technology. Currently, BIA/tribal school teachers must meet state certification requirements, but salaries are low and schools are typically hard to staff.

The development of tribal schools was an important outcome of the ISDEAA, which allowed federal agencies to distribute funds to tribes, under contracts, to provide tribally controlled basic services such as education, health, and law enforcement. Tribal control of health services has had a measurable positive effect on Native American people as shown by increased average age and lowered infant mortality rates among tribes; however, education is a longer process, and it is arguable that while there are scant indicators of improvement at this time, the full impact of tribal schools on the achievement of Native American students has yet to be realized.

The U.S. Department of Education annually aggregates academic and social factors as well as attendance and graduation rates for all Native American students—on and off the reservation. These aggregated data have shown some improvement on academic and social indicators for Native American students in the 40 years since the passage of the IEA and ISDEAA; however, overall school success for Native American students remains below that for non–Native American students in most areas. Although one nongovernment report examined graduation rates specifically at BIA schools, finding that 60% of students graduated in BIA schools compared to a 70% national average (Faircloth & Tippeconnic, 2010), no data were reported specifically for tribal schools. No research was found that compares Native American students' achievement in BIA/tribal schools with their achievement in state schools.

The majority of research on Native American education focuses on programs and strategies effective in enhancing student engagement in school and increasing academic achievement among Native American students in both on- and off-reservation schools. The research points to three critical factors: culturally sensitive school climate, culturally based instruction and curriculum, and parent and community involvement in schooling. This essay argues that tribal schools are best situated to implement these strategies because of their geographic and cultural closeness to the tribal culture.

CULTURALLY SENSITIVE SCHOOLS

D. Michael Pavel (1990) asserts that schools enrolling high numbers of American Indian students "provide fertile ground for . . . exemplary programs that have advanced Indian Education" (p. 2). He attributes the improved achievement in some of the tribal schools to ties to traditional cultures. Ties to the culture demand that schools create a culturally sensitive environment that is caring, trusting, and respectful of students; provide an open and welcoming climate for parents and community members; offer curriculum embedded in the cultural context of the community; and use instruction that encourages culturally based strategies that meet the learning styles of American Indian students. A culturally sensitive school is one that fosters caring, trusting, and respectful classroom environments, which increases the learning of American Indian students. Perspectives of American Indian students on the positive and negative aspects of schooling point to the need for small, community-centered environments.

In addition, teachers are critical players in the development of a positive culture for Native American students. Teachers of Native American students need to understand and be responsive to the learning needs of these students. Robert Havighurst's (1971) *National Study of Indian Education* suggested that teachers of Indian children be systematically trained in order to consider the sociocultural processes operating in the American Indian communities. Teachers must learn about the culture of the community where they teach, consciously develop caring and trusting classrooms that are respectful of Native American mores, and engage in ongoing self-reflection on attitudes and beliefs that may be ethnocentric.

PARENT AND COMMUNITY INVOLVEMENT

Active involvement of parents and community members in schools is critical for the success of Native American students. A body of research has determined that the engagement of parents, families, and communities in schools was most closely correlated with higher achievement among Native American students in Montana. Community involvement outweighed teaching, leadership, and curriculum. Successful schools for Native American students consistently include members of the community and incorporate Native American culture, knowledge, and expertise into the daily life of the school. Parent and community involvement in schools improves both behavioral and academic outcomes for the children.

Community involvement in the design and implementation of school programs can increase the low high school graduation rate of Native American students, and when families provide positive messages about school and maintain high expectations for achievement, students persist in school.

CULTURALLY BASED CURRICULUM

Culturally based education refers to curriculum and instructional strategies that are embedded in the context of Native American culture and consider the language and learning styles of Native American students. Literature on the influence of culture on learning supports the need for culturally based education for Native Americans: "Culture shapes minds, . . . it provides us with the tool kit by which we construct not only our worlds but our very conceptions of ourselves and our powers" (Bruner, 1996, pp. x–xi).

William G. Demmert, Jr., and John C. Towner (2003) conducted an exhaustive review of research on successful interventions for Native American students and argue that "knowing, understanding and appreciating one's cultural base are necessary starting points for initiating a young child's formal education" (p. 5). Aside from the need for knowledge of and sensitivity to tribal culture, they stress the importance of recognizing and using Native languages, using instructional strategies that are congruent with tribal culture and conform to the traditional mores for adult-child interactions, and using curriculum contextualized in tribal culture such as art, legends, oral histories, spirituality, and activities that emphasize community.

The impact of Native languages in Native American instruction has become a central concern of education since 1970 as the opening of tribal schools on large reservations has promoted education in Native languages in areas where many students speak Native languages in their homes. These include Navajo and Cherokee reservations, the Hawaiian Islands, and remote areas of Alaska. Other tribes have implemented programs to reintroduce or expand the use of Native languages. Bilingual education for Native American students is critical because Native American students often enter school with a smaller overall English vocabulary than their non–Native American peers.

Absenteeism is another factor that has a large impact on Native American student achievement. Students must be present in school—physically and cognitively—for learning to happen, and culturally based curriculum can increase student engagement in learning and reduce alienation from school. A strong link exists between culturally based curriculum, student engagement, increased attendance, and improved achievement outcomes.

High achievement for Native American students requires a combination of quality academic curriculum, culturally based instructional strategies, and culturally based curriculum. Without all three factors, little progress is made. Culturally based curriculum alone is inadequate for academic success for Native American students, and success also relies on the use of culturally sensitive instructional methods including scaffolding new knowledge on the culture and experience of Native American students.

CULTURALLY BASED INSTRUCTION

In addition to relevant curriculum for Native American students, often Native American students learn differently from non–Native American students. Roland G. Tharp and Ronald Gallimore (1988) point out that in Native American culture, learning in the family is largely accomplished through role-modeling or storytelling rather than explicit, verbal instruction. Various studies emphasized the unique learning needs of Native Americans, and found these students thrive in classrooms with a focus on social and affective learning, including an emphasis on cooperation over competition; a holistic approach to knowledge; use of creative expression and visual, over verbal, representation of information; and opportunities for reflection as a means of processing information (Pewewardy & Cahape, 2003).

Often what is interpreted as Native American learning style is more accurately the manifestation of both culture and experience, and Native American students thrive in an environment of high expectations and quality instruction, as do any other students if curriculum and instructional strategies build on their experience and prior knowledge. Countering the theory of unique Native American learning styles, this fact argues even more strongly for teachers to be sensitive to the needs of American Indian students, familiar with the community, and reflective of the attitudes that may work against their holding high expectations for Native American students.

Native American students benefit by a school environment that is sensitive to their culture. They benefit by a linkage between culturally based curriculum and instruction in school and community involvement. These factors join together for improved student engagement, which is critical to long-term educational success.

CONCLUSION

Tribal schools are uniquely positioned to raise the educational attainment of Native American students. They are accessible to and situated within the context of the tribal community—both geographically and politically. Tribal schools are controlled by the tribal community and, therefore, can institute policies that benefit their students, and they can easily collaborate with other tribal services to meet the needs of families.

Tribal schools, located within the cultural milieu of the community, can best recruit and hire culturally knowledgeable and sensitive teachers and provide ongoing professional development on culturally based curriculum and instruction. A number of tribes, since the ISDEAA, have opened or expanded institutions of higher education that offer teacher certification to tribal members as well as provide the cultural and intellectual capital to serve the professional development needs of teachers and administrators. An argument can be made that these colleges have contributed to the increase in Native American teachers for tribal schools.

Poverty, drug and alcohol abuse, and poor health and nutrition, which continue to plague Native American communities, take a toll on students' ability to maximize their academic potential. Tribal schools are an integral part of the web of community services that support families through programs for health and nutrition, family services, and early childhood education.

Another aspect of Native American education is the need for a match between culture and assessment. Alternative assessments for Native American students can offer opportunities for Native American students to demonstrate learning within their cultural context, where standardized, paper-and-pencil tests have been argued to be culturally biased. Alternatives such as visual arts, performance, and student-teacher interaction can better evaluate students' knowledge. Tribal schools, which operate independently of state requirements, are ideally situated to provide laboratories for alternative assessments in collaboration with tribal colleges or local universities as well as to institute tribal policies for alternatives to commercially produced tests.

Furthermore, cultural, political, and physical proximity and control provide for broad community involvement in the tribal schools. These schools, controlled by tribal councils, engender student and community involvement, as they do not represent the "White man's schooling" in which so many older Native Americans had profoundly negative experiences. In addition, much like charter schools, they possess the institutional flexibility to change quickly and cooperate with other tribal programs through strong school leadership. School leaders play a crucial role in the development of quality schools, and like teachers the number of Native American school administrators is inching up slowly.

Tribally controlled schools have only existed since the 1970s, and they have inherited a legacy of alienation, neglect, and brutality toward Native American children. Even today, these schools are underfunded, operating in aging or temporary facilities, short on materials, and struggling from year to year to find teachers. The road to high quality education for the 1.5% of students who are Native American is a slow one, but the small size, institutional flexibility, and tribal control gives hope for the future of these schools.

COUNTERPOINT: Rachel Trimble
American Institutes for Research

Native American education stands as a challenge to our nation. Native American students show alienation and disengagement from school, low academic achievement, and high dropout rates, resulting in a significant achievement gap from non–Native American students. Increasing numbers of tribes are opening tribal schools to serve all-Native students, but are these schools the most viable means for improving the academic achievement of Native American students? This essay argues that state-funded public schools where Native American students are integrated with non–Native American students offer the most viable solution to improving Native American education.

THE BRUTAL FACTS

For too long, education for Native American students in our nation's schools has been substandard. Achievement data for Native American students reveal a substantial achievement gap. According to a study conducted by the National Caucus of Native American State Legislators (2008), Native American students perform two to three grade levels below Whites in reading and mathematics. Additionally, the National Indian Education Study (U.S. Department of Education, 2009) reported that the average reading and mathematics scores for Native American fourth and eighth graders showed no significant change since 2005 and remained lower than the scores of non–Native American students.

Native American students' performance on exams is only one indication of the gap between them and non–Native American students. School retention rates are low, and student disciplinary problems are high. Native students are 237% more likely to drop out of school and 207% more likely to be expelled than White students. For every 100 Native American kindergartners, only 7 will earn a bachelor's degree compared to 34 of every 100 White kindergartners (National Caucus of Native American State Legislators, 2008). These statistics represent only a snapshot of the current problems facing Native students.

While Native American education has been provided by the federal government for decades through treaty provisions to supply schools and teachers as well as textbooks and materials in Native languages, currently federal programs aim to address the unique culturally related educational needs of Native American students. The No Child Left Behind Act (2006) provides a clear direction for Native students' education:

> It is the policy of the United States to fulfill the Federal Government's unique and continuing trust relationship with and responsibility to the Indian people for the education of Indian children. The Federal Government will continue to work with local educational agencies, ensuring that programs that serve Indian children are of the highest quality and provide for not only the basic elementary and secondary educational needs, but also the unique educational and culturally related academic needs of these children. (20 U.S.C. § 7401)

Most recently, "Meeting the Needs of Diverse Learners," a focus on gaps and equity, is one of six priorities identified in the Obama administration's *A Blueprint for Reform* (U.S. Department of Education, 2010). Federal commitment to Native American education is extended through state public schools by the No Child Left Behind requirements, which enforce at a higher standard for state schools than for tribal schools.

Ninety-two percent of Native American students attend state public schools, and of these 27% are living in poverty. A need for high quality schools for these students is clear, and state public schools have high standards for accountability and adequate resources to offer the best and most culturally relevant teaching and curriculum to close the Native American achievement gap.

The next section outlines the research on strategies for high quality instruction for all students, and culturally relevant education that when offered in a supportive learning environment can successfully raise achievement for Native American students.

THE POWER OF INSTRUCTION

The greatest determinant of learning is teaching. Michael Schmoker (2006) provides an example of good teaching:

> An English instructor in a school where writing scores were well below the state average was studied. Observations revealed him to be clear, organized, and effective. He was unambiguous about the writing standards he expected students to master. He provided samples of the kind of work he expected, and he had students analyze and discuss the samples. He explained and modeled each specific skill—with students' involvement. Students practiced the new skills in pairs, then individually, while he circulated around the classroom to check on progress and correct students. He called on students, randomly, to check for understanding. When he had observed that students were ready, he assessed their learning of the new skill. (p. 7)

Good teaching plays a critical role in student learning. Research has shown that teaching had 6 to 10 times as much impact on achievement as all other factors combined (Mortimore & Sammons, 1987). Teachers working with the same socioeconomic population can achieve starkly different results: In one class, 27% of students pass; in another, 72%—a life-changing difference (Marzano, 2003). Five years of instruction from an above-average teacher can eliminate the achievement gap on state assessments, and the best teachers in a school have 6 times as much impact as the worst teachers (Haycock, 2005; Haycock & Huang, 2001). Quality classroom instruction is the most important element in student learning.

Highly effective teachers understand how to teach diverse learners. Research provides a body of knowledge on best practices for high quality teaching and learning: The teacher must communicate the expectations; understand the background knowledge and cultural experience that each student brings to the classroom; differentiate instruction, incorporating skills, strategies, processes, and approaches that address diverse learners; and frequently check for understanding and use formative assessment to modify instruction based on needs.

To further meet the specific needs of Native American students, teachers should incorporate culture, language, cognition, and patterns of activities that have a cultural basis in the learning styles of Native American students, including opportunities for active and cooperative learning, home school connections, a caring and respectful learning environment, and early intervention to prevent failure. In 46% of state public schools that serve Native American students, as much as half of the student body is Native American. An effective teacher in these schools must offer culturally based curriculum and provide instruction in the context of both high quality teaching strategies and the learning styles of Native American students.

CULTURALLY RELEVANT STRATEGIES AND INTERVENTIONS

A multitude of culturally relevant strategies can be used to create supportive relationships in which learning can occur. Indian Nations at Risk Task Force (1991) found,

> Schools that adjust their curriculum to accommodate the variety of cultures served are more successful . . . ; the perspective from which a school's curriculum is presented can significantly influence Native students' attitudes toward the school, schooling in general, and academic performance; schools that respect and support a student's language and culture are significantly more successful in educating those students; the historical and practical knowledge . . . of the community served must . . . function as a starting point for schooling. (p. 16)

Culturally responsive teaching (CRT) is a collection of best teaching practices that enhance the academic success of students in integrated classrooms. Culturally relevant teaching empowers students intellectually, socially, emotionally, and politically through the use of cultural references that impart knowledge, skills, and attitudes. Research suggests that socioculturally centered teaching results in improved student achievement and that the use of interactive teaching strategies developed with students' ethnic identities, home languages, and cultural backgrounds in mind has contributed to higher student achievement (Gay, 2000; Ladson-Billings, 2001); Roland G. Tharp and Ronald Gallimore (1988) specifically confirm this for Native American students.

Cooperative learning is particularly compatible with the learning/ interactional style of many Native American children. Studies of Native American learning styles emphasize Native American students' preference for cooperation over competition. Specific strategies for cooperative learning have been developed and researched with selected populations of students in public schools. Elements that define strategies as cooperative are individual accountability, group rewards, equal opportunities for success, face-to-face interaction, and interpersonal and small group skills. When student groups are heterogeneous for achievement, gender, and ethnic composition, the dynamic that encourages learning in the classroom is improved. While heterogeneous groups provide an environment for cooperation, flexible grouping—moving students from group to group based on ability or achievement—can be an effective strategy for differentiating instruction.

Differentiated instruction—which acknowledges and accommodates student differences in background knowledge, readiness, language, learning style, and interests—results in individually responsive teaching that is appropriate to individual student needs and is effective in meeting the needs of low-performing students. Differentiated instruction can be used to support groups of students in mainstream classrooms, who have been previously unsuccessful. However, effective differentiated instruction requires that the teacher be aware of each student's level of performance and progress toward the learning goals. Formative assessment is critical to high quality instruction.

THE POWER OF FORMATIVE ASSESSMENT

Continual feedback on performance engages students and encourages students' responsibility for learning. Formative assessment provides feedback to the teacher and to students. It is a crucial factor in improving students' achievement of intended instructional outcomes. Formative assessment must be embedded in instruction to redirect teaching and learning in ways that help students master learning goals. The primary purpose of formative assessment is to provide a steady stream of evidence that teachers and students can use to inform instruction and learning so that adjustments can be made to close the gap between students' current understanding and the desired goals.

A study of formative assessment in seven countries by the Organisation for Economic Co-operation and Development (2005) revealed, "Teachers using formative assessment have changed the culture of their classrooms, putting the emphasis on helping students feel safe to take risks and make mistakes and to develop self-confidence in the classroom" (p. 2). Formative assessment is more cost-effective than other school improvement initiatives; in fact, it is 20 to 30 times more cost-effective than reducing class size (William, 2007). Policy and practice should heighten attention to formative assessment.

Native American student achievement is negatively impacted by alienation from school manifested in high absenteeism and low classroom engagement. Perception surveys of Native American high school students point out that they feel that their teachers "don't care" about their learning, or that the students don't feel they can meet the vague expectations of teachers. Formative assessment provides a vehicle for frequent, regular communication with students (and parents) about what they need to do to succeed, while it also provides teachers with information they can use to engage students in learning.

PROFESSIONAL DEVELOPMENT FOR TEACHERS OF NATIVE AMERICAN STUDENTS

Nearly 90% of teachers in schools with high concentrations of Native American students (50% or fewer) are non–Native American (National Indian Education Association, 2008). To meet the significant social and academic needs of Native American students and to develop the skills required to deliver high quality and culturally relevant instruction, teachers need ongoing job-embedded professional development. Research supports the value of professional development in improving the skills of practicing teachers. For teacher professional development to be effective, considerable time must be allotted. To implement research-based instructional methods effectively, teachers need exposure to approaches and support as they learn to implement them in their classrooms. Teacher professional development is crucial to improve student achievement, school performance, and teacher quality. Schools that serve Native Americans are frequently small and located in remote rural areas. Teacher recruitment and retention is difficult, so quality professional development is necessary for teachers to gain the skills to provide the highest quality instruction.

CONCLUSION

State public school inclusion for Native American students can employ a variety of strategies to foster a respectful and engaging learning environment to support Native American learners in both their academic achievement and their cultural sense of self. Research and experience in state public schools that serve Native American students indicate that culturally relevant instruction and content learning are not mutually exclusive. Rather, they are complementary and equally important elements for enhancing the knowledge and academic achievement of Native American children. Culturally relevant instruction, when integrated, results in highly effective teaching and learning for improved academic achievement for all students.

State public schools provide the most viable means of closing the Native American achievement gap, first because they serve the majority of these students, and second because they are economically situated to meet the needs of these students and their teachers. The professional development required to train teachers for high quality, culturally relevant instruction is expensive. Especially in remote areas, travel or technology may be required. State public schools receive federal funds for Native American students that supplement the state and local funds, including Title I funds, and additional funding under the Indian Education (now Subchapter VII, Part A of NCLB) and Johnson-O'Malley Acts. For example, one district in South Dakota with a high Native American population receives over $12,000 per pupil on average annually compared to the state average of $10,600.

Because state public schools provide schooling for the majority of Native American students, they bear the heaviest responsibility for closing the achievement gap between Native American and non–Native American students. In addition, a significant body of research argues that low-performing students (many Native American students fall into this category) can thrive both socially and academically in heterogeneous learning environments that implement effective instructional practices. Finally, state schools have greater resources to provide the needed culturally relevant curriculum and materials and professional development to close the Native American achievement gap.

FURTHER READINGS AND RESOURCES

Bruner, J. (1996). *The culture of education.* Cambridge, MA: Harvard University Press.

Bureau of Indian Education. (2011). *Primary and secondary schools.* Retrieved from http://www.bie.edu/Schools/PrimarySecondary/index.htm

Demmert, W. G., Jr., & Towner, J. C. (2003). *A review of the research literature on the influences of culturally based education on the academic performance of Native American students.* Portland, OR: Northwest Regional Education Laboratory, U.S. Department of Education.

Faircloth, S. C., & Tippeconnic, J. W. (2010). *The dropout/graduation crisis among American Indian and Alaska Native students: Failure to respond places the future of Native peoples at risk.* Los Angeles; Philadelphia: The Civil Rights Project, University of California, Los Angeles; Center for the Study of Leadership in American Indian Education, The Pennsylvania State University.

Gay, G. (2000). *Culturally responsive teaching: Theory, research, and practice.* New York: Teachers College Press.

Havighurst, R. (1971). *National study of Indian education.* Washington, DC: U.S. Office of Education.

Haycock, K. (2005). *Improving academic achievement and closing gaps between groups in the middle grades.* Presentation given at CASE Middle Level summit. Available from http://www.edtrust.org

Haycock, K., & Huang, S. (2001). Are today's high school graduates ready? *Thinking K-16, 5*(1), 3–17.

Indian Nations at Risk Task Force. (1991). *Indian nations at risk: An educational strategy for action.* Retrieved October 15, 2010, from http://www2.ed.gov/rschstat/research/pubs/oieresearch/research/natatrisk/report_pg2.html

Ladson-Billings, G. (2001). *Crossing over to Canaan: The journey of new teachers in diverse classrooms.* San Francisco: Jossey-Bass.

Marzano, R. J. (2003). *What works in schools: Translating research into action.* Alexandria, VA: Association for Supervision and Curriculum Development.

Mortimore, P., & Sammons, P. (1987). New evidence on effective elementary schools. *Educational Leadership, 45*(1), 4–8.

National Caucus of Native American State Legislators. (2008). *Striving to achieve: Helping Native American students succeed.* Denver, CO: Author.

National Indian Education Association. (2008). *Native education 101: Basic facts about American Indian, Alaska Native, and Native Hawaiian Education.* Washington, DC: Author.

Organisation for Economic Co-operation and Development. (2005). *Formative assessment: Improving learning in secondary classrooms.* Paris: Author.

Pavel, D. M. (1990). Comparing BIA and tribal schools with public schools: A look at the year 1990–1991. *Journal of American Indian Education, 35*(1). Retrieved September 26, 2011, from http://jaie.asu.edu/v35/V35S1com.htm

Pellegrino, J. W., Chudowsky, N., & Glaser, R. (Eds.). (2001). *Knowing what students know: The science and design of educational assessment.* Washington, DC: National Academy Press.

Pewewardy, C.-H., & Cahape, P. (2003). Culturally responsive teaching for American Indian students. *ERIC Digest.* Retrieved from http://www.ericdigests.org/2005-1/teaching.htm

Schmoker, M. (2006). *Results now: How we can achieve unprecedented improvements in teaching and learning.* Alexandria, VA: Association for Supervision and Curriculum Development.

Tharp, R. G., & Gallimore, R. (1988). *Rousing minds to life.* Cambridge, UK: Cambridge University Press.

U.S. Department of Education. (2009). *National Indian education study 2009.* Retrieved from http://nces.ed.gov/nationsreportcard/pdf/studies/2010463.pdf

U.S. Department of Education. (2010). *A blueprint for reform: The reauthorization of the elementary and secondary act.* Retrieved from http://www2.ed.gov/policy/elsec/leg/blueprint/blueprint.pdf

U.S. General Accounting Office. (2001). *BIA and DOD schools: Student achievement and other characteristics often differ from public schools.* Washington, DC: Author. Retrieved from http://www.gao.gov/new.items/d01934.pdf

William, D. (2007). Content then process: Teacher learning communities in the service of formative assessment. In D. Reeves (Ed.), *Ahead of the curve: The power of assessment to transform teaching and learning* (pp. 183–206). Bloomington, IN: Solution Tree.

COURT CASES AND STATUTES

Brown v. Board of Education, 347 U.S. 483 (1954).

Code of Federal Regulations, *Indian Education Policies,* 25 C.F.R. § 1 *et seq.* (2006).

Indian Education Act, Pub. L. No. 92–318, Title IV (1972).

Indian Self-Determination and Education Assistance Act, 25 U.S.C. § 450 *et seq.* (1975).

Johnson-O'Malley Act, 25 U.S.C. § 452 *et seq.* (1934).

No Child Left Behind Act, 20 U.S.C. §§ 6301–7941 (2006).

INDEX

schools, **1:**xxiii–xxiv, **1:**22, **1:**39–40, **1:**44, **1:**98–99, **2:**199, **4:**294–295, **8:**38
See also Christianity
Roosevelt, Franklin D., **8:**248
Root-Bernstein, Michelle M., **2:**160
Root-Bernstein, Robert S., **2:**160
Rose v. Council for Better Education, **3:**181, **6:**33, **6:**64, **6:**149, **6:**169, **6:**198, **6:**201
Rosenberger v. Rector and Visitors of University of Virginia, **4:**223
Rossell, Christine H., **2:**112
Rothenberg, Albert, **2:**170
Rothstein, Richard, **1:**42, **3:**68, **3:**71, **7:**86, **7:**88, **9:**228–229
Rowan, Anna Habash, **3:**103
Rowan, Brian, **7:**170–171
Rowland v. Mad River Local School District, **8:**233–234
Rowley, James B., **9:**271
RTI. *See* Response to intervention model
RTT. *See* Race to the Top
Rusch, Edith, **7:**104
Rusk v. Clearview Local Schools, **4:**244–245, **4:**247, **4:**257
Russell, Bertrand, **9:**51
Russo, Charles J., **4:**222
Ryan, James E., **3:**172
Ryan, Jennifer, **10:**77
Ryan, Richard M., **5:**152, **5:**153

S-1 v. Turlington, **8:**94
Sacramento City Unified School District Board of Education v. Rachel H., **8:**115, **8:**121
Sacred texts. *See* Bible; Religious texts
Sadker, David, **3:**212
Safety
classroom management and, **5:**141–142, **5:**144
concerns in schools, **5:**11, **5:**24–25
dress codes and, **5:**xxv, **5:**1–17, **8:**38–39, **8:**48
drug testing and, **8:**xix, **8:**60–61, **8:**65–66, **8:**77, **8:**78, **8:**79, **8:**80–81, **8:**82–83, **8:**86
goals of disciplinary policies, **5:**197–198
on Internet, **10:**xxiii, **10:**147–148
rationale for zero tolerance policies, **5:**19–34, **5:**39, **5:**40
released time programs and, **4:**165–166

religious garb issues, **4:**267–268, **4:**277–279
on social networking sites, **10:**xxiii, **10:**xxiv, **10:**xxv, **10:**174, **10:**202–203
video surveillance and, **10:**99, **10:**101–102, **10:**107, **10:**110, **10:**112
See also Abuse and neglect; Bullying; School resource officers; Zero tolerance policies
Safford Unified School District #1 v. Redding, **5:**195, **5:**199, **8:**67, **8:**68
Salaries. *See* Teacher salaries and benefits
Sales taxes, **6:**27, **6:**64, **6:**65, **6:**66, **6:**67, **6:**68, **6:**73
Samuels v. Independent School District 279, **5:**163–164
San Antonio Independent School District v. Rodriguez
background, **9:**191
funding disparities allowed, **3:**181
impact, **3:**xxvi, **6:**147, **6:**168, **6:**172–173, **6:**184, **7:**66
plaintiffs' arguments, **6:**xxi, **6:**184
right to education not found in Constitution, **6:**14, **9:**191, **9:**213
See also Financing equity
San Diego Unified School District, **6:**230
Sanders, William, **9:**139
Sankofa symbol, **3:**241, **3:**252
Santa Fe Independent School District v. Doe, **1:**25, **1:**30, **4:**36, **4:**39, **4:**46–47, **4:**62–63, **4:**73
Santayana, George, **9:**136
Sasso, Gary M., **3:**32, **3:**33–34
SAT. *See* Scholastic Aptitude Test
Sataline, Suzanne, **7:**19
SBM. *See* School-based management
Scaffolding, **2:**11–12, **2:**15
Schaill v. Tippecanoe County School Corp., **8:**57
Schema theory, **2:**73
Schmidt, William, **9:**31
Schmoker, Michael, **1:**264
Schneider, Frank W., **1:**192
Scholastic Aptitude Test (SAT) scores, **2:**66, **9:**253
School boards
accountability, **7:**9, **7:**121, **7:**124, **8:**13
advantages, **7:**19
alternative models, **7:**10–11, **7:**121–122, **7:**126–127
antibullying policies, **5:**56